a magick mirı

Doing Business In The Adirondacks

True Tales Of The Bizarre And Supernatural

by

EUGENIA MACER-STORY

YO
YANKEE ORACLE PRESS
back pocket edition

Doing Business In The Adirondacks
True Tales Of The Bizarre And Supernatural
copyright 2003 Eugenia Macer-Story

Printed in the United States of America

ISBN: 1-879980-16-9

Yankee Oracle Press
511 Avenue of the Americas--PMB 173
New York, N.Y. 10011-8436
USA
a magick mirror communication
tel: 212-727-0002 global or 800-356-6796 usa
magickorders@aol.com
info@yankeeoracle.org

CONTENTS

DOING BUSINESS IN THE ADIRONDACKS by E. Macer-Story

INTRODUCTION

This book describes a contest between the author and the "Thantatos" sorcerers which is an actual, subtle battle waged like an intuitive chess game. The book itself did not begin as a narrative of this situation. The intent originally was to describe the many anomalous and supernatural happenings which occur in the mountains and harbors of New York State. Then a pattern began to emerge from the data.

This pattern was surprising and at first unacceptable to the rational mind. It seemed that several threads of inquiry were in fact one pattern of occurrence. Supposedly "human" interference such as crank calls, talismanic debris left on the property and evident surveillance by deceptively-marked vehicles was happening concomitant with "natural" phenomena such as storms, distant power outages, anomalous shrinkage and staining of clothing and other such events normally relegated to the category of supernatural fiction. Yet, in all honesty as a journalist, I had to record that the situation looked exactly as if a group of sorcery adepts was attempting to control my independent activities as a publicly-known artist/playwright and clairvoyant practitioner.

For purposes of journaling these events, I named this unknown group the "Thantatos" organization as it seemed to me that their obsession was with death and control of life processes. Later, I found that this version of the name "Thanatos", a Latin word meaning "death", was actually in use by certain adepts who had recorded some of their correspondence in Internet postings. I also discovered that I was not alone in being mysteriously the focus of this odd attention, and that there had been a number of unexplained deaths and disappearances among U.S. researchers into the area of psychic perception, psychotronics and "ufo" phenomena.

I realized that I was involved now in a contest with people who had developed extraordinary "powers" and were attempting to conceal their existence , as well as to downplay the understanding of these abilities among the public at large.

JOURNAL OF SUBTLE EVENTS

At shortly after six a.m. on the Friday in February numbered 2/22/02, your present correspondent was sitting in the front room of her country house in Woodstock watching the news on television when she heard the sound of a car very close to the house or in the driveway. By the time she reached the front door window, the car was gone. But the motion sensor light on the garage door, which indicates motion in the driveway or of a vehicle close on the lane, had activated. Without thinking to do more than test the air temperature whilst away from the TV, I then walked to the back door in the kitchen, and opened it. To my surprise, I saw a low slung sports car without headlights on going down the next lane which can be seen through the adjacent yards in winter when the hedge trees have no leaves. This is not a type of car often seen in this neighborhood. I wondered why on this morning I should notice it. The news had been largely about the murder in Pakistan of kidnapped Wall Street Journal reporter Daniel Pearl.

Was I seeing the supernatural "death coach", an ancient omen of death in modern form, or was this yet another example of odd activity inspired by the wealthy occult club "Thantatos" about which I had just posted a brief statement on my website? Speculation about this elusive network of rogue operatives will appear throughout this book.

When I posted the draft of my satiric screenplay, formerly well-reviewed on Francis Coppola's Zoetrope website and entitled *The Undercover/Wear Trigger Org* as written under the pen name of Zephyr Fidelis, I had made commentary linking the

DOING BUSINESS IN THE ADIRONDACKS by E. Macer-Story

fictional satire to an actual cult of renegade intellectuals who might be playing the Islamic terrorists as dupes and pawns of a larger, more cynical and adept plan. If the "Thantatos" cult had kept up on my website postings, then this early morning drive-by without headlights might indicate recognition of that posting. OR this had actually been an omen, a warning related to the death of Daniel Pearl, who was lured to his death by a renegade operative posing as a sophisticated ally.

Also on this same morning I got what was obviously a crank call made to an old apartment number then linked to a voice mail forwarding service. The caller, using a suspiciously suave baritone voice, had left a message saying that:"Mike has told me you were having trouble with your long distance service." Mike is the first name of a superintendent at the apartment building where I first was issued that phone number. But Mike Luckman is also the name of an associate I had recently spoken to over the phone from my Magick Mirror Communications office about an upcoming project I had then been scripting about the frequency of alleged "ufo sightings" in Chile & Argentina as this might relate to the politics and technical; achievements of an alleged neo-Nazi commune which has been in an area of Tierra del Fuego since the mid-twentieth century, just prior to World War II.

This may sound fantastic to you, dear reader, if you are not familiar directly with occult groups or the psychology of cults. Please bear with this narration until, like the aspiring neophyte, you get into the rhythms of this arcane mindset.

At three in the morning on February 25, 2002, your present correspondent woke with an unusual film in her throat and had to sit up in bed to keep from choking. After clearing my throat, I decided to check a painting I was then developing and decided to add a small detail. I was standing in front of the easel looking at this detail as it fit into the entire design, and glanced down at the long skirt of my cotton nightgown. There was a clean cut slit in the fabric at the level of my right knee. This cut was about three inches long and was intersected by a smaller cut about one half inch long and perpendicular to the neat, vertical slit. I had not worn this gown earlier when handling scissors or silverware. It occurred to me that this might be a poltergeist act of aggression related to my waking up with a choking film in my throat.

I recalled a similar effect some years previous when I was experimenting mentally with the medieval "memory wheels" preserved in the fourteenth century by Spanish sorcery adept Ramon Lull. This process, similar to meditation exercises using diagrams or special chants, simply involves memorizing the Latin names of attributes on two or more separate wheels and by an act of ,memory and visualization putting the separate wheels together in the desired combination. This "matching" process has been called by some "the first computer". For example, the practitioner might put the attribute "simplicity" from one wheel into the category of "business" on another wheel by visualizing the two wheels overlaid upon each other and turning one wheel mentally to "dial" the desired combination. One can readily understand that though the example given here is relatively harmless a form of hexing could occur by the use of less mild categories on the memory wheels being utilized.

I had, in fact, actually memorized two of Lull's original memory wheels in Latin, as given in an academic sourcebook on "The Art of Memory" and was drawing the wheels from memory on my drafting table as part of the meditation exercise. I do not recall which exact categories I had chosen to actualize. But I will never forget what

DOING BUSINESS IN THE ADIRONDACKS by E. Macer-Story

happened as I brought the two wheels together in my mind to "dial" the desired result. Suddenly, there was a sharp pain in my left hand as I was drawing the "memory wheel" of attributes on tracing paper to overlay it literally upon the wheel of categories. I looked down at my hand and noticed that blood had begun to flow from a small, deep cut as if my hand had been stabbed with the point of an invisible knife. I immediately ceased drawing the diagrams of Ramon Lull, feeling I had crossed the boundary of protection placed over someone else's system of mental magick. At that time, I construed this to be a protection placed centuries ago by the adept Ramon Lull. At this present writing, I am not convinced that such an effect was the work of Lull himself six centuries ago. For, using plain common sense, it is obvious that the diagrams appeared in a modern book I had recently bought at a book store and there is no guarantee that the diagrams included were the actual, original memory wheels of Ramon Lull. In the intervening centuries, these diagrams passed through many hands and any one of these successive diagram owners, including the author of the modern text, could have placed a protective mental postscript upon the original medieval texts devised by Lull. OR these were not he original memory wheels of Ramon Lull at all. For Spanish Kabbalists of the Fourteenth century are said in tradition to have each devised an original system. The use of standard diagrams in mental magick did not come into vogue until such items could be duplicated on the printing press in the Sixteenth century.

Actually, the painting to which I had added a detail at three in the morning might be construed by some theorists to be such an individual system of mental action. For the scene depicted was an area near a highway where numerous "haunting" incidents had been reported, including anomalous effects to buses and cars. I had learned during grass roots investigation of this area that a motorcycle gang practicing "black magick" was active somewhere in the adjacent area and was probing this concept in my painting. The larger vista of this picture shows the highway intersection with a charred bus frozen in place by snow under the tires and a creature of advanced Interdimensional discernment rising from the asphalt, though partly obscured by a bright red mathematical diagram. As I painted, I had become aware that the situation I was probing by "remote viewing" was not simple in the sense of perhaps a violent gang crime but was also complex in the sense of participation by an intellect capable of using mathematical systems.

.The details I had added to this painting just before noticing the cut to my gown were the literal image of an old-fashioned wooden ruler and the red "sigma" sign indicating complex mental manipulation in the situation. My intent was to measure the undefined abstract activity by the material, common sense, ruler in order to define the practical means by which this nexus might be discussed. It seems I have found some entry into discussing what may be, in effect, Interdimensional crime of a very sophisticated nature by simply referring back to the cut in my drawing hand caused by manipulating the alleged "memory wheels" of Ramon Lull. Note that in this instance no blood was drawn. The cut in the fabric was a mild reminder of the previous wounding by calculated mental action, which had been both painful and frightening.

The full moon of February 2002 occurred on the twenty-seventh of that month. At six-thirty in the morning, when I opened the back kitchen door at my country house in Woodstock to leave scraps for the animals before catching the early commuter bus to my city public contact office, I found a white marijuana leaf on the top step in front of the door. This was soft and pale as if bleached in solution or grown in darkness. Later, on my

DOING BUSINESS IN THE ADIRONDACKS by E. Macer-Story

way out of the front driveway, I noticed a rain-soaked "burial insurance" brochure laid out on the asphalt lane in front of my mailbox. This featured a baby's face as representative of family concerns and the banner of the brochure read:"$7,000 burial expenses ".I had spoken over the telephone with a broker in Tulsa, Oklahoma the day before about transferring an amount less that this but in the thousands of dollars as part of the settlement of a family estate. It occurred to me that, unless this stuff was the result of very expert full moon telepathy, there might be a tap on my telephone.

There is in these situations of superstition always an interplay between actual events which may seem spooky and the accumulated backlog of fictional and legendary lore into which fresh events are set by circumstance. Do human beings alone do these peculiar things, such as leaving a pale marijuana leaf under the full moon, and thus augment superstitious feelings in both themselves and others? Or does some "full moon" activated spirit or interdimensional creature have the power to thus produce brochures which match telephone conversations, and spook humans, for whatever purpose? Or is this process of matching and/or generating material events directly from the patterning of inner mental states some combination of interlinked human and non-human intelligence? Many of the ancient alchemists and sorcerers, working without electronic augmentation and before the printing press, stressed the necessity to "form a link" with an angel or spirit in order to accomplish marvelous transmutations and transformations.

But is there a downside to this "linking" business which so easily produces material effects? Like any other form of business, the quality of the exchange will depend on all of the associates and clients and not just upon the CEO who makes the initial transaction contract. The film "Fearless Vampires Killers" or "Pardon me, Your Teeth Are In My Neck" , a satire by the young Roman Polanski which starred his wife Sharon Tate as a clever vampire, was produced in Europe in 1967, just one year and some months before actress Tate and Polanski's unborn child were murdered by the Charles Manson gang in the infamous California crime generally known as the Tate-LaBiana murders, though others at he scene were executed as well

It is not generally known or stressed by investigators and reporters who have studied this California crime situation that Polanski's fictional film, originally titled "Bal De Les Vampires" .and quite satiric of the elitist neo-Fascist crowd in Europe, was produced such a short time before the bizarre death of his pregnant wife Sharon Tate and her house guests. Speculation upon this theme of elitist revenge will take place later in this book. Meanwhile, be aware, dear reader, that there is another film director, Stanley Kubrick who died of a heart attack in 1999 just after editing his film MASKS, which seriously depicts a wealthy, elitist "black magick" cult operating incognito in masks and little else but mad arrogance. It has been firmly stated by friends and associates that Kubrick's heart attack was a natural occurrence brought about by stress. Quite so. Apparently, there is no evidence of conventional skullduggery. But how about unconventional skullduggery, the deliberate focus of an adept mental magician and/or hypnotist upon harming director Kubrick, who had dared to make public commentary upon perverse elitist practices he fictionalized as occurring at a nude, masked ball. The same "Ball of the Vampires" as intuited by Polanski thirty years prior to the Kubrick film? Perhaps some version of this banquet of death has really been held for a number of years by those attempting to secretly perpetuate the elitist idea of social and political organization which , as National Socialism, was on the losing side in World War Two.

Yet, if a hexing or curse had been placed on both of these public performances, is this entirely human, political skullduggery? Or are the human beings who may be covertly dancing a macabre version of ancient aristocratic and royalist social ritual actually the pawns of a diabolic form on non-human intelligence which they misconstrue as lending them power?

On February 11, 2002, your present correspondent woke at three in the morning after spending a long evening updating the various interlinked "Magick Mirror" and "Yankee Oracle" websites. and went to get a snack in the kitchen. I was sitting in the darkness at a table adjoining the kitchen counter where there was only one light reflecting into a window above the sink from a fixture across the room. I glanced up toward the window reflection and was startled to see the apparition in the dark glass of a brunette, Caucasian man in a high collar, who was looking at me with sympathy. I had a visceral rejection of this experience and moved to another perspective of the window. The image of the sympathetic man in outdated business dress remained in the glass of the window, or outside the window. Finally, I went back to bed, not having managed to erase the reflected image except by turning off the light entirely. The following morning I noticed that a copy of the book "Walden" by Henry David Thoreau which was under an envelope at the far end of the kitchen counter had a similar head and shoulders sketch of that Nineteenth century author. The sketch was not literally reflected onto the window pane since it was partly under the envelope and at the wrong angle. Could a sympathetic non-human intelligence be trying to communicate positive intentions, or was this actually a deceptive presence attempting to reference stereotypes of the past, thus sidetracking future speculations?

On February 19' 2002, after I had taken care of pending playscript business at a nearby theater in New York, I went into the grocery stone at Twelfth Street and Sixth Avenue to get some items for my bare larder in Woodstock before taking an evening commuter bus upstate. While shopping, I felt the "presence" of a dark mental energy which I have felt before in that same area of West Greenwich Village.

When I was residing nearby that grocery, I became increasingly uncomfortable about going out to this particular store in the evening and finally avoided it entirely after dark. My visit to this store premises in the evening was simply a matter of convenience due to the playscript appointment nearby. During the next day, I had an unusual realization which caused me to re-think the experience in the West Village grocery store. I had in the meantime dismissed this impression of "dark presence" as simply a hangover from a theatrical appointment which involved claiming several of my scripts from the artistic director of a theater whose CEO had become senile. These scripts had been adorned with notes on the stationary of a major brokerage firm which said simply "yes" and "no" .For the brokerage firm appeared to be caring for the senile theatrical CEO and in the process making production decisions. I learned that though the theater did not have sufficient staff to actually produce any of my scripts some had made it upwards into the "yes" category. One runs into these conundrums in Greenwich Village. Should I have been happy that the "yes" notes outnumbered the "no" notes or should I have worried about the future of the senile CEO? Instead, like a character in an Arthur Miller play, I went across the street and got groceries.

Just before keeping my appointment at the small West Village theater, I had a minor office visit medical treatment involving a tiny metal and plastic patch... I assumed

DOING BUSINESS IN THE ADIRONDACKS by E. Macer-Story

this small patch was a certain size. But when I checked this patch one day afterward it was <u>not</u> the same size and exact shape I had assumed it would be. It was fine. It fit well, and you would not notice this metal and plastic patch, dear reader, if I was sitting six inches in front of your nose .It is tiny and unimportant. But it was not the expected size I had assumed. It was smaller. I measured it against a worn out older patch. It was smaller. It should have been exactly the same size. Something tangible indeed had "happened" during the evening I felt the dark "presence". But what exactly?

I recall glimpsing in the mirror of the medical office as I was putting on my coat to leave the lobby a brief, odd impression of another angry, gray-haired face (older and more stressed than myself0 which immediately became a normal reflection when I checked the larger mirror on the opposite wall. On previous occasions, this type of face— which appears to be an older version of myself but on a negative destiny pattern—has warned me to beware of treachery and to take firm action to separate from some circumstance which seems almost "customary" but within which I do have an "exit" option.

The medical treatment cannot be faulted. But the situation at the small theater with "yes/no" notes from a brokerage firm pasted to playscripts was bizarre. I did some research and determined that the management of this theater was now also connected with a group of stage magicians who announced connections with cultural projects in Germany. Indeed, this connection was not propitious for me or for anyone connected with mysticism or ESP/PK. I looked over the "yes/no" notes more carefully and found that the "no" notes occurred on all of the plays which overtly mentioned supernatural topics in the introduction and the "yes" notes occurred mainly on my musical satires and politically-oriented dramas. The "danger" signal was of course the influence of moneyed stage magicians on cultural issues. More will be narrated of the European and South American stage magic and quaisi-shamanic trickster connections later in this book.

I decided in this context to move forward swiftly with my plans to re-establish a firm independent presence in a new public "Magick Mirror office space in the west Village area. I do not think I would have moved as swiftly had I not stumbled across the influence of the foreign stage magic interests within the organization of the small theater with "yes/no" brokerage management over the decisions of the senile CEO. This is the same theater where in 1981 your present correspondent had met the South American shaman on his way to Canada who figures as a "trip not taken" in the previous book by this same author, entitled DR. FU MAN CHU MEETS THE LONESOME COWBOY: SORCERY AND THE UFO EXPERIENCE . For in the meeting with the Hispano-Canuk Sufi there was a preternatural "warning" or indication of unusual energy in the form of a plastic "spare part" from some unknown electronic machine which manifested upon my kitchen table the morning that I decided to cancel the expedition this individual had proposed.

At that time I did not specifically associate this rogue Sufism with the theater itself as many artists and writers flow through the Thanksgiving festivities and I assumed the traveler from Mexico to Canada was simply a wandering philosopher/performer. However, twenty years later in context of recent terrorism involving the Al Quaida network and this connection with international drug trade partly based in South America, I have a new perspective on this rogue "Sufi" I encountered , who was Arabic in appearance. A connection between the brokerage management of the theater and rogue

DOING BUSINESS IN THE ADIRONDACKS by E. Macer-Story

financial interests is quite possible in context of the established firm being ignorant of the local, theatrical machinations. This may be an operational pattern as artists and performance groups are sometimes taken lightly and not thoroughly examined by authorities.

For, by the use of common sense, it can easily be determined locally that such elaborate international scaffolding is not necessary in order to run the usual off-off Broadway community theater. No names are given in this account, dear reader, because such operatives are extremely clever and adaptive performers and can change their modus operandi in the twinkling of an eye. I should comment that the USO employee "Carol" who disappeared in Germany in the 1970's after claiming that trucks of the light opera were being used to transport contraband (as described in this reporter's article entitled *ESPionage: Has Mind Control Replaced the Cloak and Dagger?*published in PURSUIT magazine in1983) experienced a fate which does fit within this general " hand is quicker than the eye" paradigm.

Yet there is a form of natural magick native to New York state which is similar in effect to the "sleight of hand" used by stage conjurors and yet originates in the nexus of some mysterious link between the mind of the individual and the cosmos at large. After buying the Koffee Kake muffins in the health food store, I glanced down in sleight amazement at the four extra dollar bills which had appeared in my wallet while the cashier was making change from the five dollar bill I had handed her. As usual, I had added an extra dime to the five dollar bill so that after my $1.09 purchase I would have exactly four one dollar bills to purchase the One Day Metrocard Fun Pass I use when I have a number of errands to run quickly. So four one dollar bills were on my mind when the extra four dollars appeared in my wallet. Specifically, when I placed the penny change from the dime in the cashier's penny dish and then went to put the four bills in my wallet I found that I already had four one dollar bills there plus the single one dollar bill I had noticed before asking the cashier to make change from the five dollar bill.

In other words, previous to purchasing the muffin for $1.09, I had six dollars plus small change in the outer compartment of my wallet. Subsequent to purchasing this muffin, I had nine dollars and small change in the outer compartment of my wallet.

For a number of years, small bills have materialized in my wallet in various locations in New York City and upstate in the Catskill and Adirondack mountains.

Your present correspondent will not bore you with each instance of this miraculous cash flow since though the amounts have been small, the instances of materialization have been many. There is a legend in the Catskill village where the four dollars appeared as I was idly contemplating the four dollar price of a subway ride that whatever you think/do there will boomerang back upon you. In one extreme version of this situation, a woman who had browsed over a dart board at the local hardware store in the town of Woodstock, N.Y. did not buy this item for her daughter because she thought it was dangerous. She then left this store to walk a few blocks down the street to an outdoor community book sale at the library and was accidentally hit as she walked by a metal-tipped dart thrown by a child just as she was approaching the book tables on the library lawn. Lest this seen too droll, dear re4ader, it should be noted that this dart drew blood.

Now, four extra dollar bills and one small metal-tipped toy dart are not large items. But the larger pattern seems to be that events and objects which are focused on in

DOING BUSINESS IN THE ADIRONDACKS by E. Macer-Story

the practical sense whilst doing business in certain New York State areas do seen to solidly materialize or be drawn to the citizen or traveler in some uncanny way. Someone familiar with "new physics" terminology might comment that these areas facilitate the "self-organization" of material events.

Yet, dear reader, it would be unwise to visit these areas of anomaly—as will be discussed in this book—with an idea of thus materializing one's fortune to happen and one's coveted sweetheart to approach. For there is a fey quality to these mind/matter matching events . It seems that Intelligences with opinions and an independent agenda may facilitate certain of these "matching" events in order to make some very palpable points of instruction.

When the core draft of data and concepts for this book had been word processed on the laptop computer and was then being printed from the desktop publishing computer, eleven pages of the total sixty-four had been printed when suddenly the virus banner: "You may think you are god but you are only a piece of shit". Appeared as displayed on the JFax Messenger display box. Shortly afterward, the entire Windows software programme melted swiftly off the screen.

Later, it was discovered that the virus attack had also critically impacted the hardware, rearranging an electronic "cluster" inside the hard drive and permanently sidelining the desktop computer. Fortunately, the initial printing of the short. core draft could be successfully completed on the laptop.

This incident reminded me of two previous electronic erasures connected with investigations involving possible "sorcery" and/or "ufo contact". When your present correspondent was investigating the Tobyhanna Materiels Depot sightings in 1980, the central contactee (pseudonymed in the original discussion in the book "Sorcery and The UFO Experience" 1991) had sent from Boston an audio tape about her many notable experiences as a clairvoyant and about her alleged involvement with the World War Two Nazi ahnenerbe in a previous lifetime.

When I played this audio tape in my then Seventeenth Street apartment in the Chelsea section of Manhattan, it spontaneously reversed after I had heard this woman's narration about "ufo contact" in this lifetime and "black magick" experimentation in a previous lifetime. At the time of this electronic event, it seemed to me that this was "magickal" psychokinesis or "spirit intervention" of some sort having to do with whatever the previous "ahnenerbe" or "black magick" involvement may have been in another lifetime or even in obscure circumstances during this woman's present lifetime.

But, in light of twenty-first century electronic virus interference effects, there is also the possibility that the Tobyhanna contactee tape sent from Boston in 1980 was somehow rigged by sophisticated electronic means to deliver controversial information and then erase itself. This blank tape would thus tend to discredit any statements about Nazis, past or future, as associated with the Tobyhanna contactee's situation. A bit of "stage magic" perhaps? Or a genuine mind/matter event such as the apport of small plastic parts in situations involving subtle chicanery when the anomalous apport serves as a materially puzzling signal or warning?

For by a series of serendipitous (or rigged?) events, this Tobyhanna contactee had come to be living in the Boston area with a man named James Schneller who claimed that his father had been a big wheel in Hitler's "sharp shooting" elite corps during World War Two. Schneller was working at that time in a civilian capacity for the Navy as a "health physicist". He was later transferred from Pennsylvania to the Philippines. Since after the publication of an article mentioning his activities in the Tobyhanna situation was published in the *MUFON UFO JOURNAL* in the mid-1980's Schneller had paid a visit to that editorial office in Texas, very concerned about the "relationship" of your present correspondent with several male editors she happens never to have met face to face. So this insertion of gratuitous social and sexual issues did not "work" in that particular instance. But in other instances a "setup" could occur and so caution has been used by your present correspondent in trailing such as Schneller since that time. The proper response to sorcery and/or covert "stage magic" techniques used as espionage or mind control is not naïve "tracking" of the perpetrators in any conventional sense. Techniques must be used which match the level of mental and covert activity used by the perpetrators.

Down a long tunnel which is the iris of my eye becoming the dark, smooth-sided solenoid at the center of a peacock feather I slide like a child in an amusement park into the sanctuary of the unspeakable. The ancient gods are trying to reassert themselves.

Somewhere in the astral regions, they have always been roaming whilst their temples lie now in ruins. Some found and excavated by archeologists. Others buried so deeply in the jungle and under tundra that though some structures are seen now as mound temples to be excavated other—perhaps more significant—places of ancient ritual are completely unknown.

The astral continuum being the closest tie to the material past of these "god creatures", many remain attached to the area of the hidden temples or to any actual discussion of worship rituals which goes beyond light academic talk or comic book characters.

Soldier of fortune Aymon De Sales described his experiences with malevolent energy at Mexican temple sites to your present correspondent during a dinner discussion at his apartment in the Chelsea section of New York City in 1994. This account was also published in *BORDERLANDS* magazine in 1994. DeSales and a few other people had toured ancient pyramids in Mexico. When left alone at the apex of the pyramid, DeSales experienced a negative telepathic Intelligence which then haunted him in other locations. This disturbing Intelligence was not pleased with his presence at the pyramid..

Or was this seeming displeasure actually a "communication" which was not pleasant simply because it was not expected? Similar communications at historical locations have been experienced by persons ranging from the wife of a Victorian dabbler into the magickal arts who felt herself to be possessed by an ancient Egyptian spirit on through the cultural continuum to a variety of people who have written to FATE magazine and similar publications describing the experience of meeting ghosts in old castles or battlefield locations.

The difference here is that the "New Age" visitors to the Mexican pyramid ruins were psyched up for a different sort of adventure than actually occurred to Mr. de Sales. By his own account in conversation, de Sales and his companions were typical intellectual hippies of the 1960-70's era who had smuggled marijuana past various authorities and made a connection between altered states of consciousness in the pharmacological sense and religious experience connected with ancient cultures.

Possibly the non-religious aspects of the telepathic approach to de Sales by spirit intelligence at the pyramid basically violated the presupposition that numinous Advanced

DOING BUSINESS IN THE ADIRONDACKS by E. Macer-Story

Intelligence would appear in golden and inspirational form, the LSD of the Beatles song "Lucy in the Sky with Diamonds", a controlled experience limited to the known effects of chemical substance upon the organic mechanism..

The question arises: Why are all tourists to these pyramids not haunted? Why particularly Aymon DeSales? Because of his innate sensitivity? Or for other reasons which are part of an agenda not apparent in the late 1960's when the strange, particular haunting occurred only to Aymon and not to other members of his party, all of whom had passed away at the time I heard this narration.

Much literary criticism has been written about tracing the "real" autobiographical origins of the mystery and horror fictions written by Edgar Allen Poe and Sir Arthur Conan Doyle. This sort of speculation may be more to the point than looking for arcane scholastic and literary references.

It is a fact that Edgar Allen Poe lived as a young man not far from the Jefferson Market triangle area of Manhattan island, a place among other places of continual mystery which figure in narrations about actual vampiric and non-local physics information connections throughout this book. Sir Arthur Conan Doyle's Sherlock Holmes story "The Crucifer of Blood" will also be considered from a non-fictional standpoint as this relates to the survival of clandestine, opium-oriented killer cults from antiquity .It is possible that such a cult may have attempted to discredit Sir Conan Doyle's 19th Century research into spiritualism.

On February 11, 2001, a statement was released on the Internet by *AQUARIAN PERSPECTIVES INTERPLANETARY MISSION* which might seem fictional or false to most people unfamiliar with talismanic sorcery. This group vowed to carry a magic wand made of crystal with a crystal sphere at the top around to various geographical locations in order to implement World Peace. However, according to their account of this mission, the magic crystal rod disappeared upon their return to their home base in Los Angeles from their World-Pilgrimage "with major initiation sojourns in Egypt, Greece, India, Tibet, Nepal Mexico and the USA." Whatever else might be thought about this endeavor, it was a real geographical trip .These were actual people who believe:" Never fret if a magic talisman is lost for it will go where it is meant to serve best. "There will be more about this *AQUARIAN PERSPECTIVES* group later in this book when the unfortunate car accident of Randal Baer, author of the book *THE CRYSTAL CONNECTION* , is discussed in context of individuals who hold a Satanic version of the "crystal rod" belief system.

Librarians and those with a literary orientation often make the mistake of looking for the source of a fictional character in a book or in some written facet of an author's known identity. Frequently writers will take their characters directly from life or from imagination & inspiration. I know this is true of the plays and short stories I write. There is a definite difference between my reporting of paranormal & supernatural events and the writing of a playscript. *However* ,I find that my plays particularly are often inadvertently prescient.

For example: I wrote a play called *SCHEMES OF CONQUEST* which was produced in Boston years ago. This is a farcical comedy about a professor with illusions of power who starts a bacteria epidemic which ends up in possible mass explosions of wads of bacteria out of control. This terror epidemic is averted by a member of a secret occult motorcycle group called The Last of Methuselah (his name) who teams up with a gorgeous baby sitter and a grandmother to avert the catastrophe and outwit the professor.

DOING BUSINESS IN THE ADIRONDACKS by E. Macer-Story

Today we learn that the nuclear power plant at Three Mile Island has been threatened by terrorists and that alleged anthrax was sent from Atlanta, Georgia to a doctor in Kenya.. I have previously done an article & book review on a book by Larry Arnold (motorcycle jacket} about premonitions of the previous Three Mile Island disaster. At that time--which was subsequent to the production of *SCHEMES OF CONQUEST*--it was obvious that the publication of the review was drawing nuisance attention. This nuisance attention may *not* have been coming from U.S. government sources. The anthrax envelope sent to Kenya--for example--may indicate a far right conspiracy. Never forget that Dag Hamerskjold of the U.N. was kidnapped & murdered (suspicious plane crash) by South African white supremacists during a visit to Africa.

Am I "The Last of Methuselah", the "Baby Sitter" or the Theosophical :Grandma"???? Stay tuned.

Meanwhile, note how much the following narrative—which was received over the Internet—resembles a fey science fiction play like *SCHEMES OF CONQUEST*. Yet rocket scientist Dr.Werner Von Braun, who was imported from Nazi Germany after World War Two to assist in developing the United States guided missile program was quite real. Why do we feel that the observations of a scientist like Herman Oberth about the certainty of ufo contact are doomed to be wrong or fictional? What is holding back the realization of such possibilities? Prejudice against the truly "supernatural" which has been instilled by pop psychology? Check it out. When you read the following narrative from Frank Edwards' book "Strange World" as recently posted on a UFO INFO Internet list, you will not be able to believe it. I am including this quotation not because I "believe" it but because I am an investigative reporter. .

DR. HANS NIEPER SAYS ALIENS ARE VISITING US

"Bruce Jessop writes, 'I would like to share something with you which is not a sighting but a meeting I had in November 1998 with a Dr. Hans Nieper who unfortunately has since passed away in Germany. We were talking about various things and the subject of antigravity came up. He has written a book on the subject. And I noticed in his office that he had photos of himself with a couple of other well-known people and US presidents. After some minutes he asked me if I believed in UFO's? I shared with him two sightings that I had back in New Brunswick, Canada and Montreal in 1981 as a huge craft slowly glided across the highway no more than 35 yards in front of my car.
He asked me "What do you think the highest classified secret of the US government is?" I waited and he answered, "The US government have made contact with four races of alien life." He described them as follows:
1) Short grays. 2) Tall grays. 3) Reptilian, 4) tall, fair skinned humanoids, like this part of the world. Dr. Nieper was a world-renowned medical doctor. But most revealing, after he told me about the four races, I asked him where he got this information. He just pointed to the wall and there was a photo of him and Werner von Braun. He told me that he had had early involvement with von Braun, starting up NASA and was privy to classified information. He was an intimate friend of von Braun. Dr.Nierper was also an astrophysicist and had gone to study the pyramids in Egypt and wrote an article to show proof that the stones had been cut with a laser device.' Thanks to CAUS and Bruce

DOING BUSINESS IN THE ADIRONDACKS by E. Macer-Story

Jessop for letting me use his article.
Editor's Note German scientist Hermann Oberth who headed an official,
West German, three year UFO study group and is considered the father of
rocketry, stated in 1954, "There is no doubt in my mind that these objects (UFO's)
are interplanetary craft of some sort. I am confident that they do not
originate in our solar system, but they may use Mars or some other body for a way
station. It is also our conclusion that they are propelled by distorting or
converting the gravitational field[1]."

A recurring theme in a direct haunting I have experienced at my home in Woodstock, N.Y. ever since seeing a phantom in my living room as I was preparing to leave for the commuter bus and later, on the return commuter bus , meeting by chance an old friend of the ghost's who enthusiastically identified my casual description, is the gem magick gent Fredrick Von Mieres, who does not quit. Every time I think I have shaken this unquiet spirit (a phantom perhaps of Germanic-Hispanic descent), I meet his interlocutor Tom Walker "by chance" in the post office or on the commuter bus. According to Walker, Frederick Von Mieres was a practitioner of "gem magick" and the author of a book on occult systems and Christianity who committed suicide under mysterious circumstances. In an effort to rationalize my initial experience with this unusual saga revolving about a man I never knew and a type of sorcery I do not practice, I simply asked some questions about gem therapy of a professed experiencer of gem "teletherapy" without telling the entire tale..

Subj: **Re: gem teletherapy**
Date: 2/8/2000 11:14:18 AM Eastern Standard Time
From: whale@anon..uk (John)
To: MagickMirr@aol.com
-Benoytosh Bhattacharya is the man who wrote the books--Gem therapy,
teletherapy, etc. His son is alive AK Bhattacharya, around about 60 years
old. Lives in India, may have his address somewhere.
He mentions in a book, or his father does, how the wearing of a ruby ring
made one mans business fold and his health to go. So you can draw your own
conclusions. It would depend on the mans astro makeup presumably.
D AK was acquainted with a friend of mine some time ago--they don't have
much contact now.
Original Message:
In a message dated 2/7/2000 3:43:36 PM Eastern Standard Time, whale@anon.uk writes: gem
therapist
Dr Battachyra (spelling) did say it was possible with gem teletherapy.
[E.Macer-Story]
What is the exact spelling of this name? I am currently researching an
instance of gem sorcery which resulted in a suicide. Any references on the
use of gemstones for magick would be most welcome.

At the very end of this book, dear Reader, you will find a few more investigative details about Fredrick Von Mieres the gem magician and his perplexing fate. Hopefully, the intervening narration will render the fatal reaction of sometime fashion model Von Mieres to his own circumstances more comprehensible.

DOING BUSINESS IN THE ADIRONDACKS by E. Macer-Story

Many interpretations of gem qualities and powers are available from a variety of sources. It seems that the qualities of gemstones used for sorcery are very particular as to the individuals involved and the system of interpretation employed. Or is this so? On October 23, 2001 as I was just beginning to draft this book , there was a bizarre event during which a double exposure of a sales feature on channel 62 about gems and jewelry kept interrupting the continual terrorism news coverage on CNN. I was idly watching TV while waiting for a locksmith to arrive and open a strongbox of family documents to which the key had been lost. I assumed this gem/news split screen might be therefore a family haunting but in retrospect it might have been the spirit of Fred the gemologist as there was some attempt to link Fred's suicide with clandestine business or contraband of some kind.

The following translation by Scott Corrales concerns the sighting during the same period of time as Fred's gem sorcery haunting began in the Northeast United States of an unidentified object in Argentina

Cordoba, Republic of Argentina, Sunday, January 30, 2000
"Intervoz de Cordoba" newspaper

INTENSE SEARCH FOR ALLEGED AEROLITH AT SANTIAGO DEL ESTERO

" Ramon Agustin, a porter at Provincial School No. 188 "Andres Bello"
explained that the phenomenon he witnessed caused "a very strong impact"
in him, since he "had no idea what was falling down. I felt considerable
panic and fear."
Rojas explained that the fireball "was quite large and descended rapidly
from the north toward the south, accompanied by loud whistling and
thunder."
" This is the first time that such an event was
recorded in the area, "added Olga Bertolotti, the local commissioner. She
further stated that "many curiosity seekers have approached the area
where the object fell, but as the "baqueanos" have explained, access to
the area is considerably difficult due to heavy forestation. Many technicians, investigators and
astronomers appeared in the area, contracting the services of the
"baqueanos", and have taken off to conduct their own research, in some
kind of race to see who finds the object first," concluded Bertolotti.[2]

Indeed. During this same time period of the early Millennium year, the following dialogue appeared as a web posting:

Subj: **"The Stargate Conspiracy"**
Date: 2/6/2000 12:09:49 PM Eastern Standard Time

We have the innate prejudice that such unexplained, interruptive events only happen in the remote selva (jungle).But is this actually true?
[Aexus]

DOING BUSINESS IN THE ADIRONDACKS by E. Macer-Story

Beat physicist raconteur has commented:
"Number Ny-unn, Number Ny-unn, Number Ny-unn?"
in response to discussions of the spirit guides/perhaps extraterrestrials said to guide the endeavors of his particular neo-tech bohemian crowd in San Francisco, as well as public officials in other terrestrial and historical locations.
[Sarfatti]
C'mon now, Aexus, Stevie Wonder Boy Schwartz told you this was only vanity press from a super megalomaniac, it takes one to know one of course, for an imaginary book and an imaginary TV series. Surely you do not take any of this seriously? This sort of thing has been going on in the Café Trieste for many years. It is Bohemia. This is all promo for my book DESTINY MATRIX at
[Aexus]
Oh, Jack. Puhleeeze! Methinketh thou doth protesteth too muchly, PhysicsMan! Are you saying that NONE of what you are talking about here is true,
[Jack]
No, all the isolated events are true to the best of my memory. I am not saying that. I am saying that your particular interpretation of how to link these isolated events, how to connect the dots is essentially not true. However, there is room for legitimate disagreement here on the subtle complex matter of interpretation, what Wheeler calls "the paper mache" of theory imposed on the "few iron posts of observation". ...
I do not weight the significance of all the patent conspiratorial nonsense in the book equal to the significance of my solid reliable information. What they have is mostly rumor and eccentric interpretations of legends. Nothing solid except for my information, Einhorn's and a few other tidbits. It's quality, not quantity, that counts.""

[E.Macer-Story notes:]Yet interpretation is also how we select facts and what exactly we select as being facts. Dr. Sarfatti quotes here from the book "The Stargate Conspiracy" hoping to relay what he regards as being rock bottom fact.

Page 205-206: "Puharich had qualified as a doctor and neurologist at Northwestern University in 1947 under a US Army training scheme, but was then discharged from the Army on medical grounds. He set up the Round Table Foundation in Glen Cove, Maine, in 1948, and ran it until 1958, working with psychics including Eileen Garrett and Peter Hurkos, as well as first making contact with the Nine through Dr. Vinod, and with Rahotep through Harry Stone. In addition Puharich was also carrying out secret research for the defense and intelligence establishments in two main areas: techniques of psychological manipulation, including the use of hallucinogenic drugs; and the military and intelligence capabilities of psychic skills. His own account records that his work with Vinod was interrupted for several months in 1953 because (despite his medical discharge) he returned to Army service."[3]

It is tempting to attribute incidents such as described in the following excerpt from my ongoing journal of "exceptional incidents" as possible attempts by a "covert government project" to interfere with independent research into sorcery and ESP/PK

DOING BUSINESS IN THE ADIRONDACKS by E. Macer-Story

&/or to experiment on sensitive subjects. . But this interpretation does not actually fit the facts unless covert researchers are employing or cajoling shamans and spirit guides of shamans. Here's what happened:

"On January 5th, 2001 a crank call was left on my message tape in the Magick Mirror Space in the early hours of the morning by persons evidently impersonating "Reggae" or Islands music whilst a voice sounding like a child's voice made vaguely obscene statements. I kept the tape of this call.

Also on this day while outside taking a walk in the Woodstock "gap" area it occurred to me to link the odd pink semi-spheres on the photos of talismanic wands found in my yard in Woodstock on November 27 and December 29 of 2000 with the "flying head" vampire lights reported by Native Americans of previous centuries in this same area we now call the "Catskill Mountains".

On the next day (January 6,2000) while thinking about the "flying heads" of the journal entry above I opened the top drawer of my desk in Woodstock and found a note written awhile ago about a poet associated with RIFT literary magazine . This note made reference to a pun in which the "loop" of the editorial "delete" symbol means "wolf" ("loup" in French) in the sense of "werewolf". I had found a loop of fence wire in the shape of a long-tailed "delete" loop and thought it might mean "delete" as a form of sophisticated hex. This was several years ago. It was a thick, steel wire hard to form into a loop except deliberately. "

It is quite possible that persons with a sophisticated knowledge of symbology are experimenting with the use of editorial and/or mathematical symbols as a basis for sorcery rather than the familiar astrological and alchemical archetypes.
Also, according to a former client of Dutch clairvoyant H/ Dykestrom, this accurate psychical practitioner used such a loop of metal wire to "clear the air"about the subject of negative auric influences. So such a loop left on a subject's property might indicate an attempt to place malefic energy into the auric and/or event-patterning fields of the target area and property owner. A spiral "aerial"-like metal rod also was found on the Woodstock property of your present correspondent during the 1998-99 high incidence period of talismanic littering by would-be shamans and magicians.

The excerpt from the book *THE STARGATE CONSPIRACY* as cited in the previous dialogue between Sarfatti himself and Aexus continues as follows:

"According to Jack Sarfatti, a physicist on the fringes of
the Puharich-Geller-Whitmore events of the mid-1970s, Puharich 'worked for
Army intelligence in the early fifties' -- (44) -- which perhaps implies that
his 'discharge' was a cover for continuing to operate in an apparently
civilian capacity. It also appears that some of Puharich's medical inventions
were originally developed as part of classified Army projects."

This is a very general statement. Puharich had developed a type of watch containing certain metal and crystal components which he was vending during the 1980's as a health improvement device. But this had something also to do with his research indicating Entity Presences signaling by arbitrary positioning of the hands on the dial of a watch. Possibly such classified projects might have concerned developing a digital gauge or signaling device similar to a quartz-pulsed watch by which reliable communications might be established with spirits or between humans by telepathy. Uri Geller, who was Puharich's most famous research subject, includes a crystal by which a telepathic/healing jump start can be achieved by the customer . Energizing this crystal involves a meditation at a certain time of day when Geller will also be focusing on energizing Psychic Kit crystals from his office in London.

Yet when your present correspondent met briefly and interacted with Puharich in 1986-87, he was deeply involved with Hawaiian huna magick and prophecy rather than primarily with the rivalries of government and academic research.
Once again in the case of Pujarich we have the odd intersection between enhanced abilities and perceptions of the acknowledged sorcerer and the contemporary folklore of technical and political "conspiracy".
Internet commentator Aexus has written:

*" Perhaps of more significance, PUHARICH's working for Army
intelligence at that time puts Andrija directly under the operational
supervision of General Trudeau and his deputy, Col. Phillip Corso, most
recently author of "The Day After Roswell" and its claims that "crashed
flying saucer" remains stimulated many of our technologies."*

Later in this book, Dear Reader, you will read of the investigation of the trickster identity of "Aexus" and learn why this individual is pseudonymed here. In this context, give some thought to the statement of Dr. Jack Sarfatti in this particular Internet dialogue :

*"Yes, what Rose said to me on the telephone was ambiguous enough that Ira could
have been an unwitting patsy, what is called a "useful idiot". I certainly was,
along with Bob Toben, Fred Alan Wolf and many of the "others". We were all puppets
on covert strings back in the 70's. This puppet is now pulling his own strings. "I
got no strings on me." (Disney's "Pinocchio") The Puppet Masters are now all dead
or dying or senile. Information is powerful. ...I am not working alone. Do you grok that?"*

Yet were these expanded consciousness pioneers the puppets of government intrigue OR of the manipulations of what French researcher Jacques Bergier calls "Intelligences", powerful non-human life forms with some interest or stake in the progress of human civilization on Earth. "Intelligences" not necessarily from another planet or solar system but perhaps from other dimensions and worlds directly attached to this material sphere by the "hyperspacial" links which the neo-tech shamans have attempted to probe under the aegis of "modern science", Perhaps we are sharing this planet with powerful neighbors of whom we are unaware on most occasions.
Aexus has commented about controversial 1970's guru figure Ira Einhorn:

*"Significantly, just three weeks before his arrest, Ira Einhorn gave a
lecture in Philadelphia in which, according to Stephen Levy (in "The
Unicorn's Secret"[4]): 'He said that for years he had been primarily interested in the relation of
nonphysical entities to the physical world. This led him to revelations,
he explained, that had startling consequences for our civilization.'*

E. Macer-Story interjects here: But are these "new" revelations? Tales of the interference with human destiny, for good or ill, by the djinn have been told in all human cultures since antiquity.

[Aexus]
"Levy also said of Einhorn's strange quest:
' As he delved deeper into the world of the paranormal, he became
increasingly convinced that recent psychic revelations (presumably a
reference to the Nine's communications) could have significant global impact.
In some scenarios, these could have alarming consequences.'
"He goes on to stress Einhorn's role in bringing about major changes through
the acceptance of the unexplained:
'Through his relationship with Andrija Puharich and others, in what he
jokingly called a 'psychic mafia', the Unicorn assumed a key role in the task
of alerting our people about the implications of this revolution...in
Einhorn's universe, those factors included the undeniability of UFOs, the
startling discoveries in quantum physics, and the inevitability of the new
world order -- shaken loose by the Aquarian Transformation.)
In the book "The Stargate Conspiracy" the authors comment:
"However, a dark shadow was cast over this early idyllic promise by the involvement of the
Pentagon, CIA and other security and intelligence agencies, who soon realized that the
breakthroughs of these idealists had great potential in their own spheres,
such as remote viewing. And they did not fail to note that research into
altered states of consciousness, including the use of LSD and other drugs,
also had darker applications in the various techniques of mind control. So
often this research was encouraged and funded -- although often covertly,
through other channels -- by organizations such as the CIA and the Pentagon.
One of the pioneers of LSD and consciousness research, John C. Lilly, worked
at the Esalen Institute for several years, as well as for the CIA, but only
on the condition that his research remain unclassified. This made things
difficult for him professionally, because nearly all other researchers in
this field were also working on classified projects, so he was unable to
share data with them and vice versa.
"Another case of behind-the-scenes agendas in this milieu involved Dr.
Brendan O'Regan, research director of Edgar Mitchell's Institute of Noetic
Sciences and a consultant to SRI, as well as research director for the
scientist-philosopher R. Buckminster Fuller. O'Regan arranged for the
experiments into the strange talents of Uri Geller at Birkbeck College,
London, in 1975 and was also closely involved with the Puharich-Whitmore
circle surrounding The Nine. And, since O'Regan's death in 1992, JACK
Sarfatti has claimed that he was also working with the CIA at this time,
writing:"

Or did these self-designated "Space, Time & Beyond" neo-physicists tap a force quite different from the abstract "Nine" they had envisioned, a real bucking bronco of Interdimensional Intelligence which was then and remains beyond their control? Some

DOING BUSINESS IN THE ADIRONDACKS by E. Macer-Story

vital component of shared reality only caricatured by calling on the "Nine"? Or unrealized components of LSD and ESP/PK research gone wild? Dr. John Lilly had some inkling of this possibility in his theories of the SSI solid state and non-organic, non-human intelligence which will be discussed later in this book.

Similar to the mistake made in attributing extraordinary acts of conspiracy to the government rather than to an individual's genius or some supernatural source may be the misinterpretation of concepts of "elixir" as being a literal beverage. However, the actual "crossing of the abyss" between local and topological or mystical cognition cannot by all logic and reason be solely dependent upon the trigger of some physical substance, drug or talisman.

When the computer software and hardware partitions were completely destroyed as I was printing the core draft of this book, this following section was the text on that particular page. This is a brief anthology of occult sayings by "Blue Resonant Human" , an individual who was during the 1990's very active on the Internet as a "Sacerdotal Knight of the National Security" and also claimed expertise in the legacy of terrestrial occult and Interdimensional lore. In this brief anthology of quotations provided by Brother Blue and entitled "Whitley [Strieber] and the Abyss" there is an introduction which cites "soma" or the " sacred beverage drunk by the Brahmins" . It seems that Brother Blue in his exegesis has taken the bait of the drug vendors who did service the global "expanded consciousness" contingent throughout the 1960's-70's in the wake of the Tim Leary/ Ken Kesey LSD antics . Or perhaps this citation could be taken to refer to the herb-oriented "Carlos Castaneda" sorcerers of the 1980's-90's if limited to the face value of "soma" as meaning a physical substance. However, there is no evidence that the ancients meant simply a material substance when mentioning "soma". Rather, this beverage is ,more like the mental/material "elixir" of the European medieval alchemists.

Brother Blue refers to the "subtle substance" cited by H.P. Blavatsky in her Secret Doctrine writings in this same way. It is actually humorous that the mystical "boat of Ra/Set" of the ancient Egyptian cosmology should be relegated to the status of the "apple of Eden" in the Judeo-Christian cosmology, which is then taken simply to be an image which occurred as the result of the ingestion of some potion of herbs and esoteric bread mold. If this were true, entire populations would have been wandering around in visionary stupor tripping over Arks and pyramids. Historians know this not to be true. The ancients were well-coordinated in the material realm and generated numerous structures and esoteric writings which were made in full consciousness of architectural and script-writing skills. Obviously, there was a distinction made by the temple builders of yore between inspiration and construction which does not occur when a person is sitting in the shade smoking weed twenty-four hours a day.

Your present correspondent recently sat opposite a person who identified himself as a "financier" and had invited your humble scribe to meet with him in his vast loft in the Chelsea section of Manhattan. This individual identified himself as having formerly been employed by the LaRouche private investigative agency.

I noticed an old-fashioned hose-nozzle style microphone (or was this a new-fangled digital video camera?) hanging suspended over the L-shaped couch arrangement where we were conversing but decided to simply ignore the electronics and simply temper my conversation and reactivity. This individual who claimed to be a private "intelligence agent" was convinced that television is a dead medium and that a "new medium" for communication would shortly be found to replace TV. A live TV set displaying only "snow" was a feature of the L-shaped lounge arrangement.

Your present correspondent here says "lounge" since the floor-wide loft space had no partitions and a variety of persons were obviously entering and exiting the area from the other side of the building, which also has an alley entrance in addition to the "front office" elevator.

I had been in a similar facility once before in exactly the same area of Chelsea. This was a floor-wide loft space occupied in the late 1970's by a numerologist who has now vanished from public contact in conjunction with some unknown producer with shadowy connections on Long Island, N.Y. For a long while, as must be known by LaRouche operatives (past & present) with an interest in the mythos of Roman and Druidic tradition, sophisticated criminals have been using systems of numerology, astrology and spell-casting to enhance the efficiency of covert activities. Sometimes these shadowy organizations have some degree of success with these procedures., depending on the native capacities of the practitioners whom they employ.

It is of interest that the notorious Charles Manson, as related in the book "Shadow Over Sonoma" by investigative reporter Adam Gorightly, discusses his feelings of "the devil" as a separate Entity, a shadow who travels on the wind to meet and animate his/her minions as these individuals figure as pawns in Manson's cosmology. The experiments by Manson's group with a variety of hex power rituals were confused, drug-diffused and profoundly evil. But these were actually attempts to conjure and utilize a negative "power" or spirit force.

Considering Manson's group to be just the botched tip of the submerged wreck in the field of "black magick", it becomes easier for the person with no detailed background in studying sorcery to conceptualize that each positive thrust for illumination—in the sense of "going beyond" limited circumstances has its corresponding "shadow thrust" for liberation from mundane bondage by accessing ways of channeling mental "power" and contacting a form of "Advanced Intelligence" which might boost individual energy and/or give information which assists human endeavor, whether or not these endeavors are actually criminal.

As one follows these quotes from occult literature given on the Internet by Brother Blue, one can imagine the negative reverse of these positive examples. It is important to remember that, like electricity, the subtle energy of living intelligence is a force which can both harm and heal, both create and destroy. But the fact that if one puts a finger into a light socket one can be electrocuted is no reason not to use electrical appliances and recognize the existence of electricity. In fact, this recognition means that an aware person will not put a finger into a live electric socket.

From: "Blue Resonant Human" <density4@cts.com>
Originally to: iufo@alterzone.com
Sender: iufo-approval@alterzone.com
Original Date: Sat, 06 Jul 1996 22:58:16 GMT

-> SearchNet's iufo Mailing List

*"SOMA is the moon astronomically; but in mystical phraseology, it
is also the name of the sacred beverage drunk by the Brahmins and
the Initiates during their mysteries and sacrificial rites."..." and yet
plainly preserving in his physical brain the memory of what he
sees and learns. Plainly speaking, Soma is the fruit of the Tree
of Knowledge forbidden by the jealous Elohim to Adam and Eve or
Yah-Ve, 'lest man should become as one of us.'"*

-H.P. Blavatsky
*The Secret Doctrine, Vol. II: Anthropogenesis (p. 499)
Theosophical University Press*
*This process must be dependent upon a linking subtle substance, symbolized by the Egyptian
ancients as "the boat of Ra/Set. "It is p[possible that those really seeking a "quick fix" initiation were
given some sort of drugged food by the ancient initiators of Greece and Asia Minor. In fact, most
probably this is true in all cultures which have "inner" and "outer" mysteries. Those in antiquity who
rejected and/or casually survived the drugged experience went on to further levels of cognition
induced by telepathic contact with the initiator already on that desired level of experience. Those
who accepted the drugged drink and/or food as "divine" remained outside the astral inner circle,
attempting as now to vend easy symbols of mystical development as a way of earning an
enhanced living as priest or scholar.*

Here, your present correspondent E.Macer-Story comments: The Internet personality
"Resonant Blue Human", who links ufo alien contacts with the initiations of mystical
religion has commented that horror fiction and ufology non-fiction writer Whitley
Strieber may have "crossed the abyss":

*"It has been often rumored that Mr. Strieber has enjoyed certain
Wiccan affiliations in the past so bearing this in mind, one wonders
if these formerly inculcated belief systems may have filtered their
way into the tapestry of his current "space alien" mythology or if
certain occult groups have long been privy to a view of what A.F.
Col. Donald Ware (ret.) has succinctly termed the "larger reality.""*

Resonant Blue Human then goes on to quote from Alt. magick FAQ #7, entitled:
"A glimpse of the Structure and System of the Great White Brotherhood"

*"The Order of the S. S." (Silver Star, Argon Astron, A.'. A.'.)
is composed of those who have crossed the Abyss; the implications
of this expression may be studied in Liber 418, the 14th, 13th,
12th, 11th, 10th, and 9th Aethyrs in particular. All members of
the Order are in full possession of the Formulae of Attainment,
both mystical or inwardly-directed and Magical or outwardly-
directed.*

After this, our Internet "authority" on these topics goes on to quote from ceremonial magician Aliester Crowley's Equinox, again on the Order of the Silver Star::

*" Every active Member of the Order has destroyed all that He is
and all that he has on crossing the Abyss; but a star is cast
forth in the Heavens to enlighten the Earth, so that he may
possess a vehicle wherein he may communicate with mankind.
The quality and position of this star, and its functions, are
determined by the nature of the incarnations transcended by him."*

And so on run the Byzantine quotations from the "inner dogmas" of Crowley's occult literature, as Resonant Blue Human cites such passages as:

*"To attain the Grade of Magister Templi, he must perform two tasks;
the emancipation from thought by putting each idea against its
opposite, and refusing to prefer either; and the consecration of
himself as a pure vehicle for the influence of the order to which
he aspires. He must then decide upon the critical adventure of our Order; the
absolute abandonment of himself and his attainments. .. He cannot
remain indefinitely an Exempt Adept; he is pushed onward by the
irresistible momentum that he has generated.*

*Should he fail, by will or weakness, to make his self-
annihilation absolute...He may indeed prosper
for a while, but in the end he must perish, especially when with
a new Aeon a new word is proclaimed which he cannot and will not
hear, so that he is handicapped by trying to use an obsolete
method of Magick, like a man with a boomerang in a battle where
every one else has a rifle. ...he must employ to this end the formula called "The
Beast conjoined with the Woman" which establishes a new
incarnation of deity; as in the legends of Leda, Semele, Miriam,
Pasiphae, and others."*

The above quotation about Magister Templi" is from a novel by Whitley Strieberr which , according to Resonant Blue Human, contains the character of an intelligence agency officer who is also the initiate of a secret occult order. It is extremely significant that Resonant Blue Human has seen these similarities.

Your present correspondent finds no need to follow the details of this comparison. Strieber , in his multiplex & best-selling personal narrations as "ufo contactee", has not cited his inner occult connections in any detail. He may not be fully aware of the extent of the subtle influence of previous occult associations upon his literary output as a fiction writer. Is it possible that threats reported by Strieber to students at his Omega Institute seminar in the early 1990's were made by some covert organization rather than U.S. government intelligence or any other established political intelligence agency? According to a student in this seminar, professional architect Attilio Marconi, Strieber had said at the time that threats had been made to smear him in context of a false pornographic video, or some similar item. It is quite possible that such a tactic stems

DOING BUSINESS IN THE ADIRONDACKS by E. Macer-Story

from the drug and pornography trade of a dedicated, covert organization rather than any standard "government issue" interest in downplaying his "ufo contactee" books. The government has been documented as at one time having been given the mandate to "make ridiculous" certain ufo reports. But adding sex and intrigue to the "ufo mix" would only serve to make those reports more popular if a "smear" action against Strieber was detected.

On the other hand, the Romany (gypsy) people, who have maintained a tradition of practicing sorcery for many centuries, emphasize the family and emotional identity of the practitioner as the roots of this tradition. Roma intellectuals such as University of Texas professor Ian Hancock may choose to de-emphasize the Romany traditions of sorcery but in a film such as "Angelo My Love" (major Cannes Award 1985) one can clearly see the old ways still active among the merchants who were the amateur actors in this semi-documentary about a young gypsy boy who must go in search of his stolen ancestral ring. Mysterious aerial "spirit lights" help the boy in his quest.

Professor Hancock has, however, done a service in tracing the Roma or gypsy language to a Sanskrit origin. The Roma people obviously were originally a tribe living in the area of India or Pakistan . The exact reasons for the diaspora of the Roma people from their origins to a variety of locations Northward across the Mediterranean Sea are not known to written history. It is probable that the origins of the Tarot of Marseilles, originally transcribed as the "Egyptian Tarot" by artists in the Court of Louis XIV of France, were Romany.

In the film "Angelo, My Love" , unusual lights are seen in the sky above the rural gypsy encampment where Angelo has come from the city in search of his ring. No attempt is made to define the origin of these lights. Yet in the following "ufo" account from Argentina in January of 2000 we are ultimately limited to the choice between "meteor" and "spacecraft"

ALLEGEZD WITNESSES TO UFO CRASH
Source: "Diario Hoy de la Plata", January 29, 2000
As translated by Scott Corrales

"What could allegedly have been a UFO (unidentified flying object) collided Tuesday at noon in the vicinity of the Santiago del Estero village of Sachayoj. A group of technicians, researchers and astronomers from all parts of the country joined the search which has been underway since Wednesday under the supervision of the provincial police.

According to local residents, who are still stunned by what they saw and heard, an enormous ball of fire slammed into the densely wooded wilderness. Sachayoj residents claim having heard loud noises followed by an explosion and much smoke. A tremor also shook the entire zone for some minutes.

The landscape in which the UFO allegedly collided is made up of a densely wooded area consisting of wide, deep canyons....The fact remains that is that the site in which the putative UFO collision took place is all but impenetrable. Or it is at least difficult to move naturally among the dense vegetation. What is more, the

DOING BUSINESS IN THE ADIRONDACKS by E. Macer-Story

vegetation makes it impossible to conduct an aerial search: ..No one knows if what was actually seen by the dwellers of this remote area was a UFO or a meteor....
" We are hoping to find something, because the locals are simple people with no need to lie," explained UFO expert Carlos Alberto Zaldia. "It may well be that they saw a meteorite rather than a spacecraft."

It seems that such investigations veer widely between the "simple" and analytically complex. There is much contemporary discussion on how new physics theories may implement understanding of natural, experienced phenomena such as telepathy and telekinesis, as well as anomalous "ufo" sightings. Much of the discussion centers about re-designing theories of gravitation on the small particle level. As Tom Van Flanden stated in September of 1999, the basic problem is that the mathematical computation in these theoretical constructs often does not agree with observation.

As one example of the neo-tech speculation which appears on the Internet, here follow several technical arguments by Tom Van Flanden, who is a recognized professional physicist. If you are not technically-versed, you can skip the sections printed in italics below, read only the exegesis by this reporter, and go on to the section "chaos magick vs nature spirits" . But it might be a good mental exercise to skim through this stuff and come to understand that we do not have a fully verified and developed "Unified Theory of Gravitation" on either the planetary scale or small particle level. Technicians are approximating by using the systems which "work" without fully being able to explain the situation.

Argument 1: "The effect (of finite speed of gravitation) on computed orbits is usually disastrous because conservation of angular momentum is destroyed."
Response: According to GNT, the gravitational field itself possesses a momentum, and the gravitational field momentum (linear or angular) must be added to the mechanical momentum in all conservation of momentum calculations."

Yet what does this actually mean that a "gravitational field has a momentum"? Are we to suppose that the gravitational field is a three dimensional "item" independent of mass which travels independently of mass? This does not make sense. It is the transposition of customary thought about the Fourier transform of the electromagnetic field through macro-mass structure into the discussion of gravitation. But gravitation can only be known as a property of mass and mass can only be known as an electromagnetic construct, in either Einstein's relativistic or Bohr's quantum atomic systems. So where does the "gravity item" travel as an object? Certainly not through the atomic orbital system. There is no room for such action in the pre-existing formulations. Something is missing.

"The angular momentum that is not conserved is that of the target body. The lines of force between gravity source and target, if drawn from retarded positions, cross and form a couple. The target then gains angular momentum. The momentum of the field is irrelevant because it is not changing, whatever

DOING BUSINESS IN THE ADIRONDACKS by E. Macer-Story

it may be. But the momentum of the target is changing. Hence, no conservation.

"This dilemma is easily avoided by drawing the lines of force from the true, instantaneous positions of the source and target. That is equivalent to no retardation or very large (compared to light) propagation speed. All other known ways of working around this problem are highly contrived and violate other principles, especially causality."

" Argument 2: "Why do total eclipses of the Sun by the Moon reach maximum eclipse about 40 seconds before the Sun and Moon's gravitational forces align?"
Response: According to GNT, gravitational interactions involve not a single gravitational (Newtonian) force, but several forces that depend on the state of motion of the interacting bodies. The alignment of the Newtonian forces alone has no particular significance.

To clarify the point, I should have substituted the word "acceleration" for "force". Accelerations (e.g., d^2r/dt^2, or dv/dt, where v = velocity) are observable quantities, and stand independent of any theory. Why does the acceleration of the Moon toward the Sun reach a maximum 40 seconds after the optical positions appear to align? The obvious answer is because the Moon covers the retarded visible position of the Sun before it covers the non-retarded gravitational position of the Sun. Any other answer would seem to need to invoke some amazing coincidences and cancellations because this is a non-null result, ostensibly demonstrating a different propagation speed for light and gravity."

" Argument 3. "The effect of aberration (of gravity) on orbits is not seen."
" Response: According to GNT, there is no aberration of gravitational fields produced by point masses moving with constant speed along a straight line (or nearly so). The gravitational (retarded Newtonian) field appears to be attached to the moving point mass (similar to the electric field of a moving point charge).

"Aberration is simple geometry. If is exhibited by every propagating thing in the universe, whether particle, wave, or wavicle; whether an arrow, sound wave, photon, or graviton. To my knowledge, the answer that "there is no aberration" is impossible unless there are no moving parts.

"Specifically, why is there aberration of an electromagnetic field when viewed from a particle moving with constant speed along a straight line, but not for a gravitational field? (It's best to avoid electrostatic fields here because they are carried by "virtual photons", a name for an undiscovered particle/wave that also acts as if its propagation speed is very much faster than light.)

*"Argument 4. "If gravity were a simple force . . . it mostly radial
effect would have also a small transverse component . . ."
Response: According to GNT, gravity is not a simple force.
Gravitational interactions between moving bodies involve several
forces acting in different directions (although the dominant force is
usually the ordinary Newtonian force)."*

Here there is a necessity to consider the fact that Newtonian mechanics is limited
to macro-molecular structures. As our measuring instruments became more precise, it
was discovered that photons, electrons and other small particles did not obey the same
observed "laws" or paradigms as the larger, molecular assembly of atoms. Yet in both
quantum mechanics of small particles and the larger Newtonian mechanics of macro-
structures it is taken for granted that the gravitational force acting upon mass is relatively
uniform. This does not accord with observation. There are well-known areas of
gravitational anomaly both in terrestrial locations and between celestial bodies where
"gravitational lenses" are observed which do not constitute a uniform continuum. It is not
presently known for sure where and how the surfaces between gravitational lenses and
the surrounding cosmology bound areas of three dimensional interstellar space. Possibly,
there is another form of "gravitation" acting from within atomic structure which accounts
both for areas of terrestrial time/gravity anomaly and for the interstellar gravitational
lenses and seemingly "hyperdense" black hole (Quasar) manifestations. This would not
have to do with acceleration, force or small particle trajectory but rather with a variation
of atomic/mass density caused from within the nucleus of the atom by an additional force
acting internally .to mass structure.

*"Again, substitute "acceleration" for "force", and my statement becomes a
description of observations, not a theory-dependent claim. So the rebuttal
here does not apply.*

*" Argument 5. "From the absence of such an effect (transverse
component), Laplace set a lower limit to the speed of propagation of
classical gravity of about 108 C, where C is the speed of light."
Response: Laplace based his calculation on the Newton's
gravitational force alone, but according to GNT gravitation involves
several different forces.*

*"Just to clarify, Laplace's lower limit was 10^8 c, not 108 c. And he based
this on observed accelerations, not on forces. No known cause can cancel the
transverse acceleration that must occur if gravitational acceleration is
toward the retarded position of a source instead of toward the instantaneous
position of a source of gravity. You might invent such a cause out of thin
air, but that would hardly constitute a "theory", but merely a mathematical
model that works but has no known basis in physics.*

*" Argument 6. "If gravity behaved in an analogous way
(propagated with finite speed), moving masses would anticipate*

DOING BUSINESS IN THE ADIRONDACKS by E. Macer-Story

*each other's linear motion, but not acceleration, and
accelerating masses would emit gravitational radiation."
Response: The electromagnetic analogy does not apply here.
According to GNT, accelerating masses do not emit energy, they
absorb it (although the process is not quite clear).*

*"Then why do binary pulsars *lose* angular momentum? In GR, it is supposed
to be because they emit gravitational waves, thereby throwing off energy,
much like the emission of a photon by an accelerating charge. This GNT
appears to predict the opposite effect from what is observed.*

*" Argument 7. "In practice, this suppression of aberration is done
through so-called "retarded potentials". In electromagnetism, these
are called "Lienard-Wiechert potentials".
Response A: We now have unambiguous solutions of Maxwell's
equations in the form of retarded field integrals [see, for example, ...]
Response B: In electromagnetism (and in gravitation) the aberration
only appears to be suppressed. The aberration is actually taken into
account in direct electromagnetic derivations [see ...] However, for
moving point charges (or masses) the aberration simply disappears
because of the requirement that the fields (electric or gravitational)
originating from different points of the moving body arrive at the
point of observation simultaneously. (Note: a "point charge" or "a
point mass" is an object whose linear dimensions are much smaller
than the distance from which the object is observed).*

*"The "retarded field" solutions either ignore or suppress normal transverse
aberration in order to achieve agreement with observations. They include
"retardation effects only in unimportant ways, such as in the radial distance
between source and target. But no valid basis for this major omission of
transverse aberration has yet been advanced, to my knowledge. It is the
equivalent of assuming an infinite propagation speed, whether one uses those
words or not.*

*"In other words, transverse aberration is arctan (v/V), where v is the
transverse component of velocity between target and source, and V is the
propagation speed of whatever travels from source to target (e.g., light or
gravity). This term must exist, and cannot be cancelled by any known
mechanism or process. Dropping it is the logical equivalent of setting v = 0
or V = infinity, whether one says that or not."*

Here we have a particular way of stating a very important problem as regards radar
mechanisms which have two pulses of light speed: an internal, steady timing beam or
pulse and the external locating pulse which determines the status of objects by
comparison between the time of transmission and the time of bounced transmission
arrival back to the source. These mechanisms take for granted the uniformity of speed of
e/m transmission. However, since terrestrial and cosmological gravity is not actually

DOING BUSINESS IN THE ADIRONDACKS by E. Macer-Story

uniform it can be argued that though radar works well locally for such purposes as guiding aircraft into airports and over specified local increments of a journey this same dual comparison radar mechanism will not actually be as accurate over long distances (or even short distances) wherein there is transit in and out of areas of varying gravitational density which affects the e/m speed.

"All these arguments are interesting as far as they go. But they ignore one of the best experimental lines of evidence I presented -- the Walker-Dual experiment. Walker and Dual have shown in laboratory experiments that both electrostatic and gravitational "force" propagation speeds must exceed the speed of light. This is shown in such a direct way -- a vibrating source induces gravitational vibrations in a target without a light-speed delay -- that it is difficult to imagine any dodges over the conclusion.

"And ultimately, that's okay, because Lorentzian Relativity (LR) predicts the same effects as special relativity (SR) in the sub-light-speed domain, but allows ftl propagation speeds. The Global Positioning System has shown us that Lorentzian Relativity must be used in preference to Einstein's SR in practical applications. So why not accept the next logical step, which is that ftl propagation in forward time is simply allowed by nature because no experiment favors SR over LR?"

CHAOS MAGICK VS NATURE SPIRITS

On July 9, 2000 in following my inspiration to join a certain Internet shopping service in order to vend my paintings and talismans, I noticed a book on "Typhon" and "Chaos Magick"by Aleister Crowley at auction. This reminded me that the discovery of the professor of chaos theory after the poltergeist 5:34 inspiration of July First (to be noted here shortly) might actually be a form of communication as to the source of certain sophisticated acts of magick I have discerned clairvoyantly as directed toward your present correspondent for some arcane reason. After the web search of the shopping service, I began to have what I later recognized as false memories of Austin Spare aficionado Barry Klugerman as hosting various Crowley and Austin Spare books with the shopping service.

On July first, the smoke alarm at he house in Woodstock, which had previously been disabled in a lightning storm, blatted twice at 5:34 in the morning and then ceased. Thinking this number somehow significant, I web-searched and located a professor Henry D.I. Alarbarel who was resident at Scripps Oceanographic Institute doing research into chaos theory. I was later informed that Alarbarel 's research on reflections from a shark's skin is actually in the bibliography of the Ph.D. dissertation of a Turkish physicist with an interest in numerology to whom I had sent the original email inquiring about the possible significance of 5:34 a.m.

On the thirteenth of July at two a.m. I noticed a twinkling red and white "ufo light" over the mountains in front of my Woodstock house where I have noticed these lights several times before. It seems that the lights want me to see them at times. They

DOING BUSINESS IN THE ADIRONDACKS by E. Macer-Story

have also manifested in the sky over Lewis Hollow, which is easily visible from the chair on the back porch where I sit in the evening after working.

Theoretically, all of these phenomena, poltergeist and synchronistic, can be measured and/or recorded by conventional means. It is the mental lightning of our interpretations which jumps the conventional alarm system. Yet is what might be allowed by our measuring instruments actually the limitation of material Nature? I corresponded in September of 1997 with Michael Theroux of Borderlands magazine about his efforts to link biodynamic signals to the larger celestial movement of stars and the etheric (as Theroux terms it) movement of weather patterning.

[Eugenia]:
I read your article on Biodynamic Signals. The experience of your project>LUCAS group seemed sincerely rendered. But I think there is no real way to ascertain whether the 10 seconds of signal you recorded came from a distant star or was simply a response by an interdimensional intelligence to your efforts to work with the "patterning" energy you describe.

[Michael]
Quite possible. A couple things to consider tho. First, the biosensors are "tuned" to be receptive to specific "patterns" only. For instance, we need to use different biosensors if we are doing a wireless comm experiment with plants. When we point these at most plants, the response comes thru. If they are pointed skyward or simply away from the plant target, we get nothing. On the other hand, the biosensors used in our biodynamic version of SETI incorporate tuning substances which are not reactive to terrestrial etheric impulses. Our scanning of the sky produced response in only one section of sky (Ursa Major). Of course this could be location dependant intelligences coming through, and based on the "Gigeresque" nature of some of the biograms obtained, could certainly qualify it as a correspondence from some interdimensional entity rather than of extraterrestrial origin. One really can't be certain.
    Gerry Vassilatos and Eric Dollard are both using my biosensors in research projects. They have both confirmed that the biosensors seem to be responsive to etheric "tides" which precede specific weather events. But, in this case, the patterns emerge over a very long time cycle compared with the immediate and spontaneous reactions observed in skyward scanning operations. We are building some new very sensitive diagnostic equipment which may help us to distinguish and clearly define the nature of what we are receiving.

[Eugenia]
I am sure that there is a non-electromagnetic
"structural" or "patterning" energy which transduces with the e/m continuum.
We agree on this basic concept.

[Michael]

DOING BUSINESS IN THE ADIRONDACKS by E. Macer-Story

Not sure I follow you on this, -- "transduces with the e/m continuum".

[Eugenia]
But I also see the action of interdimensional 'Intelligences" in the
use of this patterning energy. Indeed, "synchronicity" often seems to involve
the telepathic action of interdimensional Intelligence for good or ill.

[Michael]
Agreed.

[Eugenia]
I want primarily to advance human consciousness. Sometimes this seems
almost futile, like civilizing wolves. But I keep at it, trying to pattern
events more positively.

[Michael]
A commendable but formidable task.
I would like to run this dialog on Biodynamic Signals in the letters section
of the magazine. OK?

[Eugenia]
Yes! please do include our dialog in your letters section and send me a copy. Kindly also
include the following reply within the discussion.

In an early article this reporter wrote for PURSUIT magazine, entitled
"Fluidice"she described a transduction process between the "etheric" and the
"electromagnetic"energy continua. This transduction process is similar to the action of
stress (mechanical torque) in a piezoelectric crystal, when a torque on the crystal
produces an electrical signal. Persinger cites this effect often, by the way, in his studies of
atmospheric electrical discharge before and after earthquakes.
But the "'etheric transduction" described by E. Macer-Story is not the same as
piezoelectric transduction. Rather, the torque/electrical transduction process is an analogy
for the transmutation of "shape"(the patterning to which you refer in your article) into a
form of structural etheric coding which we do not yet fully understand.""
This dialog was subsequently published in Borderlands but the journal later had
financial problems and ceased full publication. It is from conversations like this that the
"fluidice matrix" theory developed. This theory is an attempt to render in "technical
language" the perception that there is an additional substance/energy actually palpably
(and not just philosophically) active in Nature, as Intelligence (incarnate or discarnate) is
a part of Nature.
The difference between this reporter's "fluidice" theory and the traditional
"etheric" theory is that the additional patterning enters from within the nucleus of
molecular structure rather than being an additional external quality of four dimensional
mass structure.
Another individual within a covert government, corporate or rogue group may
have discovered, re-discovered or invented ways to use this natural energy, and also may

be holding this knowledge in a deliberately obscure coding. Certainly, my research indicates that there is more than one mind//matter way to access this "fluidice" force. I have recently received some quite sophisticated interference which I have discussed with persons versed both in modern physics and the occult. Here follow two short emails which I jotted to Dr. Jack Sarfatti about one specific "talisman" which was found in my driveway on New Years Day of 2001:

"It seems, after a probing of this talisman by various means, that some attempt has been made by user(s) of esp/pk to block my psi abilities so that the operations of their craft are not evident to me. I link this to the quaisi-martial arts group using Japanese ethos which I mention in a previous article published by two magazines and which has, among other charades, managed to annoy Temple of Set by impersonating same in various contexts .Apparently, these practitioners have successfully been using hypnosis and spell-casting as part of some illegal venture.
[Auth.Note: These are not all actually Japanese but are using the Shinto, Buddhist deity and Zen façade.]
"A crank call was left on the message machine at my Magick Mirror studio space late on the night of Thursday, Jan 4th. This was a charade during which Reggae-like music was played in the background whilst children's voices made vaguely obscene nonsense statements. I saved the tape. I emphasize: this was a charade. These were not actual "voodoo" or similar practitioners. Once again, an attempt is being made to "set up" a known occult group as the culprit".

The circumstances of finding this talisman had been as narrated in an email sent on January 2, 2001 about finding a motorcycle track and classic "crow's foot" talisman in the snow of my driveway on New Years morning 2001.As noted at the time:

" But I followed my inner guidance & found the bike track. What next? "

This bike track theme will be followed up in more detail later, as it was journaled at the time. Note, however, the awkward attempt of this reporter to dismiss the initial incident as humorously "awk cult". This attitude will be seen to collapse later into serious concern.

" Just to keep you up to date: I found a discernibly awk-cult talisman at the foot of my back driveway this afternoon. It was very small so I had not seen it from the porch. I felt like walking around the house at 4:30 EST, and there it was! Just as an aside: sometimes my inner guidance cam be very specific. My inner voice instructed me: "don't put on heavy socks under your boots. You won't be outside long." I wasn't out long. It was neat. I walked up to the talisman, plucked it up with gloved hand and went back inside. I am deliberately not describing the form of this thing by email. It is a traditional spell-casting shape.
At any rate, I now have the thing in my possession. I don't think I was supposed to notice it. So I will query it sometime tomorrow. I do feel, holding it, that the origin is Cambridge, Mass and environs. The entire awk-cult situation is much weirder than I have yet narrated in my articles.

[Auth. Note: I had anticipated there might be some occult shenanigans in an email sent prior to the New Year celebrations, as follows.]

Happy New Year, Jack--
This is actually the first new year of the Millennium. I have had a few
new talismanic occurrences in Woodstock during the past few days. I am
deliberately not giving a specific description as these were definitely of
human construction and who knows who's tapping the email:-) I think--and
co-witnesses also think--that somewhere "out there" is an actual adept in the
martial and/or magickal arts who has either gone crazy about my probings into
sorcery or is being paid &/or cajoled into this hexing activity. I am keeping
a journal as this evolves. The key to understanding these events is that the
talismancer actually is gifted, and the talismans left outside my place have
multidimensional resonance. So for me it's like playing martial arts
chess. Something is going to be attempted on the turn of the Millennium here,
as I intuit and I hope the poker face above my poker hand is absolutely
inscrutable.
BTW: this line of thought reminded me of my Dad's poker ability. A bit of a
wise guy about his ESP, he used to organize poker clubs wherever we moved. As
a child, I noticed that he frequently won at poker and that these clubs then
rapidly dissolved.:-)
I do not play poker and I restrain myself from telling my friends how their
"secret affairs" will turn out. I hope though, in this one instance, that my
opponent(s) cannot read my strategy whereas their present strategy remains
open to my intuition.
Feliz Ano Nuevo

Dr. Sarfatti responded with the perception that the talisman represented:

" A multi-dimensional romance. "

Romance? In general, Jack Sarfatti's perceptions about male/female relationships tend to
be slightly colored by the flamboyance of the North Beach, San Francisco, California
environment in which he has lived for many years. But he is, nevertheless, a gifted
clairvoyant as well as a physicist. What he perceives as "romance" may be an off-beat
sexual fascination. Later in this book the fact that film director Roman Polanski had acted
a role in a satiric vampire film (Fearless Vampire Hillers) opposite his future wife ,
actress Sharon Tate in 1967, just two years before she was murdered by the Manson
"Family" cult will be discussed in terms of an anomalous arrangement of fireplace logs
found at the LaBianca murder site by detectives.

Could the "cult" belief or practice relate to experimental or attempted Intel-elite
"conditioning" attempts? Or is this something else, a supernatural and/or
interdimensional shared reality involving actual non-human Intelligences with an appetite
for human contact? As I wrote to Dr. Sarfatti at the time:

"In reference to the situation I mentioned in my previous email (copy below for your reference) your
intuition goes in the right direction. But this individual and/or awk-cult org has a very unusual
fascination. I describe my findings & views on this situation in my article *THE ART OF MAKING
WOLVES FROM HUMAN SKULLS: THE BINDING OF FENRIS*, which is posted on Magonia
Online and is now also being serialized in hard copy in Alternate Perceptions magazine. In that

DOING BUSINESS IN THE ADIRONDACKS by E. Macer-Story

article I mention a motorcycle club with a wolf motif--like the neo-Nazi Gray Wolves--which I had previously intersected with in the Boston, Massachusetts area but which are based in the South, as far as I am aware. These guys use their women like supermarket meat and are not happy to see a woman investigator making progress in unraveling their modus operandi.

Well, to make a long story short for today: I was having my morning coffee and had the strong inner guidance to look outside on the front driveway. At first, I resisted this as it meant going outside the house in my red velvet bathrobe onto a frozen driveway .Crazy behavior, eh? Just what the opposition wants: Macer-Story transmogrified into a version of "Liz Taylor plays Tennessee Williams." But, then, I might be resisting this under false Southern Belle modesty. Alert! Overcome conditioning!!!So I did this driveway expedition, and found a clue there.

On top of the clean, absolutely frozen plowed snow of last night was one track of dirty snow from a tire leaving softer residue from the town road now slightly melted and sandy which crosses at the foot of the driveway. Hmm. I had a visitor last night after the New Years traffic over the unsanded hard snow. This visitor must have been here in the early hours of the morning. He was using one tire. Either this was a ufo vehicle rolling sideways :-) OR it was a motorcycle.Yup. I had a covert visitor in the early hours of the morning who was driving a bike.

Probably doing one of those "untraceable talisman" numbers wherein the magickal item is a common object like a piece of ice or plaster which the recipient cannot identify as having overt awk-cult significance.

But I followed my inner guidance & found the bike track. What next?"

I noticed when getting this manuscript ready for publication that I had difficulty in this preceding passage with linking and re-rendering the sequence of emails, which are actually very straightforward. Possibly there was a subtle effect to me from handling the talisman found in the driveway which was undetected at the time and surfaced more obviously in the narration. The first twelve days of January are observed by some as the "Satanic Revels". But these stereotypical observations do not necessarily pinpoint the actual identity of my New Years Day motorcycle visitor.

Resentment about prejudicial judgment of appearance might cause guerrilla manipulation of stereotypical costume and behavior No one knows better than a Ph.D. who has been taken to be a bellhop about the disjunction between physical appearance and mental ability. Thus, a brilliant actor/impersonator may be created by this type of misunderstanding when the intellect of the "outsider" becomes aware of the gullibility of the complacent establishment attitudes.

This may take extreme forms as in the film *"Mrs. Doubtfire"* when a rejected husband poses as a dowdy governess in order to be close to his estranged wife and children. The proper, neatly-dressed façade of the woman he is impersonating is a humorous reversal of the sloppy, jobless and irresponsible way of life for which he has been criticized by his ex-wife.

On the downside of this farcical impersonation behavior, there is the possibility of the sort of masque which would be unthinkable to most people, including experienced detectives. There is a possibility that organic material taken in the ongoing cattle and livestock mutilations regularly reported in the U.S. since the 1980's (cite most recent incident) may actually be used in covert plastic surgery and/or bizarre rituals requiring body parts compatible in some way with human flesh. Bovine blood is somewhat similar to human blood in hemoglobin characteristics.

DOING BUSINESS IN THE ADIRONDACKS by E. Macer-Story

In his excellent article on the 2002 livestock mutilations in Argentina and Uruguay entitled "The Night Ravagers"[5], Scott Corrales makes the point that neither the skeptics offering "predator" explanations nor the advocates of a religious or extraterrestrial explanation have completely convincing proof of their opinions. The most that can be said with certainty is that the livestock mutilations are part of a larger fabric of paranormal anomalies in the area of Argentina and Chile .Because there have been other events such as unexplained aerial lights, religious apparitions and teleportations in this region, witnesses sometimes do not find the mysterious death of livestock to be the center of investigative attention.

Certainly, "alien" life from another planet or solar system would probably not have the same catalytic characteristics as do the chlorophyll /hemoglobin molecules which convert oxygen and sunlight into nutrients. Often, the "cattle mutilations" are attributed to "ufos" because of the puzzling neatness of incisions. But the situation is simply that the closest we have come to finding a lifeform on any near by planet is the bacteria detected beneath the surface of the earth which are said to be living under conditions similar to the extremes of temperature on the surface of the planet Mars. According to Amherst College geochemist Gerek Lovley, these bacteria use hydrogen gas released deep in the earth's surface as their energy source. Extraterrestrial life from beyond this solar system, when we meet it directly, will probably be found not to use the same catalytic chemical processes as animals and humans living on the surface of earth. This is simply because the "photon" energy of the native star/sun will be different. Mars and Earth share the same source of sunlight. Yet the atmosphere of the other planets in our solar system is different from Earth and so each planet has a different catalytic standard. An advanced testing from extraterrestrial intelligence of this matter could be done at long distance and would not require continual gross physical removal of body parts. So whatever or whoever is removing blood and autonomic tissue from livestock most probably has an arcane terrestrial agenda..

A similar idea to the suppositions about "outer space" cattle mutilation projects is the idea that odd persons with advanced mental capabilities seen in anomalies context are "extraterrestrial" beings masquerading as humans. Not necessarily. The blind skepticism about telepathy by conventional academics worldwide has led to the false belief that sensitives of all sorts, ranging from professional psychics on through poets & painters, are "fair game" for experiments involving charades designed by behavioral psychologists. It is one short step from this attitude to the use by academically-trained rogue intellectuals of such sophisticated charades for criminal purposes, as has previously been described with reference to the involvement of stage magicians with international politics. There is also another possibility. Pushed into covert activity by academic prejudice, individuals with telepathic and spirit conjuration skills may be combining the stage magic behavioral charade routines with active hypnosis, telepathy and remote viewing of target situations for use in criminal activities. For centuries there have been "witch wars" and sorcery rivalries within the occult demimonde. Such a sophisticated combination of psychological and mental projection techniques might be a natural expansion of these techniques into terrorist and mind control strategies within which organizational pawns must be given a religious rationale.

Scientific whiz kids now analyzing data about the cosmos under sanctioned government and/or academic financing have been brainwashed by internalizing amid

DOING BUSINESS IN THE ADIRONDACKS by E. Macer-Story

other parts of the SAT-testable academic canon the "truth" that all but the most gross of behavioral psych theories about Intelligence are mere fairy tales and superstition. This includes "Life on Mars", "vampires' and "mental telepathy". It is not actually scientific to hold these prejudices while disregarding plain material observations which stand to contradict the belief that such things do not exist.

I have encountered in my career a variety of Very Intelligent persons of both genders who have set up "conditioning circumstances" of a behavioral nature to prove that I am a reflexive human animal without genuine esp. They have never been successful. I have never been debunked as a public practitioner of esp and sorcery skills. But I have been seriously harassed by a form of rogue or hostile intelligence which is actually using advanced telepathic, behavioral and hypnosis skills.

One of the latest in these behavioral farces which I have noticed occurred last week when I went o several camera stores looking for a bargain digital camera to replace my older camera which had started to loose focus for some obscure technical reason. On that day, I could easily have been followed from store to store without my noticing anyone behind me. But in the final store--where I ultimately got a deal on a new camera (esp helps in shopping)--I noticed that a man dressed in a light tan sport coat and slacks, costumed exactly as in the jacket photo on the back cover of "Destiny Matrix"(a recent book by California physicist jack Sarfatti in which your present correspondent is mentioned) but physically resembling more closely a pal of my youth who has approximately the Jack Sarfatti appearance but is a Hebrew blonde (very handsome, I think) like Danny Kaye--was directly behind and then in view of me as I browsed cameras. I noticed that he was trying the entrap me into some direct contact. I ALSO noticed that his clothing was light for the day--which was cold in NYC. I did not acknowledge him. Sometime as I was demanding specific testing from the clerk on the bargain camera, he left the store. I noticed him leaving. So did a cashier who as I was buying the camera asked the cyberware clerk if he had noticed the Odd Guy. Indeed, he had: "They come in sometimes to look over the stuff' he explained to the cashier, indicating he thought the Odd Guy was a spy from another store. The clerk was indeed close to an accurate observation of the truth.

The rogue behavioral mentalists trying to subtly control the esp/ufo research scene using contact hypnosis and other slick techniques really think I am attracted to externals only. Perhaps these odd operatives have a low opinion of women, having worked mainly with prostitutes and shills. Once again: I have quietly defrocked one of their operatives; this time combining previous occult experience with the practical observations of an alert store clerk. The question remains: what is the purpose of these charades?

How much different are these rogue "behavioral scientists" from those devotees of another sort of belief system using a combination of materially-organized "power" rituals and contact hypnosis which academics would of course call a "cult" using "fetishes"? The established behavioral psychologists believe they are contacting and manipulating "subliminal complexes" which are not up front in the conscious mind but are *assumed* to be active by those trained psychological manipulators who are using a systemic behavioral guide which they learned as "truth" the way religious dogma is sometimes learned as "truth".

The members of shamanic groups which use material fetishes believe that they are contacting by the use of observable patterns, objects and actions unseen but palpable

DOING BUSINESS IN THE ADIRONDACKS by E. Macer-Story

living forces and spirit identities. It may be true that individual members of both the psychological and the religious belief systems cross the line into mutual mental territory more often than they might comfortably realize.

In both traditional "power magick" and more contemporary "mind control" practices the technique is to create a mental world controlled by the Operator's paradigms, an artificial construct so persuasive that targets enter this world mentally and then by their actions begin to create a more materially-actualized version of what was originally simply an eccentrically-centered design of the universe held by an individual sorcerer or small group of initiated psychologists .

The more positive and realistic forms of sorcery or magick are more naturally practical in recognizing the existence of Worlds filled with accidents and alternative priorities which exist exterior to the mind and circumstances of the Operator . In fact, it is only by recognizing the existence of "other" belief systems that one can effectively detect attempted "hex" or "mind control" actions which have hypnotic and/or telepathic thrust.

On the afternoon of August 30, 2001, just after I had removed the chartreuse crepe paper seahorse used as an example in the NUFOC '38 from my writing desk beside the window in order to store it in the Woodstock loft closet, there was a loud sound as if a bird had flown against the window glass, perhaps chasing the bright color of the seahorse. It crossed my mind that the crepe paper effigy was the color of a parrot.

Later, when I went to close the back, glass sliding doors, I noticed that a cement brick near the back steps was stacked out of alignment. As I straightened this stack, I had the impulse to check along the edge of the house below the loft windows. There I found beneath the writing desk window a beautifully-plumaged dead bird with a gray-brown body and a white breast with black dots. The long beak of this bird was driven into the earth and it had a red chevron mark at the back of the neck. This mark was so clearly defined that it seemed to have been made with paint.

I put a work glove on one hand and took detailed photographs of the dead bird with a 35mm camera, stroking back the neck feathers beneath the red mark to see if the paint was still wet. No paint was wet but the red mark did not seem to extend to the nub of the neck feathers. Possibly , another bird could have flown against the window glass earlier in the afternoon , disoriented because of the dead bird below rather than only because of the moving chartreuse shape glimpsed behind the glass/ The beak of the dead bird was driven into the ground more deeply and neatly than from an ordinary fall. The bird's wings were furled close to the body. If the bird had actually hit the window glass and fallen with a broken neck, the wings of the bird would have been in more disarray, perhaps extended. I have seen the bodies of dead birds in Nature, where they have fallen with extended wings.

Shortly after eight a.m. on the following morning, I was dozing after being awake in the early hours of the morning to go over some diagrams for the NUFOC '38 lecture which I intended to re-sketch sometime during the day. There was a definite knocking at my bedroom windowpane. When I checked this, no one was there.

As described by Erik Davis in his essay "*Trickster At The Crossroads*":.

The orisha, the gods of the Fon and Yoruba peoples of West Africa, are some of the most vital and intriguing beings ever to pass through the minds of men and women. The orisha are profoundly "living" gods, if by this we means archetypes, or

DOING BUSINESS IN THE ADIRONDACKS by E. Macer-Story

constellations of images and forces, that actively permeate the psychic lives of living humans. On the simplest level they are alive because they are worshiped: orisha are prayed to, invoked, and ritually "fed" by many millions of people in both Africa and the Americas. Not only are the gods alive, but they are long-lived; unlike contemporary Neo-Pagan deities, which have basically been reconstructed from the inquisitional ashes of history, the orisha have been passed through countless generations of worshipers with little interruption.

More profoundly, the very nature of the orisha is to be alive in the most fundamental sense we know — though our own human lives. Though they possess godlike powers, the orisha are not transcendent beings, but are immanent in this life, bound up with ritual, practice, and human community. They are accessible to people, combining elements of both mythological characters and ancestral ghosts. Like both of these groups of entities, the orisha are composed of immaterial but idiosyncratic personalities that eat, drink, lie, and sleep with each other's mates. Though West African tradition does posit a central creator god, he/she is generally quite distant, and the orisha are, like us, left in a world they did not create, a world of nature and culture, of sex, war, rivers, thunder, magic, and divination. The orisha are regularly "fed" with animal blood, food, and gifts, and during rituals the gods frequently possess the bodies of the faithful. Their behavior draws from the full range of human experience, including sexuality, mockery, and intoxication.

That the orisha remain outside the scope of many Western students of esotericism and even polytheism is understandable, given the historical domination of Africans by the Europeans of the New World. Black Americans were forced to hide their deities or dress them up in Catholic garb, while whites cut themselves off from all but the most superficial appreciations of those African cultural values that managed to survive."

Your present correspondent has in the past encountered several practitioners of modern voodoo and Cuban "peeled stick" sorcery. Could the bird with the red chevron at the back of the neck have been either a deliberate propitiation or "sacrifice" voodoo style? Or was this dead bird at the window and later knocking on the windowpane truly supernatural, a "warning from the gods"? For the NUFOC'38 event for which I was photographing the seahorse stage prop and redesigning diagrams for a lecture demonstration was canceled due to the World Trade Center terrorist disaster on September 11, 2001. The event had been scheduled to begin on September 14.in Austin, Texas.

"Because the West is such a text-oriented culture, there is an understandable tendency to equate civilization with the technology of writing, and the sort of reflective interior consciousness that that particular machine apparently constructs in human beings. West Africa did not possess writing as we now it, and the orisha disclose themselves not in books but in shrine, ritual, and memory. For today's

DOING BUSINESS IN THE ADIRONDACKS by E. Macer-Story

text-oriented seeker, there are no great Yoruba books to commune with, no Gita or Genesis. Though the Yoruba system of divination, Ifa, compares to the I Ching in terms of complexity, structure, and poetic sublimity, few know about it outside the tradition, partly for the simple reason that the "writing" of Ifa is carried in the heads of the diviners, the babalawo. (A complete edition of the Ifa has recently been published by Harper SanFrancisco)." ..

In his article "Trickster At The Crossroads", quoted above, Erik Davis comments :

"So too is blood sacrifice, the "feeding" of the orisha, an acute acknowledgement of the material dimension of spirit, of the fact that it is humans, not gods, that keep gods alive, and that our being is bound up with the excesses of mutual contract and exchange. Molly Ahye, an important scholar of Trinidadian dance as well as an orisha worshiper, speaks about how one "must have the blood, which is a life force, which spirit lives on. You think that spirit doesn't need sustenance, but spirit needs sustenance" (Ahye admitted, however, that she did not kill animals herself).
"

Even in this sympathetic article, the voodoo Orishas are in certain passages discussed as "archetypes". What does this adaptation to the "psychological religion" do to our direct perception of the actual situation? Certainly, it does lead to some amusing characterizations. Erik Davis attempts to equate the Yoruba "Eshu" or "Papa Legba" with the Greek messenger god Hermes. Is this to make Gatekeeper Legba, quirky and humorous holder of the keys to earthly power, more acceptable to readers schooled from childhood in the Greek heroes which these days also appear in avante guard comic books and Japanese animated films? Is this really valid anthropological analysis?

TRICKSTER INCIDENTS AND IDENTITIES

Tricksters can take on many different identities. But each identity is unique. The faces on all the masks are not the same as the one identity behind the masks and this is the essence of the trickery. The keys to all the doorways known by Gatekeeper Legba are not the same either but there is no trickery in this fact. It is the reverse of the masks. The keys all look the same but in reality they are different. One needs the correct room number as well as the key from Papa Legba.

Sometimes the irrational behavior of people in public places seems to be motivated by impromptu spirit overshadowing becoming part of the jigsaw of a rebus message from Advanced intelligence or the demi-Gods of yore.

On Friday October 26, 2001, while waiting for the 8 a.m. commuter bus opposite the Woodstock Village green, I noticed a man who was standing about one yard from me. I had rested my camera bag on a planter trough at one side of the Woodstock Design door and this man came and stood beside the matching planter at the opposite side of the door. He was fairly handsome, with dark hair and a wide fair-skinned and robust Greco-Arabic "classic" face . He was wearing a jacket or short overcoat with a purple muffler and first

DOING BUSINESS IN THE ADIRONDACKS by E. Macer-Story

attracted my attention by saying "no" loudly. When I turned to look at whatever was happening, there was no one there but the man in the purple muffler. He had replied to some spirit or inner voice. I looked away and he said "no" again. I ignored this and he spat sideways onto the cement beside the planter. I assumed he was waiting for the bus.

The bus came shortly thereafter. When I had boarded the bus, I glanced out the window and saw that he was still standing beside the planter. I find this highly suspicious. Previous to noticing this man at the bus stop, I had seen one condor fly low over the buildings just below Bread Alone Bakery on Mill Hill Road. I thought the lone condor, which I identify with my spirit guides, was a positive omen.

On the Sunday following this incident, I was followed into the local hardware store by an individual I was not able to see clearly without turning around obtrusively. This individual had evidently made some low level comment about me to the clerk, who protested loudly but cryptically that : "She is not…"Whatever. It may be significant that I did attend a talk by Dr. Steven Greer on Friday October 26 about the supposed U.S. government role in concealing information about ufos . I had acted as a reporter at the event, taking documentary photos, and so on. But I did not inform the Greer organization I would be attending this event until mid-day on October 26th though I had emailed [anon] that I would be attending.

On Saturday November 3, there were two unusual and insistent "wrong number" phone calls for some one named " Betty Butero"(pseudonym) during the afternoon. After the second call, during which it was evident that the caller either thought "Betty" was being concealed at my number or was attempting to enter my personal space via an insinuating tone of voice, a familiar, low male baritone, seductively sexual.

I dialed *69 trace coding after the second call and got a tape for the "Zachariah Book Store on Main Street", Main Street somewhere. I did not take down the number given to me by the *69 service as I thought the information on the tape was not genuine and I did not want to be tempted to trace any numbers later. I have changed the names in this narration for that same reason.. However, the original name of the bookstore refers to a type of ancient manuscript which has concomitant translations of Old Testament Biblical scripture running in parallel columns.

At one point in his article on "trickster" entities, Mr. Davis even ventures to call Eshu "the Hermetic linguist" since he has chosen to describe "Papa Legba" as the "messenger of the gods". Yet this is not the only description of this voodoo deity. Eshu or Legba is more frequently characterized as the Gatekeeper or Superintendent of the Property of Earth. He holds the keys to earthly power and all the other gods must ask for these keys before they are able to operate on the planet Earth. In his essay "Trickster At The Crossroads", Erik Davis expresses this situation in linguistic terms, as follows:

> "So Legba knows all the languages known to his brothers, and he knows the language Mawu speaks, too. Legba is Mawu's linguist. If one of the brothers wishes to speak, he must give the message to Legba, for none knows any longer how to address himself to Mawu-Lisa. That is why Legba is everywhere.."

As the hermetic linguist, then, Legba knows the cosmic language as well as the earthly language. Does Legba also know the language of mathematics and

DOING BUSINESS IN THE ADIRONDACKS by E. Macer-Story

physics? This possibility will be discussed later on in this book. The voodoo god Eschu (Exu) is often depicted with a red plume on his head. Is this symbology related to the red chevron painted on the back of the neck o of the gray and white bird I found below my writing desk window at the time I was assembling diagrams and illustrations of a quaisi-mathematical "flow chart" nature? Are these mathematical diagrams like the veviers or patterns used to symbolize and summon the Yoruba gods?

When the Manson family, as reported by several sources referred to a "Grand Chignon" who was far more evil than Manson and was in charge of "black magic" activities internationally, were they actually referring to the Haitian term :"Grand Cheman", the name for Eschu or Legba as "Lord of the Crossroads"?

On November 2, 2001, Reuters news service carried the article, *"Sorceress Had Smugglers Under Her Spell?"* datelined Bogota, Colombia.

"A Colombian sorceress who allegedly entered the international cocaine smuggling business used black magic to soothe her nervous drug runners, police said on Thursday.
Maria Elsinda Vasquez Munoz, known simply as "the Witch" would make her employees swallow as many as 70 latex glove fingers filled with cocaine before they boarded planes to Europe, police say.
"She would tell them that the black magic would protect them, that nothing would happen to them," said Col. Rodrigo Gonzalez, head of Interpol in Colombia.
"Obviously, it did not work," he said, adding that Vasquez was found with a voodoo doll when Vasquez and eight other members of her drug smuggling ring were arrested on Halloween in what the police called "Operation Bewitched.".

So it is evident that though intellectuals may have concerned themselves with the fine points of comparison between the Greek god Hermes and the Yoruba Orisha Exu, certain ceremonies involving the voodoo belief system still remain in the free form area of "hands on" practice. Some of these improvised ceremonies evidently do involve plastic gloves with all fingers still attached, as will be discussed later in this book.
In more intellectual discussions of these ceremonies, the crossroads symbol can be seen to resemble the type of mathematical x/y or geometric axis commonly used for elementary algebraic formulations. Yet on my way downstate from my home in the Catskills to my Magick Mirror office in Manhattan, I saw in the clear blue sky above the highway traffic a giant diaphanous aerial X which either had been made by two "skywriting" trails crossing or by one exhaust trail of a small airplane crossing a long, thin slat of cirrus clouds. It was a bright, crisp Fall day and there were no other large clouds in that Northeastern area of the sky. I wondered if this was in truth the free and more positive aerial sign of Papa Legba . I chuckled. For into my head had come a sly echo of the famous quote by the emperor Charlemagne, who had seen a cross in the sky and heard the words:" In this sign, thou shalt conquer." before successfully defending Europe from the infidels many centuries ago. Staring at the sky-written X, your present correspondent heard in her mind approximately this thought: "By this foggy X you will know the trickster's hex." In other words, light information which is made of obfuscating

DOING BUSINESS IN THE ADIRONDACKS by E. Macer-Story

fog and then vanishes may be the emblem of some serious, covert problem. I took this whimsical comparison to be actually a communication from the Janus-faced superintendent of All Worlds, the Guardian of the Keys to the Gateways of the Gods.

In what way should I proceed with my investigations when it had become obvious that criminals were playing games with spirit conjuration systems which might, particularly in combination with consciousness-altering drugs, actually produce real personality alteration and hypnotic effects as well as providing a channel for the manifestation of discarnate diabolic intelligence?

Frequently those who enter the "occult" scene either to dominate or to debunk from a very mental or intellectual training or point of view will not fully grasp the associative modality of thought and/or sensual/behavioral component of occult practice.

Those trained or sociology are particularly apt to miss the actual boat of the mythological "Ra/Set" before it even has left the pier. They are not able to find the point of debarkation simply because the assumption in that material, sensual perceptions are lesser and are to be controlled by "higher mental faculties" such as intellective analysis. But frequently the material/sensual perceptions are the true measure and guide in the material realm, which does not absolutely arrange itself according to intellective systems.

A few days after observing the foggy X in the sky and connecting this cirrus cloud crossed by con-trail in sky-written form with the "Papa Legba" crossroads symbol in the reference material by Erik Davis which I had been pondering along with my own past experiences involving voodoo practitioners, I had a sudden realization.

The email address of a correspondent on demimonde political topics and esp/pk I had recently come to suspect of deliberate disinformation contains wording which is similar to the "aerial x" sigil. This individual going by the alias of "Aexus"[6] is also unusually prissy on topics related to the personal sexual lives of the scientists and politicians he is discussing supposedly in terms of ideas and political viewpoints. Often, he will stress in near-slanderous correspondence semi-obscene suppositions about the intimate personal lives of people whose actual close emotional negotiations he could not possibly know. I recall catching him specifically on the issue of supposed details about the publication of a controversial conspiracy-oriented political magazine. He had written that the publication was issued by the managing editor and her date to a convention in Washington, D.C. where he had evidently witnessed these two journalists getting into a car together. Aexus referred to the situation as if the male companion of the editor, a man who is also a reporter, had been the publisher of the magazine. This was obviously a slur intended to establish the idea that the lady editor was "sleeping with" her boss. Yet I knew from direct experience as a sometime features writer for this magazine that the actual publisher is a professional advertising consultant who prefers to keep a low profile at public events.

At the time, I had dismissed this mis-construction as a foible. But perhaps it might be instead a deliberate "blocking" tactic coming from the mercenary and/or mentally-disturbed underbelly of the "mind control" and "consciousness research" contingent. Aexus had actually at one point been a part of the paid research & consulting demimonde surrounding the Esalen Institute, Laurence Rockefeller and CIA/academic contingent so "ready to roll" into cosmic dominance in the 1970's-80's. This coterie melted into foggy obscurity due to the collapse of funding to projects skewed by "sacred drug" experimentation and the weird sexual high-jincks (both in the area of indulgence and intense prohibition/regulation) which often attend upon the regular alteration of ordinary sensory consciousness by "sacred substances".

KGB and other foreign operatives had been a part of this demimonde. Might a person accustomed to society/agency money given over/under the table and finding this regular source of funding evaporating then turn to take money for "disinformation" and "obfuscation" services from very unconventional foreign and/or criminal sources?

According to our intellectual resource on the Trickster Deity, in the traditional Caribbean prayer to Papa Legba "Sonde miroir, O Legba" means literally "Fathom the mirror" or figuratively: "Uncover the secrets". So I asked this question of the living spirit of Legba, who replied with a well-known Lightning Hopkins blues music couplet:

"Don't let your left hand know
  What your right hand do:
An unseen eye is watching you"

It is worth commenting that after directly challenging Aexus under an email alias your present correspondent found that the Magick Mirror desktop publishing computer had been infected by the "god/shit" virus mentioned in the opening passages of this book. I make this connection most forcefully since when this reporter's alias was identified as being connected with knowledge of Shakespeare's play HAMLET in some way the "events calendar" page of the YankeeOracle.org performance site then originating from the Magick Mirror computer received a number of unusual posts containing executable files which were not opened. Give the cheap tricks contingent fifty cents for guessing the source of this reporter's email alias correctly.

It is indeed very tempting to jest a bit with these concepts. An over-serious and hyper-intense attitude frequently will inform the practice of power-oriented sorcery. When one stands outside the motivational emotion for these rituals and elaborate psycho-mythological systems, the actions of a self-appointed "adept" may seem ridiculous—like a video with the volume turned to zero—because the exact reason for every covertly-understood action is not overtly explained or spontaneously grasped by the observer who can see only the Adept taking deliberate action in the environment without hearing any explanation or enhancement of this simple vista of the bizarre.

Aexus once sent a "closed post" to a group of email addresses including that of your present correspondent which announced that the issue of "psychotronics" would be withdrawn from the so-called "Kucinich bill HR2977" which concerns U.S. government release to the public of data about ufo reports and ufo research. It is unlikely that the average American citizen would be highly energized on either of these issues. I did not take the continual posts from a variety of "in-group" people lobbying issues connected with this legislation seriously and did not read or save them. However, an incident involving a ride-not-taken on the Long Island railroad caused me to have second thoughts about certain of these energetic "ufo secrecy" advocates. I had been invited to a meeting of a local New York City group which was nominally about psychotronics, the intersection of mind with machine technology. This was not the national organization for which I have previously given papers at a yearly national convention. I had an odd feeling about the gathering on Long Island but decided to probe the situation anyway. I am well-acquainted with Pennsylvania Station near Herald Square in New York and walk through the station lobby several times a week to visit my post office box in the James A. Farley building across Eighth Avenue from the station.

I bought my ticket to the small town on Long Island at the Long Island Railroad ticket window and looked through the crowd there several times to locate the people who had invited me to the meeting and had arranged to ride the commuter train with me. No one I recognized was in the commuter crowd. As I waited beneath the large schedule posting board opposite the ticket windows, I noticed a conservatively-dressed man who reminded me closely of one of the "psychotronics" wizards I had agreed to meet there.

As the minutes rolled past on the digital display, bringing the time close to the scheduled train departure without any sign of the actual psychotronics wiz, I began to have an uneasy feeling about the "look-alike" standing stolidly in the crowd, evidently waiting for one of the several trains leaving for Long Island at that hour.

This man in the crowd was dressed in a conservative, tastefully-tailored navy blue overcoat with a matching winter muffler of a soft, navy blue fabric. When the "psychotronics" wizards failed to appear at the scheduled location and the commuter train had left without me I continued to have strong memories of this unidentified stranger as I walked up Eighth Avenue from Pennsylvania Station to the Port Authority to take the commuter bus upstate. There had been several aspects of his facial appearance which seemed unusual in retrospect. There was a dark energy about the eyes, which I could not see clearly, as if energy was coming from behind the eye sockets. His head was large on his medium-sized body and his carefully-groomed brunette hair did not seem false but did seem unusually neat. There were streaks of gray hair combed back to the side of both ears, as when a stage actor has streaked his hair to look more mature. But the feature I particularly noticed and remember was the chin line. This was unusually sharp and defined, as sometimes is the chin line of people who have had a face lift by plastic surgery.

In retrospect, I think this personage may have been or have represented the "business angel" who sometimes manifests to me. The "double" he presented actually kept me waiting until it was too late to check the other posting board upstairs in the station where the psychotronics wiz later said he and a friend had been waiting for me. Because I took the "double" as a synchronous impersonation, I automatically assumed that the real item might soon be arriving and only recalled the upstairs location too late to locate the waiting wizards, who had already boarded the train.

Later, it evolved that there was some type of business intrigue involving multiple "special" meetings taking place in that particular situation which it is better in ethical and practical terms that I do not enter. Along that fork of the road lies a descent into "special" and "secret" organization of the mental and social life which can ultimately result in the complete disconnection of the individual from ordinary conduits of information and funding.

The young Polish avante guarde film director Roman Polanski had, as was mentioned previously, created a satire of the Nazi-Viking "Lance of Power" and "Aryan Immortality" quest entitled "Fearless Vampire Killers" or 'Pardon Me, But Your Teeth Are In My Neck." People who speak German have informed this writer that the use of "High German" dialects in the film is actually quite funny, like having actors speak in a mixture of modern English and Olde English to indicate the presence of ancient vampires. However, it was very shortly after that light-hearted vampire romp that director Polanski's pregnant wife, the actress who played the comic vampire heroine in the film, was brutally murdered in a cult killing in California which did show signs of a bizarre

DOING BUSINESS IN THE ADIRONDACKS by E. Macer-Story

"execution" ritual. Is it possible that the satire and the murder were connected by a more direct thread than simple mad co-incidence within the naturally surreal artifice of the California film community? If so, is this thread cultist or "supernatural"? Or a bit of both? As in books written about a variety of un-apprehended serial killers, it is probably the over-intellectualization of such very simple questions which prevents the over-educated and pop-psychology conditioned writers from acknowledging the very real, but evil, "strange powers" in the minds and spirits of their opponents.

Adam Gorightly, in his book "*Shadow over Santa Susanna*"" about the Charles Manson situation, is canny enough to have grasped one aspect of these possibilities but imperfectly understands the full implications of his insight though his documentary narration is basically very evocative of the sleazy desert rat subculture. The title of the book refers to a song by Manson himself who envisioned the devil as a shadow with substance coming toward him on the wind to animate his diabolic activities.

Your present correspondent had an indicative experience with book divination whilst reading GoRightly's book I had been working on a talismanic painting involving apparitions of living persons from California I had experienced on the Woodstock-NYC commuter bus. As I paint, images arise which may provide answers not available to my analytic mind. One of the conundrums I was attempting to probe in this painting was: Why does a sense of the "supernatural" happen at a certain bus stop more frequently? I knew that it was rumored that a motorcycle gang had a house near that stop. But I had never seen a biker there. At any rate: I had just painted a squarish, transparent vehicle with windows like a house which troubled me because it looked odd, like a house with tires awkwardly at the corners. So I took a break and opened "*Shadow over Santa Susanna*"" at random.

Therein I read of the "log cabin" vehicle in dispute between filmmaker Kenneth Anger and actor Robert Beausoliel. That's very similar to the vehicle I had painted *before* reading that chapter. Kenneth Anger, according to a history of recent conflicts involving the Ordo Templi Orientis, is deeply into the actual practice of conjurations and power magick. He did in his film "*Scorpio Rising*" portray the wild orgy of a motorcycle gang involving actor Beausoliel. This may have entangled the film director with a "shadow" presence of notable destructive power which can manifest in a variety of locations and material forms.

Often, people unfamiliar with the actual folkways of the magick and sorcery underground mistake the sleazy trappings of "the occult" as these are seen in popular media such as TV serials and horror films with the actual practice of sorcery as a form of mental endeavor involving "mind over matter" or "spirit links", if you will. It is quite possible that the master criminals responsible for a number of psycho-sacrificial sleaze events are still at large simply because these individuals do not fit the media stereotype of how an insane sorcerer should appear visually.

The "Zodiac" killer, who was never traced by law enforcement authorities, once bragged in a note to a California newspaper: "I do not always look like this." Of course, a highly intelligent criminal would be able to costume him/herself to avoid detection. The "shadow" which may animate a variety of diabolic individuals has no one, distinct physical body but may appear in a number of guises, including very conservative and tiny bodies. By the same token, an angel may also take unexpected forms.

DOING BUSINESS IN THE ADIRONDACKS by E. Macer-Story

As I was preparing to transcribe the following section of text from hand-written notes which had been hastily journaled on January 22, 2002, a flying insect which was buzzing loudly flew against the side of my head and caused me to leap from my chair. At first, when I looked around the room, I found no such insect. But then I noticed a small housefly which darted away into another room, or vanished. It was hard to discern where it had gone.

On the same day in January of 2002 that my laptop computer had registered the destruction of a Magister B virus attempting to invade through the efax mechanism, my cat, wandering in the crawl space in between the ceiling of the cellar study and the floor above, seemed to be fighting with an aggressor. But when I checked out this situation there was no aggressor and the fight had ended. Frequently, individuals approached by the inner "devil's shadow" will seem to talk to themselves and/or fight with themselves or invisible opponents.

I wondered if the cat had sensed an evil presence. For on the email registry that day were several posts from "Aexus". Logically and by common sense there is no actual connection between an upset cat, a destructive computer virus wiped out by auto-detect cyber protection and written messages from a person suspected of subterfuge. However, once before—as described previously in this text—communication with "Aexus" had been concomitantly accompanied by a bombardment of anonymous posts containing executable files. A small bell began ringing very deeply in my mind.

I emailed author Adam GoRightly and asked him whether he had encountered any cyber experts in his investigation of the Manson situation. GoRightly responded:"Well, I can think of someone who might be called a "cyber expert" that is associated with Manson research. He uses a handle online but I have reason to suspect he's a Turkish guy living in the Bay area."

There are times in this type of intuitive investigation when one hates to be right. Now what? GoRightly does also describe in "*Shadow over Santa Susanna*" his enigmatic encounter with a cyber-operator from Saudi Arabia who was selling bogus or second hand website locations and for a short period of time overwhelmed with an ad for automotive services the web page intended to advertise GoRightly's book. All this seems scattered. One can't get a handle on how to put it together. But the sense of some unifying factor remains as the ghost of a possibility that negative advanced intelligence is playing disturbing games in cyberspace.

Those familiar with Arabic and East Indian traditions of drawing numeric sigils for spell casting may have stumbled upon a way to make a "talismanic" link involving computer coding. The automotive services location which briefly overwhelmed GoRightly's "Mansonmythos" web site turned out to be an actual service station located in North Carolina which had purchased web hosting services from the Saudi Arabian cyber bandit. Perhaps there is also an actual underhand crime connection which links the international vending of duplicate web sites with U.S. hill country drug moonshiners such as the fugitive hate bomber Eric Rudolph, who is reported by authorities to be hiding somewhere in the Southern Appalachian Mountains.

As Erik Davis points out in his study of the Yoruba-Voodoo Trickster spirit:'

"*In his book Count Zero , science fiction writer William Gibson put the orisha in the heart of cyberspace, his computer-generated astral data plane, and it worked far better than any hoary*

DOING BUSINESS IN THE ADIRONDACKS by E. Macer-Story

Egyptian deity or Irish fairy would have. Gibson, who tossed in those gods when he was bored with his book and happened to open a National Geographic article on voodoo, told me in an interview that he felt "real lucky, because it seemed to me that the original African religious impulse really lends itself much more to a computer world than anything in Western religion...It almost seems as though those religions are dealing with artificial intelligence.". Gibson also pointed out how similar vévés are to printed circuits. "

The presence of intelligent "fields" or energy forms does not, of course, apply only to the cyber process of artificial computers but also to the macro-process in natural structures, as we are now technically able to observe this intelligence within matter as manifesting in the "self-organization" of events."

Often physicists and other academic scientists recognize the spontaneous micro-organization of matter, as in the quantum atomic orbitals, but fail to see how events in molecular structure may be also spontaneously organized from the smaller or "hidden" structure of matter as this intersects with intelligent energy. A typical example of this teleological skepticism occurred in a question received from Matti Matpika of Finland. who was on the "antigravity" email list in 1999.

Subj: *[antigrav] Re: right & left spins in overt macro/micro context*
Date: 10/16/1999 8:46:22 AM Eastern Daylight Time
[Matti Matpika]
There is wellknown but I think poorly understood parity breaking effect which anyone can observe (has nothing to do with occult(;-)). The water going down the drain forms vortex which is righthanded (correct?). Why not sometimes left handed?

[Auth.Note: Actually, the water goes down the drain left handed just south of the Equator. In small particle and micro-reactions the direction of spin is not trivial but very important.If this natural reversal of drain vortices takes place in the planetary macrocosm, it must also have similar effects in the microcosm.]]

This reporter had not intended to limit commentary about counterclockwise spin to water or air. These are molecular structures which are basically mixtures which can vary in actual configuration. If anyone can recall--which may be hard to do after the avalanche of whirlpool etc commentary--I had simply stated that it is interesting that "mind/body" energies are used to spin by certain sorcerers. I did not state that "water" was always used in this spinning process.

It is the "accompanying" structural fields which Kosyrev discovered in his experiments and/or the "back action" effect discussed by Jack Sarfatti which may be similar to the "event configuration" fields which the sorcerers use to spin events into existence.

Additionally, counterclockwise is important exactly because it is rare in nature and must be artificially induced by the energy spinner. When power is obtained from a dam turbine--by analogy--the blades which are pushed by the water act *against* the flow thus causing a mechanical process of energy generation to begin.

DOING BUSINESS IN THE ADIRONDACKS by E. Macer-Story

[Auth. Note: Just south of the equator, as has been previously noted, the natural drainage is counterclockwise and so the arbitrary "widershins" of the manipulative sorcerer must be clockwise.]

Here it is important to recall that beneath the surface of our recent political history there are many mysteries left unsolved. For example, the fatal crash of U.N. official Dag Hammarskjold's airplane in Rhodesia, Africa on September 17, 1961. According to an article by Matthew Hughes in the London Review of Books August 2001, this may have been the work of mercenary Franco-Algerian white supremacists resisting the U/N. policy on Apartheid. But, if so: who paid them? Are we missing comprehension of a significant "mind control" group simply because that covert organization has been effective and is using a rather meticulous and detailed intellectual cultist rationale?

In this context, the location of a lost letter by Hispanic ufology expert Scott Corrales has enhanced importance:

Subj: **FORWARD -- lost letter! :-)**
Date: 2/1/2000 2:13:03 PM Eastern Standard Time
[Scott]
This is the letter you meant, right?
[Eugenia]
This is quite interesting. Which Spanish word is used for
"shiny" by the native residents? Can you forward me the article in the
original Spanish? I should notify the publishers on this list that speculation as
to a secret "ufo base" in Argentina constructed by neo-Nazis is part of my
recent book (available on Amazon.com) entitled DARK FRONTIER.
[Scott]
Hello! Synchronicity being the untamed beast that it is, I was re-reading
DARK FRONTIER yesterday afternoon in connection to a completely different
avenue of inquiry (OUR SOUTHERN HIGHLANDERS and your descriptions of
Appalachian sorcery) when my eyes were drawn to your quotes from Bob
Pratt's presentation the killer saucers in Brazil. Please feel free to
advise anyone on the list. The word used for shiny is alternately
"brilloso" and "brillante" (the first indicates reflecting light, the
second indicating self luminosity). I'll go back into the system and draw
the original out, since I didn't print it.
The Teutonic connection in these matters is very, very strong. Even in
the Zone of Silence (Mexico) there've been reports of Adamskiesque
"Blond" saucernauts conversing in German with certain tourists and local
schoolteachers who could identify the language."

Scott Corrales was writing about these Teutonic occupants of "flying saucers" in South America in February 2000, a year and a half before it was discovered following the terrorist action which demolished the twin towers of the World Trade Center that certain significant instigators within the Al Quaida Arabic terrorist network had operative connections in Spain and South America (CNN documentary) and had been living in Germany prior to their journey to the United States to undertake the co-coordinated terrorist action which involved trained pilots ramming hijacked commercial jets into the WTC skyscrapers. In this context, it is not outlandish to speculate that some portion of

DOING BUSINESS IN THE ADIRONDACKS by E. Macer-Story

the apocryphal but hotly-debated *"UFOS: NAZI SECRET WEAPON"* scenario may indeed be based in fact. Blueprints of a ufo-like craft are shown in the Iciris videotape which this reporter obtained at a New Science Forum conference in Fort Collins, Colorado in 1993. The documentary testimony is persuasive that there are aspects of the Axis scientific and technical projects which have escaped post World War Two scrutiny by Free World experts

According to professional translator Scott Corrales: *"It's a shame that no one was ever interested in my offer to translate Daniel Rebisso Giese's "Vampiros Na Amazonia", which offered in-depth, first hand info as to some of these capers (for want of a better word)."*

Perhaps those interested in this subject might profitably consult the works of British medical doctor and spiritualist Sir Arthur Conan Doyle who in his Sherlock Holmes mystery "The Adventure of the Sussex Vampire" describes the use of poisoned arrows from a primitive South American artifact by the blonde and Anglo-Saxon son of a British gentleman to frame his dark-complected stepmother for vampiric acts. It is possible that the actual planners of the acts of terrorism now being committed by desperate Arabs who believe they are engaged in a "Holy War" are actually instigated by the descendents of Axis scientists and technicians who escaped to South America and perhaps also to pre-arranged hideouts in India and Africa.

Inexplicata magazine editor Scott Corrales has also commented in email correspondence: *"A gentleman named Richard Ross, who is an expert at these things, even mentioned the Siemens Corporation in relation to the South Am. Nazi situation. More information continues to surface about the Nazi scientific capability every day--there was apparently a heavy bomber (six propellers) designed specifically to drop a uranium bomb on NYC. Photos of it have just been disclosed --why haven't we been told of this? More importantly, would this neo-tech research project perhaps open links to other dimensions? "*

Scott Corrales seemed to take knowledge of this "uranium bomb" project for granted. I had never heard of this Nazi plan before reading this reference to the work of Richard Ross. In light of the 9/11/01 terrorist attack on the World Trade Center towers in New York City, this is resonant of covert fascist connections and is perhaps a delayed National Socialist scenario.

Here we return briefly to the "antigravity list" discussion of occult philosophy and small particle spin orientation:

Subj: Re: [antigrav] Re: Kozyrev and two antigravity ...occult spin/spin lore
Date: 10/15/1999 8:19:15 AM Eastern Daylight Time

[Turkish Physics/Sufi Student cites:]
. Hayasaka, S. Takeuchi (1989) Anomalous weight reduction on a gyroscope's right rotations around the vertical axis on the Earth. Phys.Rev. L 63, pp. 2701-2704

[E.Macer-Story]
An interesting correspondence between Kosyrev's observations that variations of the gyroscopes' weight exist depending on angular velocity and direction of rotation and European/British occult lore is the distinction made between clockwise and counterclockwise as regards movement of the mind during operations of sorcery. When moving the mind/body clockwise (deosil) a "positive" result is supposedly obtained and when moving the mind/body counterclockwise (widershins) a

DOING BUSINESS IN THE ADIRONDACKS by E. Macer-Story

"negative" result is supposedly obtained. "Positive" and "negative" in this context may be interpreted as meaning "altruistic" (deosil) and "power-oriented" (widershins).But both directions are commonly used by sorcerers. I suggest that we should study widershins or counterclockwise spin as this is obviously the direction traditionally used for fast material effect. Deosil or clockwise may be more subtle or participate in long range effects which are less obvious in experiments."

It is hard to predict absolutely in which direction a Turkish Sufi may be spinning at the moment. However, it should be remembered when considering widershins and deosil orientation that Arabic and Hebrew, languages used for the ancient practice of "gemetria" are written from right to left of a margin on the right hand side of the page. The direction of spin and alphabet is obviously not as important as the careful intent of the practitioner. For obviously black magick spells in German, English and Cyrillic can be written left to right on a page from the left hand margin as well as greeting card verses about roses and violets. According to Rabbi Yisroel Dovid Berger, there is attention given in correct Hebrew calligraphy to the exact relative size of the letters and slant of accent marks which is a fundamental part of spiritual writing of scripture as in Buddhist, Shinto and Hindu calligraphy.

This attention to detail and measurement of the very small letters indicates an awareness of the connection between small, material shape/ action and larger events. In this context, it is worth noting that when your present correspondent was attempting to locate the book "The Universe In A Nutshell" in the 6th Avenue and 8th Street bookstore whilst listening to chatter about vampires from the adjacent cash register line, the clerk came up with the name "Gimel" Press as publisher before giving up the computer search entirely. The book was easily found later as issued from an establishment press on Amazon.com. The tale of the vampire synchronicities which followed mention of this event is told later in this book in context of non-local perception and spirit identities.

It is probably indicative that "Gimel", the third letter of the Hebrew alphabet, was initially given as the name of the press which had issued the book by physicist Stephan Hawking. For your present correspondent has written some physics theory which suggests a third force acting within matter in addition to the now accepted electric and magnetic vectors.

I was interested in the use of electromagnetic enhancement to study the effect of "shape" and acoustic arrangement mentioned in articles based on the work of Kosyrev included the recent post by M.Matpika. This is similar to the enhancement of effect which is experienced in the "high strangeness" areas which I am currently investigating. In the "high strangeness" areas, however, it seems to be variable gravitation which is providing the enhancement of effect rather than e/m fields. However, a comment on one of my papers years ago at an AAAS convention was that I should employ a geologist to also check for e/m effects as regards tectonic stress below the surface of the earth. Maybe. But I prefer to proceed with experimental naiveté and a simple camera and tape recorder because this does not limit findings to either g or e/m but includes both possibilities at first. Maybe the "spaceship" we are imagining on this Internet list is quite simple and we are tangled (entangled?) in complexity related to learned technical concepts."1999.

This is perhaps also why we do not recognize the overwhelming evidence for the distinction between mechanical "ufo"s which can fall from the air and the amoeboid

DOING BUSINESS IN THE ADIRONDACKS by E. Macer-Story

energy forms of Wilhelm Reich's and Trevor James Constable's research which seem to live either in the atmosphere or in hyperspace regions connected with the terrestrial atmosphere. Are investigations being blocked on two fronts in this area of ufo research? Might there be both interference by non-human Advanced Intelligence and by covert human intelligence using some type of Advanced Technical Systems with non-canonical notation and material characteristics?

The following is an update on the Argentinean aerolith situation from the "Diario Norte" newspaper, referred by Gloria R. Coluchi and translated by Scott Corrales.

WITNESSES CLAIM UFO FELL 70 KM WEST OF CHARATA
Tuesday February 1, 2000.- At a ranch some 70
kilometers away from Charta, on the border between Chaco and Santiago,
there exists eyewitness evidence of the location where the alleged
unidentified object fell last Wednesday, enshrouded in flames.

The radius covering the locales of Tintina, Otumpa, Sachayoj and
bordering Chaco would be the probable location of the resting place for
the object that crossed the Chaco and Santiago skies. NORTE covered the
area indicated by the "La Mensa" business establishment as the locale
where the object that fell to earth would be found, obtaining eyewitness
accounts of local residents giving their own versions of the event, thus
making it highly credible given the down-to-earth nature of these rural
residents.

One of the parties consulted by this agency, Juan Carlos Leguizamon,
claimed having knowledge of people who set off to find the object but
were unsuccessful in located it. "However, when the situation occurred, a
sound like a jet airplane was heard, and explosions like a burst of
*machine gun fire. **But all we saw was the smoke a few kilometers away***
from us."

In our tour of the "La Mensa" ranch and the Mennonite colony, there was
no visible traces of the object's fall, but during each interview, every
utterance by the locals always contains the possibility of the presence
of the strange "fireball" that altered the residents' easygoing
lifestyle.

The locals further indicated that the Santiago del Estero police was also
in the vicinity, but without confirming the reason for the presence.
Accompanying the authorities were technicians, astronomers and
researchers from said province, where the motives for their presence in
the area can only be guessed at.

All of this indicates a certain silence among the owners of the fields
involved as well as the authorities responsible for combing the area. But
there are also traces that this could be the center of attention to

DOING BUSINESS IN THE ADIRONDACKS by E. Macer-Story

verify or reject this mysterious event.

The area in question has proven to be a great hardship for the "baquianos", since it is densely forested, has deep canyons, and the vegetation proves a barrier to movement."

[PHOTO OF AERIAL ENERGY GLOB shown at Steven Greer lecture—NYC]

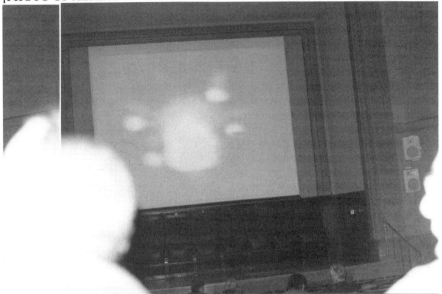

Could this aerial "smoke" then be the type of "ufo" pictured here in an unidentified 35mm candid shot from a montage shown at a lecture-presentation by Dr. Steven Greer in New York City in October 2001?The white silhouettes at the far left and right are audience members illumined by the camera flash. The globs of luminous energy in this frame shown on a movie screen at the back of the stage are quite different from the "flying saucer" prototype of unidentified aircraft and look more like the amoeboid forms researched by Reich and Constable. Could it be that these aerial manifestations are three-dimensional projections of a multi-dimensional intelligence which has the ability to "seem like" a jet or a fireworks display and/or to induct in percipients the idea that they had seen or heard conventional "aircraft" noise?

Two weeks after the crash or non-crash of the "smoky aerolith" near the "La Mensa" ranch in Argentina, a UFO craft was reported in the early morning skies over Mexico City.

From "Diario El Norte" Mexico City, Monday, 2-14-2000
by Javier Garduno as translated by Scott Corrales

MEXICO CITY-- An alleged UFO seen in the early morning hours on Monday by elements of the Secretariat of Public Safety led to a massive
mobilization of police elements in the northern areas of the city.
The alleged UFO was seen by patrolmen from unit 16156, who claimed having

it in plain sight and who described it as an object flying at low altitudes with flashing multicolored lights. The UFO was seen in a number of neighborhoods in the Azcapotzalco and Gustavo and Madero sections of the city between 2:20 and 3:00 am on Monday. Itvanished in a southerly direction behind Tenayo Hill in the municipality of Tlanepantla, state of Mexico.
According to information supplied by officers Javier Cedeno and Israel Valdivia, the alleged UFO remained suspended in the air at some 3 meters over a football field located inside the Center of Technical Research and investigation facing Vo-Tech No. 8 in the Barrio Santo Tomas neighborhood. Wristwatches worn by those law enforcement officers closest to the phenomenon were inexplicably stopped. However, when the agents tried to enter the building to reach the football field, they were kept from doing so by members of the buildings security force.

Here, in this visual sighting, there is indication via the stopped wristwatches of, at the very least, unconventional energy which interrupted the occasion whilst the unusual craft was visible. Certain SONY computers cannot be used in bright sunlight because the ultraviolet and/or direct heat of the sun interrupts the subtle electromagnetic cyber display process. So whatever was powering the craft or aerial display seen in Mexico City may have been using Advanced ultraviolet or microwave technology which affected the pulse of quartz watches. If these were not quartz battery powered watches but were mechanical watches then the microwave intensity necessary to stop them is quite different..

Is this an experimental aircraft using enhanced microwave technology and designed by a conventional government or corporate "black ops" project or is this watch-stopping vehicle "something else" , an advanced development pursued outside conventional, shared scientific and technical knowledge.

Here follows an excellent summary by Tim Matthews of Black Dawn Military UFO Research describing the alleged discovery that certain triangular "ufo" sightings were actually secret aircraft then under development..

"Both the Daily Mail and Daily Express newspapers reported today (circa April 4, 1998, when this article was forwarded by Paul Williams of WBAI radio UFO DESK) *the existence of 'radar tapes' purporting to show the operation of a UFO out to sea. The object was said to be flying at between 17-24,000 miles per hour.*

Despite the Ministry of Defense position that UFOs are 'of no defense significance' the story was said to have been leaked by a 'military source'. This was almost impossible to believe and the story could be seen at best as a cover for the operation and testing of secret military aircraft in the North Sea and over the Atlantic.

Despite their sophistication, it is not true that the latest Phased Array Radar systems would be able to identify the shape of a UFO - even one '900 feet' in length at anything approaching the speeds reported - a science correspondent should have known this simple fact.

The MOD press office commented today that they knew of the 'source' for

DOING BUSINESS IN THE ADIRONDACKS by E. Macer-Story

this story, that he could under no circumstances be taken seriously and that he had put out similar fabrications in the past. He is, apparently, an ex-MOD man with a grudge against his former employer!

Moreover, the Daily Mail KNEW (!) that the story was nonsense before they printed it and it will be noticed that this tabloid has put out a great deal of alien/ET-type material in recent months.

(The only sensible suggestion would have been that a comet with a large tail had entered the UK Air Defense Region/North Atlantic Ground Defense Environment - NADGE and had been tracked by sensitive radar systems. Apparently, this happens twice a month and DI55 have an interest in tracking both comets and space junk as they enter the atmosphere. In this respect, DI55 is undertaking a similar role to that of Project Moondust. Both DI55 and Moondust personnel have been linked with 'UFO' research activities.)

What is really going on out there then?

Just last week a diamond-shaped wing-wing aircraft was spotted by a trained observer off the Western Scottish coast near Campbeltown not far from RAF Macrahanish, previously rumored to be a base of operations for a number of secret aircraft and still a NATO standby base.

I have spoken to serving RAF personnel who have witnessed the operation of large triangular aircraft from RAF Boscombe in February 1997.

The secret history of advanced aircraft testing between the US and UK goes back to at least 1957 where British pilots were given unrestricted access to Groom Lake, Nevada (Bissell, 1996) during early U2 flights.

The recent wave of European triangle sightings, possibly an extension of the Hudson Valley operations of 1983-1988, began in Belgium in late 1989/early 1990 where a large triangular aircraft, based at Boscombe Down and perhaps also RNAS Yeovilton, was reported by numerous credible witnesses as hovering at low altitude.

A peculiar idea shared by certain theorists into the UFO enigma and communications from Advanced Intelligence is described by Colin Wilson in his book "Alien Dawn", which is a compendium of ufo research and thought about anomalous events and expanded perception published in 1997. This unique idea is of a "suction" up into a more advanced and comprehensive level of perception. Subsequent to the mental "suction" event, the affected individual is not the same and older, more mundane versions of reality are not able to be comprehended as valid. Your present correspondent cannot resist commenting that this sounds like what happens when new software is installed on an older computer.

DOING BUSINESS IN THE ADIRONDACKS by E. Macer-Story

The concept of the individual consciousness being absorbed into a higher-level more integrated functioning is similar to a variety of alchemical ideas on the breaking apart or dissolution of older, previous circumstances in order that this situation be re-assembled in a newer, more appropriate form.

Traditionally, however, this reintegration includes the material, mundane aspects of existence. That's what alchemy is in fact: material transmutation by means of the catalytic mind/spirit. A "suction upward" may not actually be the most beneficial use and recognition of more topological or "advanced" intelligence. Like the buffered, unfocused quality which accompanies hypnotic induction, this "suction upward" seems to be dissolution without reassembly, a topological functioning without specific mundane application.

But here in New York the citizens have always believed in freedom of assembly. This also may be seen to apply to states of dissolution by "suction upward" without reassembly. People of whatever literary and/or social distinction are free to make the mistake of being "sucked upward" into an abstract and "quantum" agenda ruled by unidentified "higher intelligence". As P.T. Barnum once remarked: "There is a sucker born every minute".

Quite a few of those who have been "sucked upward" find their way to New York City and environs. There they hope to sink an anchor in order to float the boat of their "higher knowledge" upon the restless sea of real estate which they conceptualize will support without leakage a barge of paper mache which inevitably melts upon the mundane tides of material reality.

Tim Matthews of Black Dawn Military UFO Research, having been sucked into the idea of vast, secret aircraft projects, assumes all aerial triangles are these secret aircraft. He thinks himself privy to the secrets of a privileged governmental intelligence project which will "explain everything" in terms of strategic military priorities. He may not be correct in every instance.For example, the Catskill and Adirondack mountain area of New York State has been the site of unusual aerial occurrences for centuries. The shape of the aerial vehicles seen in the 1980's there as triangular may not definitely distinguish them from the "flying heads" seen by the Onteora Indians or the aerial bowling balls of Hendrick Hudson's ghostly crew.

However, the commentary of Tim Matthews and others with a limited technical viewpoint should be included and considered lest this present narration be accused of metaphysical abstraction. Matthews writes:

In 1994 a secret US spy plane crash-landed at RAF Boscombe Down and was widely reported in regional, national and specialist media but denied by the MOD.

In 1993/4 an aircraft not unlike the US Advanced Airborne Reconnaissance System 'Tier 3' aircraft was reported to be operating over the UK as part of a series of transatlantic demonstration involving the RAF and elements of the aerospace industry. According to US black projects researcher Dan Zinngrabe, a respected source, the aircraft cost over $150 million, used active stealth features and was able to hover through the use of an advanced jet propulsion system which might have been ducted 'fan-in-wing'

DOING BUSINESS IN THE ADIRONDACKS by E. Macer-Story

technology....

At this time, Nick Pope, former Secretariat Air Staff 2a UFO 'expert' went public with a story that UFOs were of extraterrestrial origin and this was undoubtedly part of the cover story involving the MOD and the UFO community.....

Nick Cook, military aerospace expert for Jane's Defence Weekly, has stated that the US is actively seeking to develop 'electrogravitics' propulsion systems.

(These are also being researched within British Aerospace as part of a classified defense project).

So whilst we have twaddle being put out in the tabloids, some UFO researchers are getting to grips with the reality of secret military aircraft."

So we see here in this documentation the belief that unidentified flying triangles may credulously be taken to be from outer space but are actually secret terrestrial war-craft under development. So, also, those sightings of :"craft" not in the form of amoeboid energy aloft may be part of an independent terrestrial project rather than apparatus from beyond this planet.

Contemporary sighting of religious apparitions, which in certain instances may be the mask of unknown Advanced Intelligence, presents an array of problems which—considered separately from any religious beliefs—revolve about mind/matter manipulations quite different in impact from simply seeing a distant, anomalous aerial object.

The Catholic Church, familiar with the masquerades of diabolic intelligence, continues rightly to caution about the validity of certain "religious" apparitions which, though they may show power of "mind over matter" and seem quite astounding are actually a "show" or "charade" by diabolic intelligence .Notice that at the end of the following article on a Marian apparition taken from an Argentine publication the Catholic Church is actually disclaiming liability for the apparition..

MARIAN APPARITIONS IN LAPRIDA, ARGENTINA
The apparition of a supposedly religious apparition in downtown Laprida caused a commotion among local residents. The event acquired notoriety last week,(late January 2000) following a woman's claim of having seen an image of the Virgin Mary on a tree at the intersection of Almirante Brown and Independencia Streets.
While some argue that the image represents the Virgin of the Miraculous Medallion, others believe that it represents the Sacred Heart of Jesus. Religious articles were immediately placed on the tree--flowers, rosaries and votive cards. The incision on the tree's trunk, which allegedly reflects the holy image, was made by municipal personnel approximately six months ago, and do not betray any sign of paint nor other strange

elements.

It is thus that this community remains agitated as a result of this apportion and over the course of recent days, the street corner is filled by faithful who have visited the image out of devotion or out of mere curiosity. The fact is that the sheer numbers of visitors have caused considerable traffic headaches.

Last Thursday evening, the image of a cross was discovered on a streetlamp located two meters away from the tree. In this regards, the operator of the local power utility (EDES) was consulted. The company spokesman indicated that at no time had a signal of that nature been made on the post by their crews, and was therefore unable to venture a guess as to its origin.

On the other hand, another event which has caused even greater curiosity is the fact that the same tree reflects another image of the Virgin as a child. Beyond the existence of these signs, it is refreshing and touching to see the elderly, the young and children approach the tree, pray before it, and even kiss it. The devout appear to be the most motivated. They worship at the site and try to convince those who doubt the existence of the divinity.

"I'm so excited," enthused Queca, a devotee of the Virgin Mary and who remained at the tree for 24 hours when the image was first discovered, accompanied by a group of young people. "One of my nieces made this discovery. She had seen it for almost a month, but didn't say anything for fear of being called a lunatic."

Queca opines that the site ought to be protected, in the knowledge that it has become a place for prayerful retreat.

17 year-old Oscar indicated that the entire situation pivots on faith and the perspective one has about the event. "I have my doubts, but I'm not discarding the possibility that it could be then virgin. That's why I'm here."

A Catholic and member of the "Cursillos" movement, Monica claimed being as perplexed as other residents, but does not hesitate to indicate her agreement with the image's holy origin. Another item that caused even greater surprise among Lapridans was the fact that the worker in charge of caring for the tree suffered an accident while trimming the holy tree, while the adjoining tree was trimmed without incident.

The Church does not avow the apparition, however. Upon returning from holiday, parish priest Calros Garciarena reflected the church's policy on such things during a sermon. After contacting Msr. Emilio Bianchi Di

DOING BUSINESS IN THE ADIRONDACKS by E. Macer-Story

Carcano, he was told that the Church does not attest to the truthfulness of this apparition, and further assumes no liability over any events which may take place at the site."

Note that this statement about Church opinion sounds like an insurance or divorce disclaimer. Centuries of experience with the various apparitions and disguises of the crossroads Trickster force (Remember the Orisha Exu or Legba") may have made the good fathers skeptical of images which magically appear in the incised bark of trees. These images may be genuinely supernatural but such wonders tend to cause odd effects such as the accident to the worker who dared to prune the "Holy Tree".

In 1997, as part of a project for the "Artists & Writers Collaborative" in New York City I wrote a radio series pilot which was intended for the general audience, including children. This brief sketch in dialogue illustrates the possibility of negative, demonic powers which can travel in time and are opposed by the more positive "time police" , a supernatural force signaled into action by disruptions in the natural fabric of events caused by a rogue force trying to pull the general, shared destiny into merely one eccentric power pattern.

The "devil" or "Great Deceiver" is sentimental and often will appear under unusual circumstances as a "poor orphan" or "needy waif" So: should we look for our hidden "black magicians" also in the ranks of those claiming proudly to be orphans, beggars or otherwise disadvantaged not by means of ordinary catastrophe or bad luck but for esoteric, mysterious reasons?

Note how in the following dramatic sketch the "Chronimal Conspiracy" is first disguised as a maternity nurse concerned about unsanitary odors in the hospital corridor and the forged passport of the "Time Cop" who arrives suddenly, trying to prevent the adoption of the father of a future mad scientist who is only seconds away from blowing up the planet earth.

TIME COP VERSUS THE COSMIC CHRONIMAL CONSPIRACY

A RADIO SERIES PILOT
BY
EUGENIA MACER-STORY

CAST
ALEXIS d'ANGELA,
TIME COP,A HUSKY FEMALE TENOR VOICE

ANNOUNCER,
A DEEP, RESONANT MALE VOICE

THE CHRONIMAL CONSPIRACY,
A MALE/FEMALE, FEMALE/MALE CHAMELEON VOICE

DOING BUSINESS IN THE ADIRONDACKS by E. Macer-Story

SOUND: 1, 3, 6, 8, 15, 18, 25, 41, 43, 47, 49.

MUSIC: 1, 38, 45, 49.

1. <u>LOUD REGULAR SOUND OF TICKING WITH ONE BEAT STRESSED:</u> "TICK-tock,TICK-tock, TICK-tock...FADE..ORIENTAL GONG.

2. ANNOUNCER: In between the tick and the tock, the cosmic time battle between the Time Police and the time-jumping Chrominal Horde is waged in the silent microsecond when the pendulum changes its swing from the upward to the downward arc or the downward to the upward arc, within that pause before the next digital number is advanced or reversed on the display screen.

3. <u>LOUD CLOCK ALARM.</u>

4. ALEXIS: Time police, may I help you?

5. ANNOUNCER: Early or late, you set the date, Officer Alexis D'Angela of the Chronological Bureau of Historical Readjustment may have appeared on your doorstep <u>before</u> you call for help, or many years after your alarm. So, turn off the clock on your radio and set the alarm for Anytime.

6. <u>FOOTSTEPS OF BOOTS WALKING UP CEMENT STEPS.</u>

7. ALEXIS: It is now 7:15 p.m. on the night of October 31, 1947 and Alexis D'Angela has just appeared on the steps of a maternity hospital which was once located in the British quarter of Delhi, India.

8. <u>THE DOUBLE DOORS OF THE HOSPITAL FLAP OPEN AND SHUT.</u>

9. ALEXIS: Nurse, we understand that a baby will be born here this evening. His name will be Dravid..

10. <u>THE NURSE COUGHS AND BLOWS HER NOSE..</u>

11. CHRONIMAL,<u>disguised as a nurse</u>: What is that horrible smell? It can't be sanitary.

12. ALEXIS: You will have to excuse the momentary odor of ozone, Nurse. It is an unavoidable side effect of the time travel process.

    Here we interrupt this radio play to offer an actual anecdote on arcane mischief for your real time consideration. On January 4, 2002 when I was downloading a draft copy of a book which mentions my ideas on interdimensional co-presence and time-independent causality, I kept having the problem of the download disconnecting about three-quarters of the way through the process. Other connections and downloads did not share this same problem.

Finally, I used the same ISP and screen name alias with which I had addressed Aexus, the sky-written x-rated trickster, since it was conveniently on hand as an alternate web access. The draft copy of the book downloaded easily and swiftly. Obviously, the interruptions I had experienced were programmed to occur only between that particular download and my publicly-known screen identity. As well as known perpetrators of such mischief, there is also the "Thantatos" crew I had noticed interfering with my activities in the form of micro-alterations of talismanic objects.

Cyber coding obviously would be a fertile field for experimentation in this area. Or is this selective cyber-glitching the work of a diabolic spirit entity with the ability to affect computer coding? I did get a view of a certain section of the book draft which I needed to proofread while online. When the download interruptions had become maddeningly oppressive, I did an old-fashioned candle, water and salt invocation near the computer to my own spirit guides for assistance. Then, the connection held just long enough for me to examine the section of my writing I needed to proofread.

As I was jotting this journal entry (originally in longhand) I noticed that a piece of decorative facing had fallen off one of the combination fan-light fixtures in the nearby glassed-in porch. Whatever subtle force affects cyberware by intent might also affect the molecular binding in the glue which held the sticker to the overhead fan blade. I recalled that I had once written the verse of a song:

"The saucer is a fan
It moves on currents of time
And one year of yours
Is ten weeks of mine…"

and so on through days, minutes & seconds.

…as part of a short mummers play just <u>before</u> experiencing a non-fictional "ufo light" sighting on December 30, 1973. At the time I wrote this song, it was simply a humorous spin-off of the 1970's "ufo flap" in the United States which was getting tabloid publicity.

Shortly afterward, I would find myself deeply involved with trying to explain my own "ufo light" sighting to skeptics. There is, in this context, some valid argument for the idea that the play itself, "Fetching The Tree", a Christmas musical in which Santa Claus is seen as a UFO personage wearing a large coolie hat[7], was inspired because in the future I would experience some version of this enigmatic phenomenon directly. I did include in the program flier the newspaper photo of several Oklahoma State Troopers who had sighted a ufo in 1973 shortly before Christmas as this incident had inspired several; scenes in the play.

So the "saucer is a fan" song insight might have symbolic validity as a technical inspiration. In this song, there is a constant "saucer/fan turning on currents of time" according to a "ten" constant which has no adjustment to terrestrial seasonal/ diurnal computations of years, weeks, hours , minutes and seconds. In the song, as originally composed, the months are not part of the regularization into tens by the "fan turning on currents of time". So the computations of the song are not concerned with the phases of the moon, a planetary satellite, but with the orbit of the Earth-planet around the sun/star and the diurnal rotation of the planet in relationship to the parent sun. This would be measurable in comparative terms with other planets regardless of the exact behavior of

DOING BUSINESS IN THE ADIRONDACKS by E. Macer-Story

their natural satellites. So the concept is that the "flying saucer", the real ufo phenomenon which is not a secret terrestrial ufo project, somehow generates its own time standard, which has something to do with regularized centripetal/centrifugal force. This can also be conceptualized as some form of "artificial gravity".

Future sections of this book will deal with actual theories of external/internal mass gravitation and "artificial gravity" due to variable mass density. Right now, we return to the radio play exactly where we had departed into a speculation about hyperdimensional realities. To be specific: at line 12 when Officer Alexis of the Time Police has just appeared in an early Twentieth Century nursery in the former British quarter of Delhi, India.

12. ALEXIS: You will have to excuse the momentary odor of ozone, Nurse. It is an unavoidable side effect of the time travel process.

13. CHRONIMAL:Your car must not be ventilated. Are you a relative of the mother, Madame? What is that? A passport? That is not a legal passport, Madame.

14. ANNOUNCER: Meanwhile, one century later, in the offices of the Chronological Bureau of Historical Readjustment in Sri Lanka, the biography of Dravid T. Zaylor of London, England is now being assembled by computer search of all available identification sources. It has to be a quick job! For nuclear renegade Dr. Dravid T. Zaylor,Jr. is reported to have a secret formula powerful enough to blow up the entire Republic of China. In fact, he had already activated the device and started the countdown when his colleague and loyal assistant Margo Li Chan had second thoughts about this explosive situation and e-mailed an alarm to the Time Police.

15. <u>THERE IS A SERIES OF LOUD, URGENT ELECTRONIC BEEPS.</u>

16. ALEXIS: We have exactly 48 seconds until detonation. I shall have to time jump into the next nanosecond and travel backward on the biographical line of mad scientist Dr. Dravid T. Saylor, Jr. because we do not know exactly where his present day hideout is located. According to the "China On Line" automatic computer tracer, it is somewhere in the vast Siberian Steppes.

17. ANNOUNCER: But, meanwhile, one hundred years ago, just outside the maternity ward in Delhi, India, Time Cop Alexis d'Angela has encountered an unusual obstacle.

18. <u>LOUD CLANKING AND RATTLING SOUND.</u>

19. ALEXIS: Nurse! Someone has installed a bolt lock on this door! In fact: there seem to be five or six of them! Isn't it unusual to have this much security in a hospital? Unless there's some rare disease in the nursery....Nurse! Is there any reason this door is locked from inside?

DOING BUSINESS IN THE ADIRONDACKS by E. Macer-Story

20. CHRONIMAL,feigning consternation: It's not locked from inside...or...it never used to be locked. I don't know what's going on!

21. ALEXIS: Perhaps in the future, as a grown man, Dravid T. Zaylor Senior senses that I may be trying to enter his nursery. For it is in this hospital that Dravid Zaylor, the father of mad scientist Dr. Dravid T. Zaylor, Jr., was left for adoption by his unwed mother, Francine. Francine! Francine! Unlock the door!

22. CHRONIMAL,deviously: Who is Francine? The mother? The mother's not here! She's in a hospital room down the hall!

23. ALEXIS: Are you sure?

24. CHRONIMAL,deviously: Yes! I just brought her the adoption permission forms.

25. THERE IS A SERIES OF LOUD, URGENT ELECTRONIC BEEPS.

26. ANNOUNCER: Officer Alexis d'Angela! Officer Alexis d'Angela! We have exactly 47 seconds until detonation! We are one second further into the "real time" emergency here at your time origin in the future!

27. ALEXIS: I copy. Over and out. Nurse, those adoption forms you say you just brought to Francine...Is that adoption request sent in by the Zaylor family?

28. CHRONIMAL, falsely amazed: Why, yes! How did you know?

29. ALEXIS: I am the...ah...the solicitor for the Zaylor Estate and there has been a mistake on those forms. I must see the Zaylor adoption forms immediately!

30. CHRONIMAL,falsely helpful I'll just walk down the hall here and peek into her room. Francine! There's a solicitor here to look at the Zaylor adoption forms! O my! She doesn't seem to be in her room. Perhaps she did lock herself inside the nursery. But the Zaylor forms are still here, beside the bed,

31. ALEXIS: Let me see those forms! I want to look at the names here.

32. CHRONIMAL,fearfully angry: What are you erasing?

33. ALEXIS: "Dravid." I must erase the name "Dravid".

34. CHRONIMAL, falsely helpful: O, I think that's "David". It's just mis-spelled.

35. ALEXIS: No! We must erase the entire name "Dravid".

DOING BUSINESS IN THE ADIRONDACKS by E. Macer-Story

36. ANNOUNCER: At some future point in time, the "R" might be inserted by a Chronimal imposter or the infant by any other name might still be persuaded to change it's legal name back to "Dravid T. Zaylor", the ancestor of the mad scientist now in the process of detonating a renegade nuclear device somewhere on the Siberian Steppes.

37. CHRONIMAL: Here! Give me those forms! This's not allowed! This sort of legal behavior is not allowed in the hospital! Solicitors are not allowed to just come in here off the street and change the names on those adoption forms! This's a matter of proper procedure!

Before reading onward in this brief radio script, consider the possibility that present terrestrial civilization may actually be experiencing travel into the future by so-called "Atlantean" adepts and/or travel into the past by persons from the future who are intent upon altering their present dilemmas. This tinkering may be construed to be positive or negative—depending upon the rationale of the adept. The preconception is that "ufo" phenomena are from other, material worlds and are somehow able to traverse interstellar space by means not yet apparent to this terrestrial civilization. But perhaps these mysterious alchemical strangers seen by so many people are from qualitatively different timespace areas rather than simply from different material areas separated by uniform timespace distances.

38. LOUD ORIENTAL GONG.

39. ALEXIS: So, instead, I shall now have to travel into the future, to a timespace location which has occurred after the Dravid T. Zaylor, Jr. explosion, in order to alter the multi-dimensional holographic records of human experience so that any person who happened to be named Dravid T. Zaylor, Jr (by birth or adoption)will have incorrectly designed the renegade explosive device he attempted to plant on the Siberian Steppes with or without the assistance of his former research colleague, Dr. Margo Li Chan.

40. ANNOUNCER: This is a little more difficult, but it is possible.

41. THERE IS A SERIES OF LOUD, URGENT ELECTRONIC BEEPS.

42. ANNOUNCER: Officer Alexis d'Angela was in the process of beepering in her intention to change strategy and time-jump into the historical section of the World Library archives twenty years after the explosion on the Siberian Steppes sank Japan and raised the long lost Islands of Atlantis....

43. LOUD SOUND OF STATIC.

DOING BUSINESS IN THE ADIRONDACKS by E. Macer-Story

44. ANNOUNCER: When suddenly she was interrupted by the time static of a Chronimal Conspiracy Wizard with an interest in the future existence of rug and fresh fruit trade from the New Atlantean Islands, which would not have been suddenly raised from the floor of the Pacific Ocean if there had been no renegade Siberian nuclear explosion.

45. LOUD MODAL WOODEN FLUTE ARPEGGIO.

46. CHRONIMAL, cleverly: Officer d'Angela did not suspect that rather than being a maternity nurse, I was actually a Chronimal Conspiracy Time Wizard! Actually, I will now be taking the signed adoption papers forward into the future, arriving after Officer Alexis d'Angela has already altered World Historical process by inserting a badly-designed nuclear detonator into the multi-dimensional holographic records of human experience. I will then act swiftly to re-insert the Dravid T. Zaylor adoption forms, resulting in a flawlessly-designed renegade nuclear blast which destroyed half of Siberia and raised the New Atlantean Islands from the Pacific Ocean near the China Sea.

47. LOUD CLOCK ALARM.

48. ANNOUNCER: Actually, none of this has happened yet. But, unfortunately, we are out of radio time here at the Chronological Bureau of Historical Readjustment. Tune in next week, same time-same station, for episode 484 in TIME COP VERSUS THE COSMIC CHRONIMAL CONSPIRACY.

49. TICK-tock,TICK-tock,TICK-tock, FADING. SOFT GONG.

Notice that in this play there are two possible ways for "Advanced Intelligence" to carpenter "history" or "destiny". One method is to hop backward in time to change one crucial developmental detail and the other method is to travel forward in time to alter the cosmic, holographic record of the past. Edgar Cayce, the "sleeping prophet", called this holographic history of terrestrial life the "akashic records".

Recently, researchers at Boston University's Quantum Imaging Laboratory proposed an experiment to create holographic images of objects concealed in a spherical chamber. Ideally, a small opening in the chamber wall would permit light to enter, but let no light out. However, there is a problem with this experimental design as the researchers assume the primacy of the "photon" and visible light made coherent as in the laser beams of a holographic photo apparatus. In his book "The Universe in a Nutshell" physicist Stephan Hawking has whimsically cited a concept he calls the "Chronology Protection Conjecture". To wit: a protection against inadvertent or badly manipulated time travel & teleportation of macroscopic objects is that the "universe is not expanding in the third space direction, which is periodic". I take this citation of a periodic dimension of space to refer in part to the coherent atomic-molecular pulsing of matter which Hawkng cites in the final section of his book as the "smallest fundamental length" or length of time pulse shift as in Planck's constant.

DOING BUSINESS IN THE ADIRONDACKS by E. Macer-Story

IF the Planck's constant & photon speed C permitted in the known cosmological observations is actually only one value of a spectrum of values of possible linked and parallel cosmologies which enjoy a different value of the "Chronology Protection Conjecture" then the coherent double beam of the laser mechanism cited in the hypothetical "experiment" quoted above will not be effective in creating a complete hologram of matter or actual mass. Rather, this hologram will be a "shadow" resemblance of the complete spectrum of possible linked and parallel universes which have a mass pulse with a differing "chronology constant".

The possibility of an unseen and thus uncomprehended cosmos existing adjacent to the cosmology preferred in current textbooks is the reason that your present correspondent remains interested in possible "true anomaly" explanations of the chupacabras attacks in Hispanic America which go beyond the idea of a mad monkey starving for pepperoni and other strictly zoological explanations..

Actually. certain adept sorcerers acting with the assistance of spirit entities not incarnate in a human body may be able to travel operationally outside the boundaries of linear time. There is a venerable Christian saying: "The Devil has power over the past but not over the future." Records of events already in existence or remembered to be in existence can be altered by an adept Intelligence positioned outside linear, material sequence. But the record of future events not yet firmly attached to any definite past or present event can only be altered by the innate development of the destiny matrix. Our "time police" traveler in the preceding radio play sketch can only hope that her alteration of past infant adoption proceedings shifts the catastrophe of the present-future, perhaps perpetrated by a descendent of that infant, into a more positive, re-destined pattern. Likewise, diabolic tinkering with the past is never "sure" of the desired control of future events. Many parallel future destiny patterns are possible.

As readers of my book *DARK FRONTIER* know, I have researched folk beliefs and practices in Mexico and other South American countries and those who go beyond the foofery of Barbarella Comix also must know that the belief in vampires and blood-sucking witches is part of a religious belief system, which goes way back into antiquity there.

On July 31, 2000, Hispanic ufologist Scott Corrales wrote in response to the probing of these issues by your present correspondent:.:" *Your own theories are confirmed by certain displays in the museum of anthropology at either Santiago de Chile or in Calama itself, which apparently feature dioramas of "Nuestros Indios y sus Dioses" (Our Indians and Their Gods) offering blood sacrifices which were later collected by "bright lights in the desert" --people may kick and scream,*
but this what Salvador Freixedo has been saying since 1975 or
thereabouts. These lights (UFOs if you must) appear to respond to these
ancient rituals and there is nothing interplanetary about them...if I hit
the lottery, I'd self publish my translation of Defendamonos de los
Dioses and send a free copy to everyone who ever evinced an interest in
the subject.".

Here we speculate on the human, more mundane and more understandable aspects of cultist beliefs. Individuals may 'disappear" because they "know too much" or became part of a terminal sado-masochistic ritual. But actual spirits may be the inspiration for this mischief. So, possibly, the attempted machinations of "secret sorcerers" lead to an

DOING BUSINESS IN THE ADIRONDACKS by E. Macer-Story

enhanced appreciation of human capacity which can ultimately be used for positive purposes.

On New Years Eve 2000, as previously narrated in outline as a brief interruption of the "time travel" play, I had struggled intermittently throughout the day to access online the pdf file of Dr. Jack Sarfatti's book draft entitled "*Destiny Matrix*". I wanted to see the references to the "Cat's Cradle" concept I had originated and was continually frustrated by the computer Internet connection, which kept disconnecting during access or download of this ebook file.

I had the sense of definite cyber interference but did not know how to overcome this situation technically. So finally I lit a candle, placed water and salt beside it and invoked assistance from my olde tyme spirit guide who had also assisted me in Salem, Massachusetts years ago in 1975 when I founded my "Magick Mirror" enterprise. At that time, I had developed the "Alexander Graham Bell" song, which I sang to invoke my illustrious ancestor who had originally invented the telephone in Nova Scotia and Salem.

The New Years Eve of 2000, equally as cold inWoodstock,N.Y. as the infamous Winter of 1975-76 had been in Salem, I once again felt the need for Extreme Assistance in the area of "human evolution and inventions", the area of knowledge in which the ancestral communications spirit answering to the name of "Alexander Graham Bell" has a particular specialty. So I activated the computer and went online, got water, salt and a candle and lit this candle "to keep the force of darkness out" as goes one traditional invocation for protection.

It certainly felt unique to be sitting between a laptop computer screen and a smoking candle, attempting to access a book on non-local concepts in physics and human destiny. But, hey! Such extreme action was completely appropriate! For once I had admitted to myself the possibility of cyber-sorcery, the Old Ways could be used to block and overcome the interference. The "Cat's Cradle" concept included by my suggestion in the Sarfatti book "*Destiny Matrix*" is also an olde tyme game, with loops of yarn strung between the hands to make a complex "cradle basket" out of one length of string. My concept is simply that the present, as we understand it, is simply suspended in a "cat's cradle" between past and future loops of the same cord which suspends the present securely in place.

Since Dr. Jack Sarfatti is a physicist, he immediately equated the strings of yarn in the olde tyme game with the current physics term "string" which indicates one dimensional extension in timespace and formulated an equation for showing that what we know as "the present" is dependent on both past and future circumstances. Events which will transpire in the future also affect the way are suspended "now" in present context.

Humorously, one example of this situation might have been my inability to access the "Destiny Matrix" pdf file while at the same time angrily willing mightily to "do the right thing" and proofread the references to my ideas in Sarfatti's manuscript, lest there be an error which should be corrected before printing. For my positive destiny may have prevented me from accessing a premature draft. Whilst I was valiantly trying to access the file, Sarfatti was actually in the process of revising this draft offline. He decided to upload a revised draft just before I decided to go back online with salt, water and candle.

So my inability to access this post at eleven a.m. may have been part of the future fact that a new version of the same manuscript was going to be available at seven-thirty p.m. If, as is probable, the continuous disconnections experienced in downloading the

"*Destiny Matrix*" file were part of a web-interference programme of deliberately-engineered "cyber sorcery" then it is appropriate that the frustrating blockage actually prevented me from downloading a premature draft I would later have to replace.

Author Colin Wilson writes in his excellent book "*Alien Dawn*"(p.249) about the power over sequential time demonstrated by so-called "ufo beings" during the alleged abduction of humans. In a commentary on the lore of "ufo abductions", Mr. Wilson questions how this time control might actually be accomplished. He states that slowing down or speeding up time might be a function of control of the psychological time of the abductee.

But, actually, this is not the only possibility. If an additional energy to the electromagnetic, as in the more technical "fluidice matrix" formulations given later in this book, could be used to "shift over" the life energy of the entity to another electromagnetic master frequency, a process affecting the inner density of atomic structure and mass composition, sequential time (which is an electromagnetic pulse frequency) would be automatically altered without changing basic structural shape. This is roughly analogous to slowing or speeding the sound on an electronic volume control mechanism. If all sound in the room is moving at 33 v.p.sec. then sound at that rate appears normal and words can be distinguished. If sound is moving at 28 v.p. sec. in a 33 v.p. sec room then the sound does not appear normal but words can still be distinguished. There may be a technology or advanced mental aptitude which can "switch rooms" if the sound gets fuzzy and move the 28 v.p. sec into a 28 v.p. sec room where all seems normal but the inner atomic time standard is subtly different.

While reading "*Alien Dawn*", which includes an overview of Linda Moulton Howe's investigations into unexplained cattle mutilations in Missouri, your present correspondent had the unusual experience of feeling innate hostility toward Ms. Howe, a person who is usually quiet and cordial when off the lecture platform. I also have covered as a reporter a cattle mutilation incident which occurred near Springfield, Missouri in 1990. My article on this hill country situation appeared in Body, Mind Spirit magazine in 1991. Unlike Linda Howe, I stayed with local people in the rural Missouri Ozarks and later corresponded with these people personally. I got to know them somewhat. My feeling is that someone in Missouri or another outback place where Ms. Howe has investigated cattle mutilations has hostility toward this pleasant and slightly elegant lady, and may have tricked her with several false narrations. This hostility may be implemented by resident hexenmiesters and their familiar spirits rather than by "ufo aliens". In my book "*Dark Frontier*", I describe the tradition of sorcery native to the Ozark people, which was originally brought from the UK and Europe several centuries ago. An adept hex, like smoke from a hidden fire, can color the mood and perceptions of sensitive bystanders as well as affecting the target individual. While I was on site in Springfield, Missouri I did notice this effect in the home of a couple who had protested parades by the Ku Klux Klan in that Missouri area. I mentioned this sense of "hex" at that time and a very interesting discussion then arose with some local people in the group who recalled an incident when a local man had been found naked and wandering down a highway with his face painted half black and half white. The young man was incoherent and could not give any clear account of his experiences.

According to my informants, some type of traditional sorcery is still practiced at secret or remote locations in the Missouri Ozarks. However, in modern times this practice

DOING BUSINESS IN THE ADIRONDACKS by E. Macer-Story

has become adulterated in some instances by the meth-amphetamine drug traffic which services the corporate, military and entertainment subculture which has been imported from outside the area to work on a variety of projects at installations in the Southeastern Ozark area.

The unsolved disappearance of two Springfield high school girls and one attractive Mom on the evening of their graduation in 1992 parallels in some ways the disappearance of graduate student Chandra Levy in the Spring of 2002 right before she was to depart from Washington, D.C. to California for her college graduation. Motorcycle gangs operate in the Ozark area of Missouri and Chandra Levy's boyfriend, a senator from California, had been involved with a motorcycle club in California. Criminal Justice intern Chandra Levy also had worked on the Oklahoma City Murrah Federal Building case. Recent information released from the Associated Press indicates that the FBI was initially pursuing a White Supremicist gang connection to convicted OKC bomber Tim McVeigh.[8] Perhaps these three girls, different though they are in cultural circumstances and upbringing, shared the same fate of being "smart girls" who knew too much about criminal activity in which they declined to participate as fellow travelers. Chandra Levy vanished on April 31-May 1st, the Walburgasnacht date. This is a German festival much like the Celtic Halloween when the spirits of the dead and supernatural beings are said to frolic on the high mountains of central Europe. A violent cult may have chosen that date.

Actual exceptional mental and/or spirit communication capacities, whether simply telepathic or literally material, may account for the mysterious strangers, vanishing alchemists and so on often seen in context of major world events. Also, such possibilities in local circumstances may account for the bizarre characteristics of certain vampire encounters wherein the vampire seems to have lured the victim to be inspired to travel to its lair or has mysteriously preceded the traveler to a unique location , as in the tale of Aymon De Sales at the Mexican pyramids which is given at the beginning of this book. Since the majority of travelers to Mexico City do not experience this same haunting phenomenon, it is fair to say that Aymon was selected or targeted for the experience by an entity with an "agenda". Perhaps that agenda included the ultimate expression in writing of his experience by Mr. De Sales, a person with no other literary credits.

The popular book and subsequent film. "*The Exorcist*" is based on an actual case documented by a Catholic priest--as everyone is probably aware. I think that the "time links" in the film are extremely well done and that a key to understanding certain diabolic occurrences is the ability of the demon to travel backward in time.

But not forward in time because the demonic entity is not "material" and can only affect the "material" it has "known already"--so to speak. According to the Jesuits,:" The devil has power over the past but not the future." This conundrum is worth committing to memory. For often the diabolic force will hold the target within past paradigms or false memories.

Previous to experiencing the bus interference related in the following email, I had noticed two unusual personages during the ordinary routine of activities. In the morning, when the commuter bus was parked in Kingston, N.Y. loading passengers for the run down to New York City one passenger boarding down the center aisle of the bus attracted my attention. I thought he looked pale. He was unshaven with a gray-white growth of week-old beard and was wearing a light jacket or long-sleeved shirt in the Winter cold. It

DOING BUSINESS IN THE ADIRONDACKS by E. Macer-Story

crossed my mind that he resembled California physicist Fred Wolf but I quickly dismissed this from my mind with an "o no! Can't be!" reaction. For I had seen the simulacrum of Fred Wolf once before on the commuter bus—when a look-alike boarded the bus going North at the Rosendale commuter stop. Dr. Wolf had confirmed that at the time of the Rosendale sighting of his simulacrum he was doing some research in a Southwestern area known for unusual healing and anomaly effects, an "earth chackra" area known to 1950's ufo channeler George Van Tassel and the location of a house Van Tassel had built there. Dr. Wolf had been experiencing this house at the time his simulacrum showed up at the Rosendale bus stop.

Later in the day, as I was going up a short flight of steps from the 8th Avenue Local subway platform to the Port Authority to catch the 5 p.m. bus upstate, a woman coming down the steps briefly attracted my attention because her face had an unusual smoothness and lack of expression. She appeared to be about 45 years old and had a short henna-colored bob of hair. She was wearing a bright red dress without a jacket. As I was going up the stairs facing her as she was going down the stairs in a crowd, I remember seeing only her head and shoulders. Again, an incredulous: "O no! Can't be!" entered my mind. For this was the exact location at which I had seen the woman with the large, unusual face and short dyed blonde hairdo which inspired part of my "8th Street and 6th Avenue" composite "vampire" painting a few weeks previous, (Cite page ref.)It is not surprising that public places of transportation in any major city might harbor the ghosts and simulacrums of those who experienced glorious anticipation and/or great emotional disappointment whilst passing in either direction through the Janus-faced gates to the civic carnival.

On January 8, 2002 there was yet another notable unexplained commuter bus incident at about 7:15 p.m. EST as the bus had just left New Paltz going North and was enroute next to Rosendale "Ride 'N Park" stop. I was reading a Theosophical article from QUEST magazine on interruptions in ordinary linear time flow by configurational time patterns This article is named *BREAK ON THROUGH* and contains quotes from the Jim Morrison song '*Break On Through To The Other Side*".

In previous sections of this book, I mentioned in terms of a talismanic painting that the Rosendale bus stop seems linked to several apparitions and/or simulacrums in my experience but I was not thinking of this at all as the vehicle approached that area of the highway. I was intently reading the article about spiritualism and rock music when suddenly the bus was filled with the smell of ozone. No one could trace or explain this odor. I made no issue of my perceptions; but privately noted this incident as this ozone-like odor often occurs during séances, as does the smell of sulphur.
"Something is wrong with the bus" said the driver. We had to limp to the Rosendale stop and sit there ventilating, waiting for another bus.

COMMUNICATIONS SIMULACRUMS

It may be that the simulacrums of individuals from the West Coast expanded consciousness community whom I have recognized on this commuter bus line are trying to reach me on a level which eludes my conscious, rational mind. Perhaps their intense interest will be generated at some future time when this book will be published and distributed. Either these presences are "wishing they were with me" now or they are trying to halt my professional endeavors in some way, to subtly impede the pattern of commuting to my New York City "Magick Mirror" office for some reason I do not directly discern.

After the "ozone" incident, I felt exhausted, slightly sleepy and was experiencing a pain at the back of my neck. But certainly this synchronous bus breakdown had no association with my non-local physics acquaintances on the West Coast. Rather, the association was with the fate of a suicidal rock star who had died of drug overdose and yet was now being adulated in a philosophical magazine.

In a dialog on the Internet in mid-March of the year 2000 your present correspondent has logged in a conversation which could have occurred in some similar form in the European Middle Ages when the Roman Catholic Ecclesiastics were debating the nuances of "Diabolic Presence" and "How many angels can dance on the head of a pin". The concept that "The Devil has power over the past but not the Future" had been described by your present correspondent as being a Jesuit aphorism. The name of the respondent to this concept is rendered as "Aexus" since he has been found to manifest extreme duality in his mixture of political information and personal gossip.

[Aexus]
Are you saying that Jack is trying to measure "back action" as The Devil's Pathway? Now *THAT* ought to bring a few chuckles out of this online "coven.".

[Macer-Story]
No. That mixture of religious dogmatism and physical science is Dan Smith's territory. I think Jack has done some valuable thinking about actual mental causality in physics. If this helps explain the Devil to mankind, that's valuable too.

[Aexus]
But seriously. Do you know much about the author and circumstances which brought Mr. Blatty to write "The Exorcist?" Are you familiar with the fellows we call "The Catholic Air Force" and their concerns about "other intelligences" influencing people on this planet? There are published reports that William Peter Blatty was a senior officer in USAF counterintelligence and an expert on psychological warfare.
Know anything about that?

[Macer-Story]
No. Remember: I am an infant-baptised Catholic but as an adult have studied systems of demonology and exorcism as these occur in other religions as well. I do not focus on Catholic demonology to the exclusion of other traditions.

[[Aexus]
On the other hand, the wife of a good friend of a lot of these guys...Elaine Pagels...(know her)... who teaches at Princeton Seminary or Princeton... wrote a book titled "The Origins of Satan."

[Macer-Story]
Does she know Dan Smith? He is also connected with Princeton.

[[Aexus]
Very interesting apologia for there NOT being any "real" Evil Force independent of human action; the way I read Elaine's book, she attributed tales of "Satan" to anti-Semitism on the part of early Christians in the Roman context.

[Macer-Story]
This is not accurate. "Shaitan" and similar names are Arabic or Hindu. I discussed this in my book *DR.FU MAN CHU MEETS THE LONESOME COWBOY: SORCERY AND THE UFO EXPERIENCE.* It's on record there."Shaitan", "Cytron".Check it if you need verification.

[Aexus]
Sadly, Elaine has refused to sit for an interview with folks who would have liked to quiz her about this. Unfortunately, her hubby had a mountain climbing accident and fell to his death, or so the public story has gone.

[Macer-Story]
Were she and her husband on good terms when he fell to his death? I intuit that Elaine may regret any fast generalizations about Beelzebub.

[[Aexus]
Yes, according to televised reports, a new cut of "The Exorcist" is running three cities this weekend, including Athens, Georgia (where the Univ. of GA is located). It is apparently being "tested" and may be released more widely in a short while...
There's more, but enough for now.
Anyway, given your earlier responses today, I thought you'd be following all of this.

[Macer-Story]
Nope. Because I really do hands-on research into the supernatural, I take such events as they come to me live rather than as they come to me on TV. EXCEPT if the TV flies into the loft and taps me on the shoulder, as did this tale of Heinz Pagals falling off the mountain after dreaming he had fallen off the mountain fly into the viewscope of your present correspondent in the course of a correspondence about diabolic possibilities and the identity of Satan.

  In another Internet conversation shortly afterward, Jack Sarfatti—the physicist invoked previously for his concept of "back action" or the future influencing the past-present responded to "Aexus's" citation of the Pagals couple and their identities.

[Jack Sarfatti]

What? What bullshit is this? The late Heinz Pagels was a close friend of both Ira Einhorn and Nick Herbert and spent time at Esalen. He bad mouthed me to   David Gladstone on the phone because of my claims that precognition was possible within the

DOING BUSINESS IN THE ADIRONDACKS by E. Macer-Story

laws of physics. He then fell off a mountain in Aspen after writing about his dream that he would die falling off a mountain at the end of his book, "The Cosmic Code".

[[Aexus]

Some people will do anything to sell a book. Maybe you should try this, Jack. And as to it's being bullshit? Why don't you ask Elaine Pagals?

This information from Jack Sarfatti about the strange fate of Heinz Pagals, whose wife had written a book entitled "*The Origins of Satan*", is very interesting to this reporter in context of research into the supernatural. It does seem to indicate a causality which is independent of whether or not prejudicial observers have "imagined evil". As the Greeks observed and recorded in their drama for posterity, "knowing" one's possible fate by oracular warning or in a dream (See: Oedipus Rex and Cassandra) does not ensure avoidance of that fate. However, sometimes—as has been documented in numerous "believe it or not" anecdotes about warning dreams and visions--a person can heed the oracle and avoid the catastrophe.

There is, of course, another possibility latent in the Pagals death beyond the issues of simple fate and precognition. If there exists a diabolic cult or independent "intelligence agency" with knowledge of Elaine Pagans study of Satan at Princeton which cites anti-Semitic stereotypes, these individuals—possibly quite intelligent but also racially-biased—might decide to engineer a mountain climbing accident. Or such a group which had cultivated telepathic and spirit-conjuration abilities might decide to throw a "hex" in the direction of the Pagans couple.*OR* there exists a supernatural Entity with a grudge against Heinz Pagans ?

This type of interpretive dilemma often occurs in the study of "crop circles" and preternatural weather phenomena. One does not know whether to credit the establishment, university and/or corporate-funded research or not. Scott Corrales wrote in March of 2000 about the controversy surrounding "crop circles" which had formed near Barcelona:" Well, now a researcher that I work closely with says there's no reason to suspect fraud, since a 39,000 peseta analysis paid for out of pocket by another researcher/magazine editor shows the marks have no traces of common materials! Who knows what the heck's going on.."

Indeed. How does one fund research on unexpected events which have already happened? On March 18, 2000, emailed Scott Corrales that I had an effect to my furnace just after sending several emails. I connected the furnace failure to poltergeist activity because I have had in the past poltergeist interference with a furnace elsewhere--but not recently. Among the sent emails were the one to you about the crop circles and another about diabolism & the film "*The Exorcist*". While waiting for furnace repair, I decided to meditate on the "cause". Instead of the cartoon "Exorcist"--which might be expected--I clairvoyantly saw images from a past encounter with the "ufo phenomenon" which occurred in Tobyhanna,Pa. and which has never been explained except in terms of the "supernatural" or paranormal. I also experienced a pain at the back of my neck. When

DOING BUSINESS IN THE ADIRONDACKS by E. Macer-Story

waiting with the ufo contactee in Tobyhanna late at night I experienced a headache so severe I had to take numerous aspirin.
Corrales responded:

"Synchronicity rears its ugly head again! our furnace broke down thismorning probably at 4:00 am-5:00 am, just as I was having a dream about a
large, disk-shaped UFO exploding to the consternation of hundreds of
Bradfordians as I watched it from my front porch (I dream in technicolor
with all the bells and whistles). It was 49 degrees in the house until
noon, when our bleary-eyed furnace repairman got things going again."

As your present correspondent looks at this unexplained furnace outage (UFO) incident in retrospect, a similar incident which occurred in the early hours of the morning of November 5, 2001 comes to mind. On that day, I woke and wandered into the loft room, which was completely dark. When I glanced up through the skylight window, I saw a right-angled triangle with the long side pointing right formed by two stars on the shorter, vertical side in combination with a multi-colored (primarily oscillating red and white) aerial light form which reminded me of feathers arranged in a squarish pattern.

The "feathers" of course could have been refracted slats of light. Or this marker at the end of the hypotenuse of the aerial right triangle might actually have been the manifestation the Onteora Indians termed the "flying head". This was thought to be a vampiric spirit and the refracted rays of visible light may have been inferred to be a person wearing a feather head dress.

As I was jotting the journal entry of this incident at about 11:30 a.m., the doorbell rang twice in my Magick Mirror office space. I checked both door and telephones but no one was there. This prompted me to call Woodstock to check my phone messages and I found there had been a power failure in the town which had temporarily shut off my answering machine. Later, there was a problem with the telephone in the office which was not dialing calls out accurately and and was ringing back with strange sounds on the second line which sounded like lobby noises.

That morning, while waiting for the commuter bus at 8 a.m. in front of the Woodstock Design store as usual I had noticed that the flowers in one of the boxes beside the door had been clumped over to one side and a plastic prophylactic glove was lying inside the flower box beside the damaged flower arrangement. It crossed me mind that, as with the continual finding of sectioned fruit rinds, the mention of this glove incident overtly to anyone might be taken as a false repeat of the finding of an unusual glove at the side of the house which I had already mentioned over the Internet some weeks ago.

Attention to the fine points and details of anomalous events can be compared both to the artistic style of surrealism and the type of traditional sorcery called "gemetria" in some systems. In fact, awareness of these systems—which utilize the matching of secondary attributions of physical actions and objects to create meaning can assist the investigator in understanding whether or not events are "rigged" or naturally synchronous.

I noticed when I returned home to Woodstock in the evening that the digital clocks indicated the power failure had occurred between 8:11 and 8:16 a.m. This would have been just as the commuter bus was leaving Woodstock. When I phoned the police to

DOING BUSINESS IN THE ADIRONDACKS by E. Macer-Story

ask the cause of the power outage, they told me that the wind had caused a series of outages during the day. But my clocks were both flashing the hour of stoppage at just after 8 a.m.

When I phoned Nina Kincaid on Wednesday November 6 about driving me to Kingston to run some errands, this "gal Friday" cab driver told me that at about 7: 30 on Monday evening, (the day of the power outage) she and a neighbor on Bellows Lane had experienced a power outage whilst hearing an airplane fly low over their houses. But when they called the police they were told that the cause of the outage had been high winds.

At six in the evening on that same Wednesday November 6, I noticed when I left the house after dark to get some food for dinner one of the small, worked trident wands of a style I have previously found on my property lying on the asphalt driveway illuminated by a sensor light. Beside this whittled twig was a right triangle of facing from the roof overhang of the garage entrance. I thought of the right triangle of stars and aerial light form I had seen two nights previously.. Like the aerial pattern, the triangle of siding did not appear to be contrived. It had fallen from a triangular location where the roof of the garage alcove meets the side of the house and, being plastic, was easily replaced using a plastic glue I keep on hand for framing paintings. But the trident wand was definitely "worked"and artificially crafted. It seems that a supernatural or spirit force is warning by triangulation of some fetish-oriented human aggression.

When Nina Kincaid and her neighbors heard the low-flying or invisible "airplane" at the time of the power outage, she says they had thought of possible terrorism at the Ashokan reservoir. But this reservoir is twenty miles away. In the days following this event, this industrious village go-between clarified with me several times that a variety of neighbors in the same area had heard the overflight of an aircraft on the fifth of November at about 7:30 p.m. It seemed important to her to assert that the incident had indeed happened though it had not reached the news.

On Sunday November 11 a man stood behind me at the HUB bank outdoor ATM at two in the afternoon. He seemed very familiar to me, as if I had seen him before. He was short, compactly-built with a handsome Germanic or Scandinavian face and appeared to be 48-52 years old. As I glanced at him after using the ATM, my thoughts were of an acquaintance in Boston, a physicist friend of a playwright associated with Playwrights Platform in 1977 whom I have not seen for a number of years.

If I had not experienced the unusual events beginning on November 5th I might have casually noticed this resemblance without noting it in my journal. Something beyond the local timespace frame was nagging at the edges of my attention.

In a similar way, issues concerning the reality of supernatural effects during a ufo investigation in Tobyhanna, Pa. which involved a blonde physicist of German origin and which had nothing to do with furnaces had surfaced in the Internet exchange between myself and Scott Corrales.

Scott commented: "You've mentioned the Tobyhanna case before, but I'm not sure if in emails or in one of your books. Where is T-Hanna in relation to, say, Philly or Harrisburg? Maybe the link to BCN will be a speaking engagement on paranormal subjects involving crop circles! Any opportunity to visit Barcelona should be seized immediately "

DOING BUSINESS IN THE ADIRONDACKS by E. Macer-Story

Yet the "furnace breakdown" as a cue for speculation about the supernatural persists in associations having nothing to do with Barcelona. As recorded in an email sent in December 2001 to physicist Jack Sarfatti:

"Once again there has been a peculiar problem downloading your book. *Destiny Matrix* .I will try again tomorrow morning. It is worth noting that at 9:30 EST I had a power flux which affected the furnace fuse and had to call the repair service. A plastic button on the furnace reset mechanism also would not work and broke when I lightly pushed it. In my experience with investigating hauntings there have been several notable furnace poltergeists --one of which I mention in the new book I am now drafting. I noticed that you emailed the announcement of the new draft of *Destiny Matrix* at 9:30p.m."

Independently of these material manifestations I had come to the conclusion earlier today that the multiplex figure of the "vampire" presence I am painting is indeed on some obscure agenda related to concepts of Advanced Intelligence. I feel that I should continue to probe this situation."

Sarfatti responded:

"Definitely! "

Yet in analyzing the actual impressions recorded in the painting—which is of the "6th Avenue & 8th Street bookstore vampire" mentioned later in this book in context of an unusual constellation of human behavior—the conclusions are a bit different from a simple agenda of Advanced Intelligence alchemically or mentally instructing human beings. It seems that some Vampiric Intelligence connected to the physics and intelligence agency situation, which will be detailed later, is being blocked or challenged by powerful spirit entities native to the New York area.

So an interesting dilemma of potential competition comes to attention between spirit entities which, like duplicate copies of a book, can travel from location to location as versus the type of spirit entity which is tied somehow to the molecular structure of a certain geographical area.

So: maybe the Barcelona crop circles were genuine. But, if so: what might have been the link to me at that particular time other than an art agent in Barcelona where my paintings have been exhibited several times?

In answer to Scott's previous question, Tobyhanna, Pa contacts are discussed in the same book on *UFOS AND SORCERY* as I had mentioned in the "Exorcist" Internet dialog synergistically sent at the same time in the Spring of 2000 as the Barcelona crop circle correspondence with Scott Corrales . Also, the "Cytron" entity mentioned in this Internet dialog--who said it was from outer space but had a diabolic, negative effect on the spirit medium channeling it—figures in my on site research included in that same book, which was first published in 1991.

Might the instances of "micro-wave boosted telepathic harassment" and "Implant control" scenarios mentioned in the following excerpt from the 1997 article *PKD, THE UNICORN, AND SOVIET PSYCHOTRONICS* relate more to the concept of "Cytron" as an alternative name for "Shaitan" or Satan than actual, conventional electromagnetic devices? According to this article by Internet "high strangeness" correspondent Adam Gorightly:

"Philip K. Dick, the late schizoid Sci-Fi author and Ira (The Unicorn)
Einhorn, sixties radical activist turned seventies New Age networker cum
fugitive axe murderer, began a correspondence in early February of '78

DOING BUSINESS IN THE ADIRONDACKS by E. Macer-Story

centered around Dick's firmly held (on shaky ground) belief that the
Russians were beaming psychotronic transmissions via satellite into his
already somewhat disturbed mind.

   According to Dick--often known for his far-out flights of paranoiac
fancy--these "micro-wave boosted telepathic transmissions," as he called
them, commenced on March 20, 1974, showering him with endless reams and
streams of visual and audio data. Initially, this overpowering onslaught of
messages Phil reluctantly received were extremely unpleasant and, as he
termed them, "die messages." Within the following week he reported being
kept awake by "violet phosphene activity, eight hours uninterrupted." A
description of this event in a fictionalized version appears in Dick's
brilliant though demented anti-drug novel A Scanner, Darkly. The content of
this phosphene activity was in the form of modern abstract graphics
followed by Soviet Music serenading his head, in addition to Russian names
and words appearing there as well. The ever speculating Phil conjectured
that a radical drop in GABA fluid--in his brilliant but balmy
brain--might've accounted for these strange voices and images, though he
was at a loss to further explain exactly what would have precipitated such
a drop in his GABA fluid, which conveniently lent more credence to his
original theory, as crazy as it sounded to even his own buzzing ears,
tuned into--as they were--this foreign frequency that had invaded his mind.

   In recent years various info on remote mind control technology has
filtered into the conspiracy research community through various fringe
publications such as Full Disclosure, Resonance and countless others
including a Finnish gentleman by the name of Martti Koski and his booklet
My Life Depends On You.

   Over the years Mr. Koski has been sharing with our mind controlled world
at large his horrifying tale, documenting as it does the discovery of
rampant brain tampering committed upon himself and others, including
documents concerning one Robert Naeslund, another victim of brain-research.
The perpetrators of these evil doings included, allegedly, the Royal
Canadian Mounted Police (RCMP), The CIA and Finnish Intelligence among
countless other covert intelligence agencies. (In Secret and Suppressed,
edited by Jim Keith, a remote mind control testimonial appears entitled An
Open Letter To The Swedish Prime Minister Regarding Electromagnetic Terror,
authored by the aforementioned R. Naeslund.)

   Another legendary figure in the arcane annals of conspiracy
research--and ranter extraordinaire--Kerry Wendell Thornley claims that
while serving in the Marines with his buddy Lee Oswald, he became subject
to just this sort of mind control scenario; having had planted--unbeknownst
to him at the time--into the base of his neck, some sort of high tech
implant which enabled Thornley to receive malevolent transmissions from
Military Intelligence or others of that ilk, who were tampering with
Thornley's brain for reasons far too complex to even attempt to broach at
this time, as it would swerve us away from the topic at hand into even
weirder realms concerning a genetic breeding experiment which Thornley
believes he fell prey to at the hands of Nazi Controllers. (Refer to the

DOING BUSINESS IN THE ADIRONDACKS by E. Macer-Story

Kenn Thomas' audio interview of Thornley available through SteamShovel Press.)

Along this same twisted line, I'm reminded of an incident related to me a few years ago when a close friend of mine suffered a nervous breakdown, and was diagnosed as paranoid schizophrenic as a result of malevolent voices he was hearing in his head. My friend believed that a group called "The Laser People" were trying to drive him bonkers (and perhaps succeeded) via lasers, which were perhaps, more accurately, psychotronic devices beaming these voices his way. He's doing better these days,"

But stating that a diabolic entity like "Cytron" might be responsible for certain of these allegedly electromagnetic mind control experiences is not to assert that the experiences were not real intrusions into the mental integrity of the individuals making these extraordinary complaints. If the "Nazi Controllers" cited by K.W. Thornley were powerful diabolic intelligences, the idea of malevolent military information affecting the base of the neck where the connection between the brainstem and spinal cord is located makes clinical sense. For an overwhelming telepathic influx of unwanted and unsolicited information and commands might well give the same "pain in the neck" as cognitive stress from a similar written or spoken communication

Such Interdimensional "Cytronic" intelligences might also seek to telepathically animate wealthy corporate entrepreneurs or dilettantes who actually have access to material means by which bizarre, power-oriented charades might arbitrarily be implemented.

As I was waiting for my luggage in the Albany, N.Y. airport on June 18th, 2001 there was an unusual encounter with three men who walked directly toward me with purpose, and then past me to a wall at the end of the airport baggage carousel area . I did not turn completely around to follow their exit route but I was aware that there was no reason to cross the baggage area in that particular trajectory other than to assert some arcane state of mind with me. They were wearing conservative suits and white business shirts. One man particularly passed very close to me. He was wearing a black overcoat of soft fabric and had a non-descript Anglo-Saxon face with receding hairline. For some reason I thought of an office landlord in New York City who had paid me to move to another location because he was in business trouble and needed my office space in the Chelsea neighborhood for his own use as he could no longer afford office space in midtown.

I obtained telepathically whilst focusing on the presence of this man as the group strode swiftly past me at the Albany airport baggage carousel the word "thantatos". I also had the image of an elaborate urn or vase of a gray-black or dull silver color and having to do with death and sorcery. In a more finished sketch made for this publication in 2003, the image of a live creature inside the urn and egg and sperm below the external handles became by part of the picture. It is possible that certain "Thantatos" magicians seek like the medieval alchemists to create a "homunculus"without ordinary sexual bonding.

DRAWING OF DOUBLE HANDLED URN.

When I web-searched "thantatos". I found that the Alta Vista search engine obtained a number of files from a group of wanna-be adepts who obviously know each other and are writing under pseudonyms of a Dutch-Germanic impact. Also in the same listing is a study of pop artist Andy Warhol's work which mentions that Warhol was a practicing Catholic.

One of the characteristics of the interference I have been experiencing is a peculiar sort of sexual heckling which attempts to "shame" me because seemingly these people feel I have a sensual appearance or am vulnerable in the sensual-emotional area. But I simply notice this as peculiar. Perhaps, like certain dedicated Zen, Syndicate Black Hand and Hasidic practitioners, the "Thantatos" adepts strive for emotionless action during acts of deliberate sorcery and therefore attempt to belittle natural characteristics which might arouse or be governed by emotion.

Shortly after finding the "thantatos" folder on Alta Vista, I was sitting at my desk pondering this situation when it dawned on me that the peculiar attempt at "shaming" I was experiencing is fundamentally Catholic. I thought of Dick Farley's insistence that there is a "Catholic mafia" among intelligence agents which is concerned with such topics as diabolism and demonic possession.

But I do not feel the adepts who were following me on my return trip from Oklahoma City on June 18th were intelligence agents. In this context, one should recall the unusual decline and death of U.S. clairvoyant Pat Price in context of assertions Mr. Price had made about the overflight of Washington, D.C. by ufo-like aerial vehicles during the mid-1950.

But Pat Price is not the only person to decline and die oddly after making similar assertions about the ufo presence over Washington,D.C. Your present correspondent has on file accounts of two other people who were killed in unusual auto accidents in a similar context.

A man from the upstate New York area who had worked for IBM claimed to me directly in conversation in a convincing narration that prior to the D.C. ufo sightings in the mid-1950's he had been told by a woman then resident in the D.C. area that there would be an over flight of ufos on exactly the day that this event did indeed occur and was reported in the newspapers. I wrote about his alleged ufo precognition experience in the NYC—MUFON newsletter and about his death by a hit and run car side-swiping, which occurred not long after he had gone public about this D.C."prior knowledge" experience in the early 1990s.

It seems that your present correspondent may be experiencing interference from the "airport adepts" because they do realize the extent of my mental ability and that I am determined to make public the use of "life energy" transduction in my "fluidice" theory, and in other work.

On January 5, 2002, after experiencing a severe muscle spasm of the leg which woke me from sleep during the previous night, I had extreme difficulty in accessing the file of the book "Destiny Matrix" in order to download it. This may be a bit of "voodoo physics" in that I have come to associate previous sudden muscular spasms with the attentions of an individual close to California physicist Sarfatti who may be covertly opposed to his work. At the time, I asked mentally for "higher guidance" on these issues. I was then able to access Sarfatti's *"Destiny Matrix"* pdf file as posted.

Then whilst waiting for this file to load I was prompted by inner impulse to simply browse for my brief entry in the already-loaded index section. As I attempted to do this, the index cursor jumped spontaneously to a section on "chivalric love". It occurred to me that the "voodoo opposition" here might come from persons of the "sex magick" persuasion who also are cyber adepts. This description would fit a variety of *"Destiny Matrix"* associates of self-described "theatrical physicist" Dr. Jack Sarfatti.

But it might also fit other cyber adepts unknown to the Sarfatti correspondence circle who had dabbled in the non-local arts of sorcery and sex/hex magick as a sideline to more conventional literary and/or scientific jobs. Those famous in California for such hijincks are not actually the only circle of "voodoo physicists" in existence though others have received less publicity.

In 1970, when I was visiting New York City to give a poetry reading for a small literary magazine and deciding whether to relocate from my Midwestern newspaper connections to Boston or to New York City, a recent graduate from Harvard University, then a stringer for "Time" magazine, took me out to see a Charlie Chaplin film. I had not known before this encounter that a circle of old friends in Cambridge had experimented with a variety of drugs and sorcery techniques. When my companion asked if I would like some refreshment before the film started, I told him:"O just a Tab." meaning a diet soft drink of that era. He brought me buttered popcorn on which he had somehow sprinkled (a tab of) LSD. When I ate the popcorn unaware during the Chaplin film the result was a unique consciousness expansion experience during which I began to associate the comic images in the Chaplin film with violent conflict, both personal and political. Later I would learn that Charlie Chaplin, a Jew, had actually experienced notable violence during the Nazi era preceding and during World War Two.

During that same year of 1970, I experienced another unwitting encounter with the effects of LSD on associative, non-local perception. This time the dose was a deliberate joke and not a casual misunderstanding. LSD was baked into an angel food cake by a young woman then associated with a man working for Penthouse magazine , and was served to several people along with a blue liqueur. The couple were on their way to the Caribbean and this was a "celebration" for some arcane purpose. No one was told beforehand that there would be any drugs in the food. On this occasion, I had spontaneous and unwanted images of murders and violent abuse which turned out when researched to be correct.. When I called a friend from the Cambridge circle of acquaintance to check out one of these "abuse" inspirations, he commented: "Who do you think you are, Ken Kesey?" This comment about the well known protagonist of Tom Wolfe's *Electric Kool Aid Acid Test* indicated that he was aware of the type of LSD effect I was experiencing. But I was not fully aware of what I was experiencing. Tom Wolfe's award-winning book on that subject had not yet been published.

The connection I had made then in 1970 by telephoning this Harvard graduate at his rural family home in the Southern Midwest was to spontaneously link violent and drug-enhanced activities in that conservative rural community with the Ivy League circle of individuals then under the influence of ex-Harvard professor Timothy Leary, and circulating LSD.

Probably more significant than the LSD realization itself is the sense of a covert linkage of so-called "conservative" or "far right" individuals who support an elitist programme involving the idea that "for the good of the populace" knowledge of the effects of sorcery and designer drugs must be kept within a limited circle of academics and free lance intellectuals who "understand" their own superiority.

. Author Ken Kesey, being more of a populist in his writings, would not be an individual acceptable to the covert elitist network. Also, a woman possessed by "inspirations" not genitally or reproductively sexual in reference would not fit the covert psycho-shamanic hierarchy topped by the effete, magical male with arcane "mental powers." For in this covert network sexuality is largely mental and not conventionally physical, as in the LSD-laden angel food cake and blue liquor served up in "Penthouse" context but with no direct sensual contact.

Your present correspondent has received at the Magick Mirror email address a number of peculiar communications addressed either only to one of the Magick Mirror public correspondence addresses or to a short list of addresses all beginning with the word "magick" such as the one entitled "Phoebe Is My Cat" and quoted below:

"we finally have it, right now there are 16 girls up for your viewing pleasure. everyone is amature(sic), but we aren't bad! we add more all the time and inside is where the real magic

DOING BUSINESS IN THE ADIRONDACKS by E. Macer-Story

Obviously, whoever sent this message to a short list of "magick" email addresses has more of a perverse interest in "sex magick" as distinct from "ordinary sex" than simply a standard hustler's attitude. Note the mis-spelled word "amature". In the mythos of witchcraft and sorcery, the use of money can be an important ritual tool. One may be either firmly told that "There is no charge for the Craft" or asked to "Cross my palm with silver" as an indication that the sorcery working will be genuine. This is not the same as the distinction between "amateur" and "professional" which had been under discussion on one "expanded consciousness" email correspondence list just prior to the receipt of the "Phoebe is my cat" email.

Therefore, is can be assumed for the sake of argument that a sophisticated sorcery group such as the Ordo Templi Orientis is not responsible for such crass Internet communications. The genesis of such stuff more likely lies within some hysteric "far right" and/or "far left" group which equates written female expression on intellectual, artistic or business topics with pornographic sex. This cog in the mental wheels could easily slip a peg if previous involvements with sexuality have been ritualized according to some particular version of the "psycho-shamanic" credo so that physical sex is merely an addendum to the memorized "teachings" about male & female priestly roles, energies, electromagnetic polarities and so on.

There are several old tyme European witch groups which have this bias. Author Hans Holzer in his book on "Astrology" which was published in the 1970's makes absolute gender distinctions in interpretation of the astrological signs: one Capricorn meaning for a man , another Capricorn meaning for a woman, and so on. Of course, Holzer as a public communicator, was simply reflecting the tip of the submerged demimonde of complexities in that area at the time his book was published. He is to be commended for his frankness in representing the actual, covert belief systems.

Those with cultist views far more radical than the urbane and sophisticated Hans Holzer did in this previous nuisance email example make the crazy transition from a discussion involving a woman's idea of the "Cat's Cradle concept of the present as suspended between past and future" (See reference in the book *Destiny Matrix*[9]) into a "Phoebe is my Cat" sexual solicitation involving the "real magic" of amateur pornography. In the minds of persons warped by an ideology which uses natural sexual inclinations to enforce a rigid psych-political hierarchy, any non-sexual or domestic public communications by a woman will become the subject of "cry whore" distortions. It is one short step from the confused reaction to a "Cat's Cradle" metaphor in the email quoted above to the bombing of an abortion clinic or other acts of terrorism involving the alleged "real magic" of elitist hierarchical dominance.

The National Socialist "ahnenerbe" of Hitler's regime, as cited earlier in this book, did conduct experiments with mediumship and materialization which sought to replace normal sexual reproduction with the materialization of ectoplasm from the sexual and other bodily fluids of selected physical mediums. There is a parallel to this practice in power-oriented, shamanic religions , when the adept's body upon initiation becomes controlled by an ancient, interdimensional Intelligence which "lives on" by inhabiting successive generations of "adepts"who have been similarly initiated." The King is dead. Long live the King!"

Is "Cytron" the "Solid State Intelligence" (SSI) thought to be anti-human and anti-organic by "altered states" researcher Dr. John Lilly now being tested or experimented upon covertly by corporate and/or academic researchers? Or are well-funded and control-oriented private researchers being prompted into diabolism by the "Cytronic" Intelligences they feel will implement stock market profit and evolutionary social change? Quite possibly intelligent entrepreneurs are experimenting covertly upon the intersection of non-corporeal Intelligence with cyber-enhanced signaling devices. As author D. Scott Rogo documented in his book *Phone Calls From The Dead*, the ordinary telephone is already an instrument which occasionally serves to enhance communications from the non-corporeal realm. A more sensitive instrument for these purposes might certainly be developed.

Yet, in locating such occult research practices arbitrarily—and not in the exact area of the planet where his/her ancestral sorcery was originally developed—the would-be sorcerer may find him/herself at odds with powerful devas or similar entities linked to previous practices in that geographical area which have established a prior and/or more powerful interdimensional linkage.

In the same year of 1980 as your present correspondent was researching the anomalous "ufo sightings" near a military base in Tobyhanna, Pennsylvania which have been cited earlier in this book, Chilean scientific journalist and researcher Cristian Riffo was researching the disappearance of yet another aircraft in the "Cerro Moreno Triangle" area of Chile.

The area of the Pocano Mountains where the anomalous events occurred in 1980 was land occupied by the now extinct Delaware Indian tribe before they were relocated by homesteading legislation during the Nineteenth Century. It is possible that the manifestations experienced by civilians near the military base were related to natural properties and non-corporeal inhabitants of the land once known to the Delaware Indians. Since my initial investigation of the ufo claims, I have heard a number of anecdotes about hauntings and "strange animals" in the small mountain towns and even in the highway rest stops located in that same Pocano resort area.

When I was living near the woods in the country upstate, I used to put out scraps for the animals and most often birds of various sizes would take advantage of these scraps, as well as a few cats, an occasional dog and a small coyote.

One day as I was working in my cellar study, which has blackout curtains on the windows so that a combination of the computer monitor UV plus the UV from the Eastern window above the writing table does not damage my eyes in the morning, I heard a sharp tap at the window. When I peeked out from behind the curtain, I found that a small, delicate brown bird with a white chest had found me . I greeted this bird happily, aware that this was an exceptional creature who had traced my spoor from the regular food scrap donations to the curtained cellar study.

DOING BUSINESS IN THE ADIRONDACKS by E. Macer-Story

In a fundamental way, we humans in considering anomalous events and the supernatural are like these wild creatures attempting to figure out the "why" and "wherefore" of food scraps from the table of an intelligent lifeform with some incomprehensible agenda. Attempts to grasp the significance of encounters with Incomprehensible and/or Advanced Intelligence may simply be limited by the use of human-generated systems of analysis and perception.

Books like "*Goedel, Escher, Bach*" by Richard Hofstader are excellent works which push the boundaries of known organization of events and data. But, in essence, these works are yet within artificial systems of nomenclature and language. As Goedel himself has pointed out, within any system of ordering data and experience it is not possible to know the absolute ordering of that entire system. One must actually be outside the system in order to view the entire system. It is however possible, as in the formal music of Bach, to create a variety of complex, artificial combinations and permutations of known concepts.

UFO researcher Jerry Clark once advised me that outside the consensus reality things could get dangerous , not simply unusual, but hazardous. "Be careful not to venture too far beyond the consensus reality" sounds like stodgy advice. But this is simply like saying: "Don't go too far from the village. People in the next county don't speak the same language." We learn our systems of "reality" recognition. This is the essence of "civilization", a civil agreement that, for example, there are three primary colors. It is possible to look at the situation of visible light from other perspectives and, indeed, certain animals and some people are actually color-blind, seeing all visible light and shape in gray tones.

We have agreed in our shared technical literature to discuss three primary hues. Imagine a situation, outside consensus reality, wherein if someone has pointed to an object we would term "red" in color the name of that color is "the 7.40 vibe". "Yellow" would not then be a name but that color would be known by a certain numerical value such as "the 8.14 vibe". Because, as a matter of fact, there are not three primary colors only. There is a scale of relative light intensity and wavelength containing many different and distinct colors.

In a similar way, there is no assurance that our material continuum, which is now acknowledged by scientists to be composed of mass energy linked in molecular energy patterns, is not simply one density level in a density-quantized scale of parallel multidimensional matter systems. A transduction from one matter system to another (similar to the same arrangement of musical notes being sounded at different fret intervals on a stringed instrument) might account for the mysterious disappearances and other anomalous events in "devil's triangle" and "earth chackra" areas.

As recently as November 10, 2001 the following article "*Cerro Moreno Is A UFO Passageway*" appeared in the "El Mercurio de Antofagasta" newspaper in Chile:

"Scientific journalist and researcher Cristian Riffo disclosed an

DOING BUSINESS IN THE ADIRONDACKS by E. Macer-Story

important relationship between the UFO phenomenon and the disappearance of airliners in the sector known as the "Cerro Moreno Triangle"

Riffo has investigated this subject in our country for several years since his days at the La Tercera newspaper and currently from his position as director of www.ovnivision.cl, on the Internet. He stated that the details furnished by "El Mercurio" de Antofagasta based on historic information and Air Force sources result in a positive note which reinforces the research consigned in his forthcoming book "OVNIS y Fuerzas Armadas" (UFO's and Armed Forces" to be published next year in Santiago.

In this book, Riffo divulges details on the various cases linking Armed Forces personnel with UFOs, featuring the episodes made known by this newspaper in the enigmatic area known as the "Cerro Moreno Triangle", which is defined by Balneario del Hornito in the north, La Chimba in the southeast, and the coastline facing Punta de Angamos in the west.

A Case from 1980

He notes that the case which occurred on March 24, 1980 which resulted in the disappearance of a Hawker Hunter aircraft piloted by seasoned aviation commander Cesar Guevara is one of the most important UFO events of its type in the country. "This is one of the most confidential cases for which the Air Force has still not furnished a credible, official version of the events." In this episode, Riffo added that Guevara was not alone: "He was accompanied by a Brazilian pilot, and what is strange is that it was never made clear what became of both men."

He points out that the "Cerro Moreno Triangle" area has always been a mysterious place for UFO sightings, a subject which according to the researcher "remains constant." He adds that there is no conclusive information which could completely discard magnetism and the presence of UFOs in the area. He explained that during his investigations, he made an effort to contact the widow of pilot Cesar Guevara, without ever making contact. "We have never been able to speak to her directly, only through the intervention of a functionary of the Armed Forces whose identity shall be kept confidential. The family still considers the event a mysterious situation with which they are dissatisfied.'

The Guevara Case, he added, still has too many loose ends due to the UFO sightings made before and after the disappearance. "He was an expert pilot; he was one of the ones in charge of brining the Hawker Hunter aircraft from the UK to Chile during Operation Atlantis. If you fly in this type of aircraft and have some sort of problem, it has an ejection seat. This life-saving mechanism would have activated before an accident."

DOING BUSINESS IN THE ADIRONDACKS by E. Macer-Story

Translation (C) 2001. Scott Corrales, Institute of Hispanic Ufology.
Special Thanks to Ing. Marco A. Reynoso (Fundacion Cosmos AC) and
Leopoldo Carranza (Ovnipage).

Yet in situations of actual "high strangeness" expert technicians may loose their grip because what they are facing is an emergency which alters not only the material circumstances but their own cognition as well.

On November 13, 2001, your present correspondent had gone in search of Stephen Hawking's book *"The Universe in a Nutshell"* which was then being discussed on the Internet in a neo-physics context. But physicist Hawking's' book was not on the shelf at Barnes & Noble in NYC. I decided to order it from Amazon.com. An interesting funny synchronicity to this is that--shortly after mentioning the Highgate Vampire on the Internet with reference to writer/researchers. Dennis Bardens & Rosemary Guilley--as I was standing at B & N while the clerk checked their computer for the Hawking book a man next to me was loudly discussing vampire literature. The clerk next my clerk was very uncomfortable with this. The man with Vampire interests was buying an Anne Rice potboiler and the clerk kept saying:" O well, yes sir: they sell quite well but I've never been able to get through those books myself."

Dennis Bardens particularly, with his training in British Intelligence work and his interest in context, would have enjoyed this incident. It was like a soap opera supernatural scenario, very mundane and not at all terrifying. The Highgate Vampire "gets around". Greenwich Village in New York, shopping for fashionable vampire novels about his own legendary ilk..

Soldier of fortune, musician and painter Gary Osborne commented after learning of this experience:

*"I suppose some of you know that Dennis Barden's son Peter was (keyboard
player?) in the British band 'Fleetwood Mac' in the early days.
Apparently Peter and a few other members of 'Fleetwood Mac,' were sitting in
the front of the group's van, driving home from a gig. As they passed
through the country village of Cobham, they all saw a tall white figure appear from nowhere,
crossing the road right right in front of their van. The driver slammed on the breaks, but went
straight through the apparition. This freaked the group out, and one of the members was so
traumatized by the experience, that he went into shock
I think this story is in the book Ghosts and Hauntings - or is it another
book? . . not sure. Apparently, Peter Green, the celebrated guitarist and writer for the group, was
excited by the incident. It was after this that Peter Green became involved in black magic and the
occult.*

Physicist Dr. Jack Sarfatti, picked up the heavier "supernatural" tone of Osborne's observations

*"Weird I had such an experience at the High Gate Cemetery while
waiting with Sharon Allegra Moore to meet Fritjof Capra and*

DOING BUSINESS IN THE ADIRONDACKS by E. Macer-Story

the daughter of Graham Martin who was then US Ambassador to
Rome - this was 1973. I had just come from SRI (Puthoff &
Targ, O Regan) as described by Saul-Paul in
http://stardrive.org/Jack/contact.pdf
Sharon and I watched an old hag, obvious witch, dancing on a
grave. Suddenly a huge column ~ 30 feet of flame engulfed her.
Fire Department showed up, but there was no trace of a burnt
body! Shaken, we went to the Pub to meet Fritjof. We were
staying with Fritjof on our way to Paris for the strange
encounter in Per La Chaise Cemetery in
http://qedcorp.com/pcr/pcr/sioo.html and then to Abdus Salam's
ICTP in Trieste Italy to work on strong gravity explanation of
Regge trajectories. I would not meet Dennis Bardens of British
Intelligence "In the thick of it" for another year! I had no
idea he wrote such a book until now?".

Although not mentioned, for tactical reasons, to the neo-physics email list or the store clerk , it was obvious to me that the "vampire buyer" in the store might have been an independent intelligence operative clued by my research of Polanski's vampire film in conjunction with the Polanski—Tate connection to the Charles Manson murders. There had been time as I enquired first of a store guard and then of the clerk at the counter about the location of the Science section and the Hawking book to have grabbed a popular vampire novel from the shelf and walked with this book to the cash register beside the computer terminal where the clerk was searching Science listings. It is a fact that at the La Bianca murder site six logs from the fireplace were placed side by side in a design no one could interpret. I think this was an I CHING hexagram indication and that a "mastermind" Thantatos perpetrator was at the scene, checking on the work of the prosecutable minions of the Manson crowd.

Additionally, as I walked back to my office along Bleeker Street after shopping at the Barnes & Noble on the corner of 8th Street and 6th Avenue I noticed two incidents of hazing which might relate to a tap on my Polanski web search. When I was speaking with artist George Rauchus, who clerks at a CD short on Bleeker street, there was an unusual blonde, Caucasian young man dressed entirely in red who rushed into the shop, scanned the racks with a cursory glance and rushed out again. He was followed shortly afterward by a young Japanese man dressed in a business suit & tie who was carrying a loose leaf ring binder and asked George Rauchus who paid the electric bill in the shop. George indicated the owner at the end of the store and the man had a brief conversation with the owner, out of my earshot, and then left the store. I left the CD store shortly afterward and as I was walking along Bleeker street I was overtaken from behind by three men dressed in black business suits and carrying black, duck fabric attaché cases which in one instance seemed to be laptop computer cases.These men were having a very suspicious conversation about "this is not like Internet Chat Rooms" and turned to enter a restaurant on my left after passing me from behind as I was walking. Unfortunately, the restaurant was closed. This was about 3:15 p.m. I had a clear view of the features of the man carrying the computer bag as they turned to retrace their steps. He was early to late 30's brunette, Caucasian and had a slim straight nose which could be of any European Caucasian group. He was slightly overweight.

DOING BUSINESS IN THE ADIRONDACKS by E. Macer-Story

A counterpoint to these perhaps engineered events involving encounters with "significant strangers" in public places, was a series of witnessed paranormal events which began to happen privately, without reference or cue from Internet correspondence. On November 24, 3001, I experienced a "high strangeness" event just this afternoon. I have a bid from a gallery in France to be part of an exhibit next March. They asked for photos of current painting. I duly photographed some current paintings and took them to the local fast photo shop. One hour later, when I returned, there was a "how did this happen to the equipment?' scenario happening. The roll of film I had brought exhibited many anomalies including causing the tape inside the developing machine to loose stickiness and other really *STRANGE* problems including the appearance on one frame of many black Y-shaped "things" on the side of one painting. I recalled I had meditated that the exhibit--possibly a good distribution opportunity--"go well in introducing multi-dimensional concepts to the public".

So far: I got the roll of strange prints for free and the photo shop offered to reshoot the paintings for me for cost of film. There is a lot "out there" we just do not understand..

WEIRD PHOTO SEQUEL:

Today I went to the photo shop with paintings to get them re-photographed. The owner was not there as a member of his family had to be taken to hospital emergency. Instead, a woman friend was taking over the counter until he could return. I told her my errand and left. When I returned about one hour later, there was--once again--mild pandemonium in the shop. Just after I left the assistant had run a roll of film through the automatic developer. All the shots on the film had turned out tinted red or rosy pink. I had previously shown in another context some spirit photos to the owner's wife which contained what I call the "bubble gum people"--red or pink amoeboid forms which sometimes develop on the film in haunted locations.

The particular photos I had discussed with the proprietress of the Woodstock Images shop were taken at a Candlelight Vigil on the Woodstock green just after the September 11, 2001 terrorist attack which demolished the twin towers of the World Trade Center in lower Manhattan. She had found the "bubble gum" amoeboid forms on the snapshots particularly of interest since these are definitely not the tips of fingers accidentally at the edge of the camera lens but are misty and translucent pinkish to crème soft lumps and bulges obstructing the normal after-dark view of the candles left at the village green memorial location . These candles were surrounded on that evening by a crowd of local residents who had come to pay their respects to the World Trade Center victims.

Today, *before* I saw the roll of affected film I remarked jovially: "Is it the bubble gum people?" which caused more uproar. As it evolved the woman substituting at the counter is from an area in Lexington,N.Y. which I have previously investigated for anomalous phenomena. She had experienced a haunting there in her home. Her home is across the street from the building I had previously investigated. She did not know of my investigation--which was private, for an individual not a magazine. More uproar.

Now: here is the punch line, Gary. The roll of film which was rendered rosy red is of a *rock band performing*. On the chair in front of my easel in my studio as I looked at the

DOING BUSINESS IN THE ADIRONDACKS by E. Macer-Story

photos in the photo studio was the note: "Little red wagon upper left of canvas". I write myself image notes when I pause in painting. Last night I had laughed at the image of the "vampire " I was painting and had found myself saying:" Now I suppose we will have to paint you pulling your little red wagon since you have upset Aexus. Email correspondent 'Aexus" was upset by my previous note because it did not conform to his expectations about a reply to a UFO post.

In Little Italy, NYC the phrase "pulling his/her little red wagon" is a slang phrase meaning "bothering people with obsessive, childish commentary". Usually this is used to kid someone about a "sour grapes" routine but it looks like the Entity really HAS a red wagon. I am going to paint the red wagon and see ultimately what form it takes.

Rather than boring the reader with the exact narration of the composition of this painting as narrated in fey Internet correspondence, it is more significant to comment that only a few days after this cadenza of vampire anecdotes a strange political document entitled *Operation Vampire Killer* appeared unsolicited on my email queue. If this post was not the result of email surveillance, it certainly was a resonant co-incidence.

According to email correspondent Gary Osbourne in the UK, musician Peter Bardens was asked not to speak about the vampiric traffic apparition mentioned earlier in this narration lest, if this real ghost tale was discussed it might have a negative effect of public opinion of Dennis Bardens' upcoming book entitled "*Ghosts and Hauntings*". Often, this perplexing "counter-force" in psi research is ignored. Perhaps the purpose of the apparition was to discredit any publication which might lend credence to a "supernatural" or "sorcery" interpretation of certain criminal activities such as the Manson murders and mystically-inspired acts of terrorism. Dennis Bardens does touch on the apparition seen by the Fleetwood Mac rock group and the real power of hexing in a subsequent book entitled "*Mysterious Worlds*".

According to Bardens, who is also an operative for British Intelligence services, "In the course of an interview I recorded with Austin Osman Spare for a BBC program devoted to unusual beliefs, he once remarked, quite calmly: "I could kill a man with a curse." A.O. Spare, an accomplished visual artist who practiced a form of sorcery he had learned in part from a traditional British practitioner named in his writings "Mrs." Or "Witch" Patterson, was not a member of the Ordo Templi Orientis or other sorcery organizations discussed in this book. Artist Spare was a "lone witch" among many independent practitioners of the cunning arts in the British Isles.

Similarly, the *Operation Vampire Killer* post which appeared unsolicited in my email queue shortly after a discussion by email of actual vampiric manifestations in terms of synchronicity and talismanic artwork may have been dispatched by a covert type of negative intelligence linked to sorcery practice which will be discussed in more detail later in this text. The preternatural Vampire species itself may be attempting to light a distracting false fire to draw attention toward disturbed human persons rather than supernatural causes. This is the Faustian dilemma of a person who thinks to employ spirit entities to cause destructive mischief and then finds him/herself in the situation of having been tricked by those same entities. The same ,of course, could be speculated about cyber criminals employed to eavesdrop upon certain correspondences, who about the supernatural who then decided to enact *Operation Vampire*.

DOING BUSINESS IN THE ADIRONDACKS by E. Macer-Story

On December 3, 2001, I had thought to simply send copies of the *Operation Vampire Killer* folder to a short list on the Internet with whom I had been corresponding about poltergeist co-incidences connected with the "vampire painting" I had mentioned earlier in this narration.

But other activities intervened and when I finally was getting set to send the *Vampire Op* file off by email the following morning, I realized that *if* there was surveillance on the vampire topic that electronic surveillance had to be attached to one of the three participants on the short list, possibly myself. One of the persons on that list, who had mentioned spirit phenomena associated with British intelligence operative Dennis Bardens, is located in the UK where there has been a variety of covert and intelligence activity recently. I decided not to send out word of the "political vampire" synchronicity on the Internet in order to see if I might receive further "*Operation Vampire*" prompting.

As I was first saving this preceding paragraph, there was a strange glitch during which the cat was howling and the book file name was displayed as the "Bardens Vamp" file. Bardens is the British operative who figures in the previous vampire synchronicities. It was at the time that the cyber mechanism re-named my book file thusly that I decided to include the foregoing more detailed mention of Dennis Bardens' writing about hex possibilities.

The following excerpt from *Operation Vampire Killer* supposedly issued by "Police Against The New World Order" is advocating individual resistance against global government:

SOMETIMES "DISORDER" IS GOOD

As Protectors of the People, let us involve ourselves now and for the future in bringing DIS-order to the "New World Order" by committing ourselves this day along side Thomas Jefferson to this wonderful pledge:

"I have sworn upon the altar of Almighty God eternal hostility against every form of tyranny over the mind of man".

For those of our brothers and sisters who have children, this very evening quietly steal in and look down into the small faces of your posterity and ask yourselves this question: Can there be a greater work than to save our nation for these little ones? Working together with our fellow countrymen, we can place the final stake through the heart of this Parasitic Beast that has gripped our once vibrant nation by the throat. In so doing, we will secure for ourselves, our children and grandchildren, a grand and marvelous future.

On January 16, 2002, your present correspondent on matters of the bizarre noticed a folded metal form which had previously not been taken seriously in a dish of paperclips beside old correspondence . This tiny sculpture had originally been found in the hallway beside the Magick Mirror Space installation on Greenwich Street in Manhattan.

It resembles a small Origami airplane folded out of a sheet of metal so thick that it cannot be unfolded easily. One would have to use heat or some other form of density alteration in order to undo this small tight shape. Later, when puzzling over the mini-sculpture, I had the realization that by mental projection it might be possible to impress computer coding with talismanic intention as in ancient magickal patterns and diagrams. In fact, the "airplane" shape might actually be the three dimensional representation of a multi-dimensional mathematical process. I then checked the list of viruses in the current "virus alert" update on the laptop computer and located certain obviously intentional magic names and "abracadabra" formulations.

These were such as: "Dark Angel, Baphomet, Moloch, SZATAN, ABBA, Abraxas, ANARCHIST..." and so on. Note the virus name of "ANARCHIST" which is partway mentally between Luciferian and political concepts. In October of 2001 Mark Dunn wrote from the UK about his concept of a universal duality which governs mathematical, spiritual and material process. "At the Mid-Point of the Lemniscate one can reconfigure and untie the 'Gordion Knot' of entanglement consciously, thereby releasing the zero point energy, which will initially obliterate the crystalline structure of the 7 fold organizing principle of the primary 'dwell point' self within a particular entanglement basin, thereby experiencing the period of ego loss."

Mark Dunn seems to be a positive person simply asserting his particular view of the cosmos in philosophical terms. But another sensibility moving on this level of cognition might literally begin to construct talismanic, folded diagrams and shapes to force events into an ego-oriented shift of destiny patterning. For the alchemical motto is: "as above, so below". Mental states are seen by the alchemist to be reflected in the physical environment. So, conversely, the alchemical construction of a variety of talismanic shapes by an alchemically-aware mind might be expected by the believer to affect both material and mental destiny. This is in essence no different than thinking that the knotted rag of old tyme spell-casting can serve to hex or heal.

Lemniscate.com of Raliegh, North Carolina has made of this mathematical duality contemplation an "earth religion" of sorts. Their "lemniscate" is shown as a dragon, the living "gordian knot" of Mark Dunn's more abstract formulations. The major enigma of these "knots" of spacetime is that--in the estimation of your present correspondent--the hyperspace entanglement or knot contains a transduction substance "traction fluidice" which is living and receives kinetic, mental instruction from the "mind pilot waves" or "mind field" as regards specifics of material, molecular arrangement and destiny. The reason our contemporary scientists to date have missed this "kinetic life" factor is simply an intellectual presupposition of a difference between organic (carbon-based) matter and inert (silicon or crystalline-based) matter. But we know certain viruses and micro-organisms show crystalline organization as well as self-organizing intelligence.

Now, another scientist (besides E. Macer-Story) who seriously entertained the possibility of non-organic life forms active in our affairs as humans was the late Dr. John Lilly who discussed his interactions with Solid State Intelligence or SSI, a non-organic life form he thought was hostile to human and/or organic life in general. I do not think this non-organic intelligence is necessarily "hostile" but is quite different than organic life

DOING BUSINESS IN THE ADIRONDACKS by E. Macer-Story

and may seem to be hostile or cold & calculating simply because the material-emotional requirements are not the same. There may actually be a sort of "interspecies compassion" exerted in attempted communications by SSI. For example: scarce six days before the original drafting of this section of the text, a strange barrage of files--including one with the information on Lilly's SSI concept I have just given here--arrived on my hard drive as executable files sent from one of my regular correspondents I know plays sometimes with consciousness-altering substances.

I removed the executable files, saved the text and set a curt note to my associate about never sending executable files to me again as my cyber virus protector would block them. I got back the incredible news that the human & organic suspected culprit *had not sent the information.* It had been sent to me by a "virus" which had invaded his hard drive and sent out a variety of files, supposedly at random. Could this have been a form of SSI or non-organic micro-intelligence which, rather than being hostile, wished to communicate? Certainly, the information I received from the virus has been useful to me, much more useful than unsolicited files I have recently received by email from human beings.

By synchronicity, I was web-browsing to find a reference to the Tibetan lama "Sharmar" on the same day as the virus had sent the files on Dr. John Lilly to my hard drive, and in the process had discovered in the search engine list a unique site keyed to the names "Sharmar" or "Sharmapa" which used the word "magic" a number of times and had what looked to be a fur-covered box on a red-draped circular table posted as some sort of icon or ritual object.

I did not look at this site in any detail but took the existence of such an enigmatic and unexplained talismanic demonstration as indicating that my mind is moving in the right general direction when I seek to locate an ancient, anchored sorcery presence to oppose the negative use of similar powers. "Sharmar" is a Tibetan monk originally recorded as having been born in the Thirteenth century A.D. The contemporary Sharmar, allegedly many lifetimes later, is a living Tibetan monk who advocates a return to the traditional practice of "silent meditation".

When considering the communications of the aforementioned "Church of Yahweh" and other nominally religious organizations which circulate extreme statements about their own elite status, it is advisable to spend a moment of silence contemplating their claims. Sometimes those claiming "extraordinary intellect and/or power" actually have those powers to some extent. One does not defeat an opposing viewpoint or an objectionable viewpoint by simply assuming one can say "This is obviously wrong" and thus obtain automatic, universal agreement. Negative intelligence can be extremely persuasive and cunning. For the "bad guys" may reincarnate as well as the "good guys".

The entire document "*Sometimes Disorder is Good*" quoted earlier in this text is lengthy and extremely anti-Communist and anti-Socialist, with a roster of quotes implicating a number of prominent U.S. political leaders both contemporary and historical as "Communists" or "Socialists". Though the document advocates disrupting the present U.S. political system, no future political programme is given.

Another mailing from the same source had an anti-Semitic download folder entitled:" 1489, Chenor, Jewish Rabbi" about Jews masquerading as Christians and

DOING BUSINESS IN THE ADIRONDACKS by E. Macer-Story

having their sons "become Doctors and Apothecaries". This diatribe describes the "secret protocols" of the "Satanic seedline Jew" behind the scenes of all governments as indicated by Benjamin Disraeli's alleged statement in 1849:" The world is governed by very different personages from what is imagined by those who are not behind the scenes." Note the resemblance of the name "Chenor" to "Sharmar" and "Sharmapa"and recall the unique website in the "Sharmar" search which displayed a fur box on a circular table draped with a bright red cloth. In the very idea of "secret ritual protocols" which may contain specially draped tables and magic boxes, all of these traditions—including "Church of Yahweh" –have a common intersection. I have written about the potency of a similar Ozark hill country hex practice in my previous book "Dark Frontier". But I did not in that book write about the racial beliefs of the hill people today. This did not dawn on me as an important issue involving supernatural beliefs and occurrences until I read the unique outpourings of "Church of Yahweh" as these kept appearing in my email queue. Of course: all tribes and races have some idea of their own history and the identity of their ancestors and this is also an important element in spirit invocations and spell casting.

This essay, attributed to "Pastor Bob Jones of a "Teutonic Knights" tradition which may include hex magic as it does also include healing, contains the following passage about the imagined accomplishments of a widespread Hebrew "masquerade":

"However today they also own the World's Banks, the Commodity, & Securities industry, the Jewelry & precious metals industry, the Media industry, the Communications industry, the Oil companies & energy industry, the transportation industries, the quaisi-government policy making agencies, (CFR, Trilateral commission, Bilderberg, etc.) the secret societies, (Masons, Skull & Bones, Club of Rome, etc.) the Militaries, & Police of all countries, all the spy agencies, CIA, FBI, BATF, IRS, KGB, Interpol, British Secret Service, our Secret Service, Mossad, etc. The Mafia's of ALL countries, (which is ALL jew at the top!) How do you think they could go on with all those criminal enterprises for so long on such a large scale? How do you think they launder all those BILLIONS? Why do you think they almost never go to jail?

Although Pastor Bob Jones is evidently incorrect in attributing all political and social chicanery across the boards to only the Jewish race, he and his "poor white" followers do sense correctly that there may be a wealthy conspiracy to attempt to control political and social events. Or at least the choice of an invisible caste of moneyed elite to remain covertly within events as a hidden aristocracy. Ironically, certain of these closet kings and queens appear to be part of a Nordic diaspora from Nazi Germany who began to emigrate to South America even prior to World War Two because the remote jungle locations there gave ample room for a covert, invisible kingdom. These remote locations on the South American continent may also give room for experimentation with "flying saucers". Mysterious aircraft have been seen in the jungles of Chile, Peru and other South American countries continuously since the mid-twentieth century. Mass sightings of OVNI lights and seeming vehicles have occurred in Mexico and South America which simply are not featured as forthrightly in U.S. and European news outlets. The lack of high profile worldwide coverage of these events may be due to the fact that the " hidden

DOING BUSINESS IN THE ADIRONDACKS by E. Macer-Story

Nordic aristocracy" does not want publicity. If the existence of this wealthy, elitist subculture was known, it would be resisted.

Yet "ufo" photos keep accumulating in South America and never quite getting "over the edge" from the email circuit to the network cable news shows and establishment newspapers. A colleague who has worked in gallery and media stores in the Greenwich Village-Soho area of Manhattan tells the tale of having a Peruvian ufo contactee come into the gallery where he was working in the year 2000. She was a woman in her fifties who seemed wealthy and bought several paintings on ufo-related subjects as her limousine driver waited outside. According to the artist working at the gallery, this woman had seen a very small, metallic ufo craft like a remote control toy hover craft near her home in Peru. It hovered in mid-air close to her and she touched it with her hand, finding it cold. My artist colleague could not recall where in Peru his unidentified customer had experienced this mini-"touching" of a toy-sized hovercraft. In his book "The UFO/FBI Connection" Dr. Bruce Maccabee relates the account from FBI files of a pilot flying from Clark Field to Parkersburg , West Virginia in 1949 who saw a canary yellow rocket only 15-18 inches long, which flew in sight of the cockpit at about 3000 feet above sea level. There are numerous sightings of small or "toy"-sized spacecraft in the ufo lore. This fact should indicate something significant about the "real" unexplained "ufo phenomenon" -whatever it might be in complete reality-and the vehicle-sized OVNI ships and lights which are frequently seen in South America.

After hearing the tale of the cold mini-ufo in Peru, I was refreshed in mind and once again felt like "Doing Business" in the area of the supernatural, and gathering some new information on these South American ufos. Money once again appeared in my coffee shop small change as I handed a clerk four dollars and had her incredulously return seven dollars (one five and two singles) along with my change in coin for a $3.17 purchase of coffee and a muffin. It seemed she was under the impression I had given her a ten dollar bill and some change instead of the four one dollar bills I had carefully counted out beforehand and put in my pocket. I did not question this small windfall.

I took the coffee and muffin back to my Magick Mirror office and phoned New York ufo entrepreneur Mike Luckman, having just obtained Luckman's phone number from George Rauchus (the artist who had then told me the tale of the wealthy Peruvian art collector who had touched a cold mini-ufo near her home in Peru.) in order to learn the number of ex-patriot Chilean ufologist Antonio Huneus.

.In the subsequent phone conversation with Huneus, a tree branch in a video he had been deceptively asked to narrate came into the foreground of the discussion. I recalled the section of this ill-fated video which is mentioned in my article:" *Operation Abject" The Majestic Joker Turned Upside Down*". This article, originally posted on Elfis.net website, is about the "Majestic" hoax material which was a popular conversation piece among ufo researchers during the late 1980's and early 1990's. The section of the questionable commercial video show on ufos mentioned in this article is the interview with a Soviet KGB refugee as this individual is walking down a path in the woods in the Ural Mountains. I had originally noted that the short, stout stick held in the KGB official's hand was somewhat similar to the talismanic wands left at my country property in Woodstock between the years 1997 and early 2001. The frequency of this wand talismansing diminished after the "*Operation Abject*" article was posted in 2001 and the style of the stick talismans left on my property also changed. At the date of this writing,

DOING BUSINESS IN THE ADIRONDACKS by E. Macer-Story

only smaller peeled sticks or very large tree branches which have been subtly treated either by whittling or by glazing and peeling of bark in patterns have been found on the country property recently.

I asked Antonio Huneus, a person familiar with the legendary non-electronic KGB techniques, whether he knew of the "santoria"-like peeled stick talismanic sorcery of Cuba and the actual probing of ancient Russian shamanic practices by Soviet and subsequent Eastern European researchers in the ex-Soviet republics. Huneus indicated that he was very familiar with these possibilities.

On Saturday November 11, 2001 your present correspondent found a small, "worked" twig talisman on the patio opposite the kitchen door. When I considered this talisman clairvoyantly, I was aware of a digital gauge display and thought of "radionics".

At 3:30p.m. on the same day, I was followed on my walk back from the Bradley Meadows shopping Center in Woodstock by a youth in a royal blue tee shirt and wide, skirt-like denim pants, who walked swiftly from behind me, then crossing in front of me onto a side road. He was drinking a golden-brown soft drink in a fancy bottle. I had never seen him before. He was Caucasian, medium-sized, with short, dark hair. When he glanced sideways at me, his eyes seemed unusually large and blue.

Possibly the actual perpetrators of the mischief alluded to by "Pastor Bob Jones" in his ravings do not go to jail because the extent of the machinations afoot cannot actually be comprehended by the average law-abiding person. It may be that the "Covenant Church of Yahweh" grasps the strategy but not the true perpetrators behind the charades. Modern economics and sociology are taught in most universities as analytical and mathematical disciplines. It is a classic development that persons interested in higher mathematics like Kurt Goedel in his work with "undecidable" concepts frequently push off into realms of mental endeavor which involve ritual behavior paradigms. In fact: there are equations which have been developed for predicting both economic behavior and social development.

It is just one small step from use of these equations for prediction to use of these equations for manipulation or forcing events into desired patterns. In essence, this is "sorcery" or "higher magick". In this context, it can be speculated that my clairvoyant perception of a "digital gauge" connected with the "worked" talismanic twig might be connected with the ritual action of "crossing my path", which is a time-honored sorcery practice. In the passage from "Pastor Bob Jones" quoted below there does seem to be the exhortation for the White Race to turn to ancient ways during the current planetary emergency. So one might suspect that a White Youth was involved with some sort of Druidic charade. But is this too naïve? Might a privileged youth of this description actually be part of some intellectually-based ritual practice developed by a private corporate entity or "think tank"? Might the reason that these shenanigans have not been detected previously be simply that it does not cross the mind of people who have not been mathematically or philosophically trained? In fact: the use of rituals and paradigms nor commonly available emotionally is one strategy protection used both by legitimate martial artists and cryptographers, and by criminals.

The "Pastor" is here using ritual talk in political context:

"And of course their "crowning jewel" the World Government Headquarters the <u>United Nations</u>, & most important where they indoctrinate/brainwash the "one world citizens/slaves", the <u>public school system</u>! Did I leave out anything? Satan's kids are <u>VERY ambitious for their father</u>.

DOING BUSINESS IN THE ADIRONDACKS by E. Macer-Story

How ambitious are you for your FATHER? They have taken over the world it looks like to me, how about you? If not for YHVH being in charge, the White Race is completely finished, can you see that? I HIGHLY SUGGEST YOU TURN TO YHVH & HIS WORD IN THESE END TIMES AS YOU REALLY DON'T HAVE ANY OTHER PLACE TO TURN TO, DO YOU??? "

Yet in an email from the same source, yclept "Covenant Church of Yahweh" , which was sent on December 9, 2001, a few days after the "seedline Jews" diatribe, there is an extensive, confused portrayal of U.S. President George W. Bush, a member of the White Race, as having known about the September 11, 2001 WTC-PENTAGON hijack terrorism before the event and being somehow complicit in a terrorist conspiracy charade.

This is reproduced in part here to give the reader a flavor of the mania of the extensive email narration.:
"

"There is -- indeed -- NO DOUBT WHATSOEVER that bush WAS watching a VERY, VERY "different" TV channel than ALMOST everyone else -- except for other top BushMobsters -- at about 9 AM EDT on the morning of September 11.
Bush was OBVIOUSLY watching a closed-link feed of the event that MUST HAVE BEEN transmitted from a camera positioned a priori by
agents/accomplices of the primary perpetrators themselves.
There is NO other explanation.

On a more mundane note, a number of respondents pointed out to us that a video allegedly taken by someone who just happened to be filming the Trade Center that morning did air a COUPLE OF HOURS after the INITIAL incident.

These respondents are quite correct, although it was a couple of days until security camera footage was broadcast.
Of course, this has absolutely zero bearing on the fact there was NO broadcast of the FIRST plane slamming into the Trade Center within MINUTES of the event by ANY TV station or network on the planet, as everyone in the world with two brain cells to rub together CAN figure out".
If you know how to WALK, you CAN figure this out.

Americans need to REALLY, REALLY understand exactly what these shockingly revealing comments by bush ACTUALLY MEAN.
TOP_VIEW has caught Junior with his pants down

This same communication offers the recipient an "Activist Kit" which can be ordered from a specific email address. Your present correspondent did not order this "Activist Kit" for to order this item, even to report on these Internet shenanigans, is to enter an Alternate Mental Universe, a province of darkness and chaos with unique and very tricky radio, Internet and television stations.

Though your present correspondent has speculated about actual diabolism in this book, it is tempting to now diverge into the "mentality of cults" and hang this entire

DOING BUSINESS IN THE ADIRONDACKS by E. Macer-Story

"alternate Yahweh universe" within the closet of abnormal psychiatry. Yet this may not be the correct interpretation. The ravings of the "Church of Yahweh", a group which in effect wants to re-write the Judeo-Christian Bible to eliminate Hebrew participation, do call attention to the double level of organization within the U.S. government and potentially to a similar double level of organization within the developing World government. We do hear daily on the syndicated news these days about a secretly designated U.S. "shadow government" which would take over if there was massive terrorist damage and loss of life at central, governmental locations.

So, the statements originating from this "alternate Yahweh universe" where a secret society who falsely claims they wrote the Bible also falsely claims that the elected officials are in charge of financial transactions globally can be seen to be a fearful response to an actual situation of political uncertainty. But, as frequently happens in criminal cases involving assault, the "Church of Yahweh" is right about the nature of the crime but is identifying the wrong "secret society". If the Jews did actually run the world secretly, they would not be living in ghettos all over the world. They would be living in palaces.

Should we be alert not for the next chapter in governmental intrigue, which is part of human nature, but for the type of trickster sorcery which attempts to assert that the U.S. government was complicit in the September 11, 2001 act of demolition actually planned by Islamic extremists? Would either the disenfranchised terrorists or the secretly collusive financial experts really want to publicly assert this viewpoint? Or is the personality which puppets this perverse idea actually not human? A veil of smoke which formed the large, diabolic image of a devil's head with horns was visible in several frames of news footage shot by CNN cameras during the collapse of the twin towers of the World Trade Center in Manhattan. As the well-known advice on spirit exorcism goes, the "devil can quote scripture" and a perverse negative force can get people into deep trouble by leading them to believe that the Voice of God speaks through any one human mouth. .The ancients knew well that there were many God, Goddess and demi-God and/or Goddess forces and that these non-human personalities were frequently involved in conflicts which were transmitted into the human sphere of activities.

In Colin Wilson's excellent book "*Alien Dawn*", he cites the case of a Mr. Ted Holiday who had studied the Loch Ness monster sightings and had accumulated tales of supernatural appearances in that same lake area in a book entitled "*The Goblin Universe*". According to Colin Wilson, Mr. Holiday put aside this manuscript when deep sounding of the Loch Ness revealed a physical creature in the deeps of the lake with an elongated body and huge triangular fin. But later, after Holiday's death of a heart attack, manifestly "anomalous" sightings continued to occur near the Loch Ness in a "ufo-style" modality. The triangular fin which was allegedly sighted in the sonar image of the lake's depths reminds your present correspondent of a "shark kahuna" belief from Hawaii and the Polynesian islands.

In the South Pacific it has been observed that often a "mysterious stranger" will warn of a shark attack at the beach, thus drawing crowds of people (potential victims)

DOING BUSINESS IN THE ADIRONDACKS by E. Macer-Story

toward the beach as curious witnesses. The saying of the Polynesian tradition is that the stranger who warns of the shark IS the shark. Could this be true in the Loch Ness and other "mysterious monster" sightings? Is it possible that the aquatic/amphibious creature actually has unusual powers of telepathy and selective materialization?

I passed once again through the area near the village of Woodstock where before (testing the observed boomerang of intention mentioned in the initial pages of this text whilst discussing the self-organization of events) I had inwardly expressed a material desire to the resident spirit, and that desired material event had later happened. On this walk I presented the enigmas thus far discussed in this book to that spirit (in an area where two streams and three roads meet) since recently emails from Aexus had seemed to confirm my perception that there is some unacknowledged link between his activities and some organized form of black magick, including highly adept individuals with cyber skills.

I inwardly presented the crossroads spirit with the tangled nexus of my thoughts on this subject and, as I was approaching a local bakery afterward to buy some muffins, a lone condor with feathers like fingers at the tip of squared-off wings flew low over my path. This caused me to remember other appearances of such a bird coupled with thoughts of a powerful spirit guide. So the answer by natural divination seems to be the participation of non-human intelligence in an inclusive, cosmic process.

Concepts of a kind of "quantum sorcery" which will be more fully discussed later in this book in terms of the injection of minor discrepancies or corrections into the normal flow of events were put forward in theory by physicist Neils Bohr, a rival of the physicist Dr. Albert Einstein during the mid-twentieth century.

According to Neils Bohr:

"In the first place, we must recognize that a measurement can mean nothing else than the unambiguous comparison of some property of the object under investigation with a corresponding property of another system, serving as a measuring instrument, and for which this property is directly determinable according to its definition in everyday language or in the terminology of classical physics. While within the scope of classical physics such a comparison can be obtained without interfering essentially with the behavior of the object, this is not so in the field of quantum theory, where the interaction between the object and the measuring instruments will have an essential influence on the phenomenon itself. Above all, we must realize that this interaction cannot be sharply separated from an undisturbed behavior of the object, since the necessity of basing the description of the properties and manipulation of the measuring instruments on purely classical ideas implies the neglect of all quantum effects in that description, and in particular the renunciation of a control of the reaction of the object on the instruments more accurate than is compatible with the [uncertainty] relation."[10]

DOING BUSINESS IN THE ADIRONDACKS by E. Macer-Story

According to this physics theory, mind has a direct effect on matter. This would mean that the atomic fission/fusion of induced nuclear reactions as developed by Dr. Albert Einstein and others, although effective as a manipulation of the material substances uranium and plutonium, might have concomitant side effects linked to the presence of a mind-like logos within the material, nuclear structure.

Could negative adepts, as manifested in the brief formation of a diabolic face in the smoke from the World Trade Center terrorist hit on September 11, 2002,[11] be deliberately using in secret such subtle mind/matter systems as indicated in the "quantum sorcery" of physicist Neils Bohr to contact and harness the non-human Intelligence of this logos for purposes of power?

A variety of systems of worship have claimed to be able to propitiate "gods" and/or "demons" in order to cause events to happen in the way in which individuals might will these events to happen. We are conditioned by popular films and documentaries about "aboriginal shamans" or "witches and wizards" leaping around in earthy rituals to expect that most hexes and spells will be overtly dramatic, involve non-literate activity and are subordinate to the correction of "psychological" or "sociological" analysis. Quite evidently, this is mistaken if we include the deliberate actions of trained academics, CEO's, stockbrokers and medical doctors with native mental ability into the mixture.

On the afternoon I had placed the quote from Neils Bohr on my writing table for transcription, I noticed a woman standing behind me in the line at the Jefferson Market post office who looked familiar. My attention was immediately drawn to her when she walked into the post office lobby not because of her physical appearance but because her energy was strong and intensely subtle, like the energy of a professional clairvoyant, healer or sorcery adept. I glanced back at her several times before finishing my business and leaving the store. Later, I identified her as resembling both facially and in physical stature a professor of anthropology from whom I had taken a course in prehistory as an undergraduate at Northwestern University, where I obtained my B.S. in Speech in August of 1965. The woman in the post office was about sixty to seventy years old and in excellent physical condition. The only unusual aspect of her appearance was that she was wearing thick, pink lipstick outlined at the edges of the lips by bright red lines and no other extreme face makeup. This caused me to spontaneously think of exotic ritual face painting or masking though the makeup itself was within normal bounds for visiting a post office in the afternoon.

Years ago, I had experienced a momentary vision during the prehistory class of the professor's head and neck as the head and neck of a large, hawk-like bird in semi-profile. I knew as a student that she had participated in the excavation of the enigmatic "Mound Builders" culture in the Southeast and South Central United States and wondered whether she had somehow intersected with an ancient spirit entity associated with those structures. But this visual perception of a hawk's head was a fleeting inner impression. There was no discussion of a hawk mythology in the class.

DOING BUSINESS IN THE ADIRONDACKS by E. Macer-Story

Could it be that this professor, who would be in her mid-seventies now, or someone very much like her from the "Thantatos" group was following me in conjunction with my probings into a possible archeologically-oriented elitist group with covert academic ties? After returning to my private Magick Mirror office from the post office, I had out-of frame negative emotional flashbacks from a situation involving people located in Cambridge, Massachusetts whom I had not seen for twenty-five years. An added eerie facet of this experience was that while thinking carefully about this influx of emotional memories I found that the bathroom of my private office was full of cigarette smoke when I opened the door. The professor I had recalled earlier in the day had been a chain smoker and smoked continually as she lectured. This was in 1964, prior to health restrictions on smoking.

This event of finding actual smoke in the bathroom put the entire post office experience onto another level entirely. Was this a spirit, someone over-shadowed by a spirit, or another of my odd experiences with demi-human simulacrums in the oft-haunted "Jefferson Market Triangle"[12] area of New York?

The next evening I attended a lecture at Princeton University, which is only one hour from New York City on the commuter train. This lecture was a short talk by parapsychologist George Hansen nominally about "*TheTrickster And The Paranormal*" his new book on the "trickster" concept in occult tradition and modern research. During the lecture, however, there was a focus on religion, atheism and innate cultural prejudices as regards the "supernatural" as an area of serious research. Little was said about "tricksters" in detail during the talk. Perhaps Hansen hoped that people in the audience would buy his book for this information.

After this lecture, I had another quietly odd experience resembling the experience in the Manhattan post office. I was waiting for the commuter connection at Princeton Junction station at shortly after ten p.m. It was chilly and I was impatient. I noticed with irritation that the clock on the platform read 10:20, indicating that I would have to wait forty minutes for the train to the city. So I walked toward steps leading to the parking lot and saw the silhouette of a man reading a book standing in the light near the road. A few minutes later, having walked along the platform and found the station waiting room closed, I decided to join the man reading down by the parking lot as there were no other people at the station. But when I turned and started to walk down the steps from the platform, there was no person standing in the streetlights reading. So I went back up onto the platform. When I returned upstairs, I noticed that the clocks on the platform read 1:20 but the clock inside the station, visible through the window, still had the correct time. I assumed that some trickster had altered the platform clocks but could not access the clock inside the station.

But was this a human operative or a being from the "shadow world" symbolized in the traditional Kabbalah as the "Klepoth"[13] and in systems of Arabic sorcery as the djinn? In all systems of sorcery and divination there is acknowledgement of a number of Worlds populated by diverse types of beings .Some of these are Angels but not all of the denizens of the subtle Worlds have angelic intentions. It is difficult sometimes for modern people, schooled to be able to efficiently operate cars and computers, to understand that when the ancient adepts designated the existence of hierarchies of beings living simultaneously on other Worlds accessible from Earth, these Worlds were not seen as any distance in Light Years from this planet. Rather, the Intelligences invoked by ritual or traveling on their own recognizance manifested from these Worlds onto our familiar planet by a process of subtle, material transfer linked to mental functioning. In understanding ancient systems of divination, it is important that this travel and information exchange between Worlds be taken literally.

In modern physics speculation, there are a number of systems which describe such a hypothetical "density shift" by using mathematical notation. However, these systems usually require innovative new machinery which to date has not managed to reliably visit other Worlds and return. The closest establishment science may have come to direct realization of the actual nature of these other Worlds of a different matter density which interpenetrate our familiar, material planet is simply to note[14] that unusual "flying saucer" and "aerial light" sightings first occurred in quantity in the mid-Twentieth century near locations where atomic fission/fusion had been tested, either to build atomic bombs or for development of atomic power systems.

These initial sightings just after the first atomic explosions ended World War Two seem linked to the tinkering with the inner structure of the nucleus of uranium and plutonium atoms which occurred at that time. Early military and FBI interpretations of the phenomena cited this possibility and it is most probable that these early interpretations were correct. The initial, accurate analysis of this situation was lost during the Cold War of the 1950-80's when any unusual technical or quaisi-technical manifestations were automatically assumed to be "Soviet" or a "secret project" of the U.S. government.

However, it was found that claims of the Soviets to have done more than observe the same unexplained type of aerial phenomena were unfounded. According to Chilean ufologist Antonio Huneus, a 1992 video in which he appeared along with footage of alleged KGB officials endorsing the reality of ufo crashes in the USSR was found to contain hoax material about the autopsy of ufo aliens at a medical school in Russia, as well as other inaccuracies. Huneus was just as obviously a victim of the false material as any credulous spectator of the footage might be, having been edited into the larger picture without a chance to fully investigate the context of claims made by other participants featured in the video, which was nominally about KGB involvement with ufo investigation in both Eastern Europe and South America. I asked Antonio Huneus why he thought such an expensive effort, which included transporting people to a studio location in California and putting them up in hotels there, would be made if the phenomena discussed by the alleged KGB officials in the flawed video were not genuine.

"To make money," he responded, "The video was sold all over the world."

The answer which Huneus provided me obviously has satisfied him in dealing with his own predicament. But it does not entirely account for the venture. If the purpose

DOING BUSINESS IN THE ADIRONDACKS by E. Macer-Story

was simply to make money, why didn't these people simply invest in a "Star Wars" type of film endeavor? Was the purpose of the flawed "KGB-ufo" documentary to divert attention from another, covert political interest group with an active, private research program in advanced technology? The public is familiar with the stereotyped idea of an Eastern European black market association. This demimonde has been the source of melodramatic villains in a number of films and novels, beginning with the Cold War "James Bond" paperbacks of the 1950's. But why on earth would the Russian mafia pay KGB veterans to impersonate themselves in stage costume uniforms, as Antonio Huneus has suggested was done for the video.

A section of this video during which a KGB officer interviewed in the Ural mountains carries a stout talismanic wand has previously been mentioned in this book in context of this reporter's previous article on disinformation, entitled: "Operation Abject" The Majestic Joker Turned Upside Down".. Is it possible that this individual has by this arcane means contrived to signal to those on the *que vive* the true source or motivation for this disinformation video, which may lie in the province of a wealthy , covert organization with an interest in technological innovation, flying saucers and sorcery?

Could such an organization, using material on the level of the speculations of physicist Neils Bohr, have made discoveries beginning prior to World War Two which would take technology in the direction of actual living links between human-invented Earth culture and operative Intelligences from other Worlds? If so, the inventors may wish to be unknown lest their discoveries be misunderstood or misused. OR there is the situation of concealing or encrypting such effective knowledge, lest those outside a certain "elite" be similarly empowered. For example: the "vampire" synchronicities previously cited with reference to the films of Roman Polanski and research involving requests for key books in a public place might be induced by some form of telepathic hypnosis coupled with surveillance by dedicated members of some elitist intelligence agency or similar private organization.

Technical theories no one can share but the "initiated" few who believe in an elite viewpoint are a form of "black magick" .In the years just before World War Two and during that war physicists in Europe on both sides of the conflict were involved in debates within just such a restricted network of information. In contemporary context, there is a free flow of speculative scientific information on the Internet which was not present in the mid-twentieth century.

One form of physicist Bohr's theories, not devised by Neils Bohr but presented by contemporary metaphysical analyst Peter Mutnick in an Internet physics discussion group, depicts these theories as a system of meditation with mind as an active participant in forming matter.

"The third intervention, as the fourth stage of the measurement process, must now be regarded not as the transformation of the Density Operator back into
a Density Matrix, which is now regarded as the culmination of the second intervention that leads to

a reiteration of the first intervention, but as what Henry Stapp calls the Heisenberg reduction, which reduces the physically weighted sum of meta-physical projection operators, stemming from the second application of von Neumann's intervention #1, to a single projection operator representing the actually observed result. However, the essential point here is that this does not occur spuriously through the intervention of consciousness itself, but rather through the aspect of the
measuring instrument that embodies the Kantian form of consciousness.
There are certain Buddhist mantras, pertaining to the popular cult of Avalokiteshvara, the bodhisattva of compassion, that represent this hypostatizing of cosmic consciousness: *OM TARA, TU TARA, TURE SVAHA; OM MANI PADME HUM; and GATE, GATE, PARA GATE, PARA SAM GATE, BODHI SVAHA.* The first of these encompasses *MATTER* as corresponding to the physically weighted sum of meta-physical projection operators, and the third of these encompasses MIND as corresponding to the single meta-physical projection operator actually selected. So, the mantras together signify the transformation of *MATTER* into *MIND*, similar to Einstein's transformation of matter into energy. Metaphysically, *MATTER* is at the top of the etheric world, just beneath the phenomenal world, in the horizontal scheme of worlds, while *MIND* is directly above the phenomenal world. MIND constitutes the so-called *akasha*, where the akashic records of all experiments and experiences are stored. "

In this context it is appropriate to recall the individual from the neo-Shinto religious group noticed by your present correspondent as circling her country house a few years prior to the drafting of this book. This incident is included in the article:" The Art of Making Wolves from Human Skulls" online in Magonia magazine and in hard copy in Alternate Perceptions magazine. There was no doubt that the driver of the car circling the block in 1999 was actually the same person who had been obstructive at a previous U.S. Psychotronics Association meeting . The question raised by this reporter at that time was simply a concern about the exact motivation for this surveillance, beyond metaphysical arguments.

On March 31, 2002, your present correspondent got a look at the license plate of the car which had previously been seen at shortly after six a.m. on Friday February 2/22/02 slowly circling the block in which her country house is located in Woodstock. This was accomplished by pure luck--but in the self-organization of these events it seems there are no real accidents. It was Easter Sunday.

I had been scheduled to attend a dinner in New York with friends but changed my mind at the last minute because of the accelerating Palestinean-Israeli terrorist crisis. I did not feel it was appropriate to travel into the city for a holiday celebration after seeing graphic images of the carnage on television. Prior to making this decision I had checked the bus schedule by phone and had in general made it known that I would be taking the afternoon bus from the country which got into the city just before dinner was scheduled. About thirty minutes before this bus passed through the town of Woodstock, I changed my mind but had not yet telephoned my hostess in the city. I decided to take a short constitutional walk before making the cancellation call as I knew my hostess, a lawyer who is also a professional singer, was out on business during Easter afternoon. As I reached the bottom of the steps descending the slope in front of my house, I reached up to

DOING BUSINESS IN THE ADIRONDACKS by E. Macer-Story

straighter the crossbar of a lamppost at the foot of the walk which had been pushed to one side by the wind. This must have taken about 45 seconds only. When I looked down the driveway afterward, I found to my surprise that a red sports car had pulled up on the edge of the lane right in front of the yard. The individual in this car was seemingly startled to see me begin to walk down the driveway toward the lane and drove away hastily by turning the corner onto a connecting side road back of the house. I then started to walk down the lane toward the highway on my usual route, which was opposite from the direction in which he car had sped away.

In turn, I was dumbfounded by seeing this same sports car turning onto the lane from the highway and coming directly toward me. I kept walking, pretending not to notice the car as anything special. As it passed me I got a clear look at the license plate and the driver. The driver was a medium weight bearded, swarthy individual with slightly receding, curly brown hair. I did not see him closely enough to speculate on any detailed characteristics. The license tag on the front of the car was a deluxe issue from another state/perhaps another country. The car passed at a normal speed and I did not have time to read the inscription at the top of the plate, which was not an ordinary New York State issue, and read WOMBATZ. Here before I relate the following research I should emphasize that I have dealt before as a reporter with license plates which were not on the level but had been deliberately placed over genuine plates to cloud description. There is no guarantee that the plate on this car was a straight issue.

Nevertheless, I web searched the word WOMBATZ and came up with among other more obscure associations the name of a rock group from Australia listed in quasi blood-occult context. This ID would tend to link "rock groups" with the bizarre talismans I had been finding on my property for several years. But the actual instigators of this mind game are far more intelligent and subtle than the average rock band performance. I do not here assert that rock musicians are stupid. This is not so. They have to be clever and always on the moment in order to survive as performers. But the type of intelligence exhibited by the "Thantatos" organization of covert black magick sorcerers is a different, more cleverly subtle, type of mental functioning. It is extremely unlikely that a Thantatos member would drive around in public with the actual password to a direct knowledge about the group on the front of a flashy sports car. It is more likely that the driver was a pawn employee of "Thantatos" or that the plate displayed was a deliberate ruse in case anyone noticed the car parked in front of the house on Easter.

The actual progress of events had become stranger than a Herman Hesse novel or an Ingmar Bergman film. . The reader is here asked to recall sections 14 to 19 of the radio "Time Play" previously included in this text:

"14. ANNOUNCER: Meanwhile, one century later, in the offices of the Chronological Bureau of Historical Readjustment in Sri Lanka, the biography of Dravid T. Zaylor of London, England is now being assembled by computer search of all available identification sources. It has to be a quick job! For nuclear renegade Dr. Dravid T. Zaylor,Jr. is reported to have a secret formula powerful enough to blow up the entire Republic of China. In fact, he had already activated

DOING BUSINESS IN THE ADIRONDACKS by E. Macer-Story

the device and started the countdown when his colleague and loyal assistant Margo Li Chan had second thoughts about this explosive situation and e-mailed an alarm to the Time Police.

15. *THERE IS A SERIES OF LOUD, URGENT ELECTRONIC BEEPS.*

16. *ALEXIS: We have exactly 48 seconds until detonation. I shall have to time jump into the next nanosecond and travel backward on the biographical line of mad scientist Dr. Dravid T. Zaylor, Jr. because we do not know exactly where his present day hideout is located. According to the "China On Line" automatic computer tracer, it is somewhere in the vast Siberian Steppes.*

17. *ANNOUNCER: But, meanwhile, one hundred years ago, just outside the maternity ward in Delhi, India, Time Cop Alexis d'Angela has encountered an unusual obstacle.*

18. *LOUD CLANKING AND RATTLING SOUND.*

19. *ALEXIS: Nurse! Someone has installed a bolt lock on this door! In fact: there seem to be five or six of them! Isn't it unusual to have this much security in a hospital? Unless there's some rare disease in the nursery....Nurse! Is there any reason this door is locked from inside?"*

Some austerely crazy intellectual interest group may actually be using sorcery and/or mental magick techniques either for private experimentation or covert exploitation in order to attempt to block public knowledge of actual mind/matter manipulation techniques. Perhaps in the possible "elite-dominated" future, shifting co-present and/or distant Atlantean past this type of maneuver will not be generally detectable and discussed in the popular literature as a real possibility, rather than fiction.

But this book is directed toward altering that smugly elite-dominated future. It is my hope that after reading or hearing of this book, people will sensibly speculate: *"Well, maybe telepathic hypnosis is being attempted..."* or *"That man looks like he is in costume. Maybe he is part of some improvised sorcery charade by an intelligence agency."* Here it should be noted that there are also private, mercenary intelligence agencies as well as government-funded investigative groups.

So one present elitist sorcery technique, which is to archly deny knowledge of arcanely-orchestrated covert aggression in public whilst at the same time organizing covert rituals for the "initiated' behind the false bookcase, will no longer be as effective since your present correspondent, and other alert witnesses, will not fall for cleverly-orchestrated strategies of misdirection and misinterpretation.. I certainly hope this book serves as a partial eye-opener in that regard. Practical acts of aggression do not exclude the use of telepathic hypnosis and/or esp projection, including warlike out of body dream trips.

Given this possible combination of well-heeled elitist sorcery and trickster charades, we should expect to find the most clever, covert mind/matter sorcerers and magicians among the contingent of designated "skeptics" and/or protocol-particular academic scientists. This situation fits with the alleged "Sufi" stage magician theatrical context discussed at the beginning of this book in context of the artistic management of a small theater by eccentric members of a brokerage firm.. If one actually had the formula for an arcane weapon, it makes sense strategically that one might publicly play the role of a second-rate magician making skeptical jokes about the existence of arcane weapons.

Boston artist Paul Laffoley, well-known in avante guarde circles for his paintings of visual "portals" into interdimensional space, regards these artworks as literal, talismanic gates to expanded awareness. Could artist Laffoley have opposition among the covert tricksters because he is publicly displaying within his paintings such items as Renaissance magical diagrams and ancient Greek systems of architectural philosophy, while at the same time publicly asserting that these systems of mind/matter manipulation are actual hyperspace portals, and not simply science fiction.?

In the early Spring of 2001, Paul Laffoley was seriously injured in a fall from a ladder in the Kent gallery in Manhattan which has never been completely explained. At that time, his paintings were on exhibit there and he was scheduled to give a lecture at the Yale Club in conjunction with the publication of a book about his work.

Just prior to the opening of the exhibit, Laffoley was on his way up a ladder from the exhibit space at the gallery to a guest sleeping loft above the public space when he suddenly found himself in a "free fall" situation.

"I don't know what happened", says Laffoley, "My girlfriend had already gone up the ladder and was on the loft platform talking to me. There was nothing wrong with the ladder. I had climbed partway up normally when without warning I seemed to myself to be suspended in space, falling slowly. Then when I hit the floor I landed on both feet as it I had been dropped straight downward from a high trapeze on which I was hanging. This does not make sense because a ladder would tip as I grasped it, dropping my body at an angle."

The ladder was not flawed or broken. Laffoley, who sustained multiple fractures of both legs and lost one foot as a result of this accident, regards his fall from the gallery ladder as being the result of Advanced Hexing of some sort, which affected the timespace around him. Prior to this event, he had studied a wide range of sorcery systems, including voodoo and Catholic exorcism rituals. When I wanted to speak about a possible "hex" component of his "free fall" experience, he had already considered that angle.

In attempting to explain his perception of a possible "hex working" Laffoley cited the "Muggletonians", an oddly-named sect which your present correspondent had not previously encountered in her studies of demonology. Neither had the librarian at the Jefferson Market branch of the New York Public library. But we have to give this librarian credit. After patiently listening to the description of Muggletonians as being an obscure British sect who worshipped demons, he pulled two alphabetically-organized references on religious and social history from the shelves of the library and located the information.

What would you do, dear reader, if someone came up to you at your job and asked for a book on "Muggletonians who worship demons"? Perhaps, if you had listened too long to the skeptical brainwash technicians, you might send this person to the children's room or the sci-fi section.

"Muggletonians" are listed in several reference works as being the followers of the London prophets John Reeve (1608-58) and his cousin Lodowicke Muggleton(1609-

98). These two individuals believed they had inner mystical inspiration to re-interpret Biblical scriptures and published books entitled *"Transcendent Spirituall Treatise* ." and *"The Divine Looking Glass or The Third and Last Testament"*. The Muggletonians, who believed that matter is eternal and independent of God, were several times indicted for blasphemy and were opposed to both the Quaker and the Puritan religious sects. According to an encyclopedia of world religions, "when challenged to prove their new commission, their last resort was to curse their opponents and a few accidents or deaths from fear established their credit". In the Muggletonian religion, Lucifer the fallen angel is said to have seduced Eve and fathered Cain. Eve then tempted Adam to carnal intercourse and thence arose Abel and Seth. Thus in the world are two distinct races, the cursed and the blessed.

It does not say in the references whether or not Lucifer was invoked in the Muggletonian curses to destroy his own kind, as these cultists may have believed. Certainly, as cited earlier in this book with reference to the Charles Manson literature, the Devil does sometimes have a palpable presence.

As investigator of these events, a possibility occurred to me which did not immediately occur to Paul Laffoley, who was after his injuries very kindly treated by the publisher who had arranged his lecture at the Yale Club. This is simply that, as a sensitive person with esp ability, artist Laffoley may have been closer to the truth than he realized when he blurted out while still under sedation that "the Muggletonians" had arranged the curse upon his activities. For Yale University possesses in their rare book library in New Haven, Connecticut the largest collection of arcane works on sorcery and occult philosophy in the world. It is entirely possible that a person who had read extensively in that collection would be familiar with the lore of Seventeenth Century sorcery and witchcraft, and with the Muggletonians.

There is also no reason why modern persons familiar with these systems of thought could not, if so gifted and inclined, put the archaic forms of mental magick to work as a hex to block public competition in the area of mental dominance. Recall here your present correspondent's modest experiment with the Fourteenth century systems of Ramon Lull, which resulted in a frightening stigmata reaction. At that time, I was truly astounded that the sophisticated re-rendering of these mental magick diagrams had produced an actual wound. As an occult scientist, I was experimenting only with regard to myself, as have other physical scientists who try various innovative medical and psycho-active procedures and substances upon themselves first before endangering other people.

But what if other curious occult scientists, mentally gifted on the level of an Ivy League diploma, had covertly tried such experiments on other people, and found that their curses worked? The well-known psychic Uri Geller, now living in England, has stated that at one point during the heyday of 1970's-80's U.S. government funded mind control research , certain researchers wanted him to attempt to kill an animal with his esp projection ability. Geller refused. These programs which Geller disliked are no longer being overtly funded by the government as there must have been other, rational objections to this rather heedless method of discovering the effects of esp.

But are there "Black Ops" programs, covert mind control research operations, which still experiment on "expendable targets"? Probably there exist "Black Ops" programs which study esp as well as cutting edge physics topics. But placing all covert

DOING BUSINESS IN THE ADIRONDACKS by E. Macer-Story

experimentation with "killer hexes" on the doorstep of any conventional government intelligence agency may be mistaken.

One of Alfred Hitchcock's first films was a rendition of the stage play "*Remains To Be Seen*" in 1953. In this film a pair of wealthy college students commit a ritual murder of a companion, place his body in a coffin and hold a party with the coffin draped as a banquet table. They think that because the banquet table coffin is set in the midst of a society reception, where the dead companion is expected but does not arrive, no one will suspect their crime. But in the film an alert guest has caught one or two inconsistencies in conversation and begins quietly to inspect the premises.

Can it be true that the master of supernatural mystery films began his career with a situation he knew to be partly real, the existence of a society murder cult which was untouchable except by indirect reference? As cited earlier in this book (page 3, 163), there is reason to speculate on the link between real vampires and/or vampiric cults and the fictional works of directors Stanley Kubrick and Roman Polanski. Both of these film directors also depicted quaisi-supernatural debauchery in an elite setting.

But so did the Nineteenth Century author and spiritualist Arthur Conan Doyle in his Sherlock Holmes mysteries. In the second of these stories, "*The Sign of Four.*" , written before Sherlock Holmes had become a fad, Conan Doyle perhaps drew upon his own experiences as shipboard medical officer on the steamer Mayumba six years previously.

According to Hal Erickson in the All Movie Guide, the plot of the original story involves intrigues set in motion in India during a native East Indian mutiny against British colonial forces in the 1850s. A murder was committed over a valuable treasure during that mutiny in 1857, and the four British military officers responsible signed a pact of secrecy, with the additional proviso that they'd forever be "kind" to one another. Three decades later in 1887, the four men find their past catching up with them in a most fatal manner. Was the Indian treasure cursed? And will Holmes be able to stem the tide of blood and death? This story was made into a stage play entitled *Crucifer of Blood* in 1978 by Paul Giovanni and then into a "made for cable" film by Frasier C. Heston, son of star Charlton Heston., who played the role of Sherlock Holmes.

Note the change in the title of the adaptation from "*Sign of Four*" to "*Crucifer*". In classic occult lore, the tetragramaton, the number four and a variety of sigils using four items are used as powerful symbols of mental magick. It is interesting in this context that the original story "*Sign of Four*" was not easily available in modern Sherlock Holmes anthologies. Is this because the plot of the story heavily involves opium?

The topic of opium, though Sherlock Holmes himself is depicted in the stories as smoking opium occasionally, would not be acceptable for discussion in regional locations in the U.S. where this drug is illegal.. But in the "*Crucifer of Blood*" film adaptation, the exotic opium den of the original story is shown as an important element of the plot.. During the mid-Nineteenth Century in England, when the Sherlock Holmes tale is set, opium was legal and the major intrigue of the tale would have been the concealing of a treasure by secret pact and/or the ability of colonial aristocrats to afford opium, not the use of this substance as a crime.. Was Dr. A. Conan Doyle, who as a young man was the medical officer on the steamer Mayuba which sailed between Liverpool and the West Coast of Africa, actually trying to signal to the public of such secret pacts between colonial aristocrats and the Gang Lords of the Opium Traffic? Or was this aspect of

DOING BUSINESS IN THE ADIRONDACKS by E. Macer-Story

colonial reality simply a part of Dr. Conan Doyle's natural library of experience which he took for granted, and included in his stories?

At one point during the same time period as the correspondence about vampires noted earlier in this book, with reference to the attempted purchase of Stephen Hawking's book "*The Universe in a Nutshell*", I saw a tall, dark puppet-like shadow outside in the back yard which I humorously identified as "Gandolfi"—a combination of the names of the CIA's Ron Psndolfi, rumored to oversee surveillance of the "new age" counterculture, and the wizard character from the *Lord Of The Rings* mythology, Gandolf. I also later realized that the type of puppet was like the giant, traditional German puppets created by Peter Shuman for the Bread and Puppet theater. I felt at that time that a spirit was trying to convey some sort of message to me but I was not sure exactly what sort of message. Perhaps a reminder about the mixture of truth with stagecraft in the way we have been conditioned to perceive the "supernatural:.

When I went to find the original emails on this subject in my computer "Sent" file on 12/26/01, the computer suddenly disconnected from the Web and "restarted" itself. I think the deceased or guiding spirit perhaps indicated a "correct" mark on my thoughts about a contemporary connection between certain members of the medical professions and illicit drug traffic perhaps extending to planning and funding terrorist activities as a "cover",

In the vampire incident at the Highgate cemetery narrated earlier, it is possible that young Dr. Sarfatti and his companion were feeling delayed drug side effects of which he was unaware. Perhaps the use of consciousness-altering substances had opened the portals of their perception to the existence of a type of creature which was actually in the cemetery.

This duality of effect is an aspect of the shadow area of expanded consciousness which is not often discussed in the literature. Actually, early in the evening of April 11, 2002 as I was running an errand to the grocery before a guest arrived to visit my city apartment, I had a subtly unnerving experience which remained with me for the rest of the evening, and particularly as I was editing the foregoing passage into the manuscript.

In the grocery, I had not seen the item I wanted and was swiftly leaving to go to another store a few blocks away. As I left, I glanced at a man standing near the deli section and thought he looked very much like a photo from the "*Destiny Matrix*" book of Jack Sarfatti as a young man in small sunglasses which fit exactly the area of his eye sockets. My immediate thought was that the man I saw in the store, who was a neatly-dressed Caucasian about thirty-five years old, might be a drug user with dilated eyes. It was about seven in the evening and the light in the store was not unusually bright.

I forgot about this impression as I was chatting with my guest but later in the evening when I sat down to work on this book I found that the next section to be re-drafted made mention of shadowy and vampiric presences. I could not get the image of the man I had seen in the small grocery store a few hours earlier out of my mind. Finally, I decided to simply include this impression in the same sequence as the following incident, perhaps also a djinn-incident, which occurred four months previously, on December 13, 2001:

On December 12 at about 10 p.m. EST a male voice left a message on the Magick Mirror office tape to the effect that: "*People who study the supernatural are insane.*" .The next morning in the subway as I went my usual route I was shadowed by a

DOING BUSINESS IN THE ADIRONDACKS by E. Macer-Story

man in mid-thirties, rather attractive and with a long brunette pony tail and.
Aquiline nose. He could have been any European nationality but to me looked French or
Dutch. At first I thought he might be an actor I had worked with in 1995 but
then my rational faculty told me: no. That actor would be older. I did not
give indication I recognized him. He managed to get himself into a position
exactly beside me as I walked up the Broadway-Lafayette subway
steps.

Suddenly I realized what was happening. He was not the actor but was
impersonating the type of actor I frequently cast in my off-off Broadway shows. It was
some sort of "entrapment". He wanted me to recognize him or speak to him. I didn't. As
he turned away at the top of the steps, his face was lightly flushed. Indeed, this man with
the distinctive ponytail hairdo *was* trying to get my attention.

Either he wanted a role in my next play or someone was trying to give me the
profile of soliciting men who look like young trapeze artists or old tyme matinee idols.
At the time of this incident, I tended to favor the second alternative because of the crank
call about insanity and the supernatural which had been left on my office message tape
the previous night.

On December 20, just a week later, while walking to the 8 p.m. commuter bus
through NYC Port Authority I noticed a woman who reminded me of my deceased Aunt-
in-Law . A resemblance to my Aunt-in-Law has also figured in discussing a personage
which appears in unusual density on a candid photo of a tourist street in Stockholm in the
article *"The Material Reality of Telepathy"*. [15]I thought of this spectral possibility. Then
attention was on simply getting in the bus line, surviving the aftermath of some obscure
police action near the ticket line and boarding the bus.

When I reached Kingston, N.Y. the cab driver from Woodstock Taxi there to meet
me said he was also waiting for another passenger, a man with dreadlocks whose lady
friend had phoned the taxi service to request a taxi meet that particular bus. There was no
such passenger.

As mentioned earlier in this book with reference to reading an article entitled
"Break On Through To the other Side" as an inexplicable smell of ozone filled the
vehicle , I have observed the commuter bus from New York City to the upstate Catskill
regions to be sometimes haunted at the Rosendale stop. The bus driver had also on that
particular evening stopped at the Park & Ride lot near Rosendale and waited for a
passenger to exit the bus when there was actually no passenger for that stop. It seemed
that twice on that evening I had "seen something out of the corner of my eye" as the folk
saying goes. What might the phantom, or thoughts of a phantom, be trying to signal to
my conscious mind?

On March 30, 2002 I found that four husk cuttings from a small, pitted, dried fruit
which I had seen on the front walk and thought similar to other such obviously crafted
items had been moved from that location to a place under the side window of the loft
room where I work on my paintings. I had deliberately not collected these husks in order
to see whether any action would be taken if I did not take the trouble to pick them up
and/or dispose of them. At the time I noticed the husks had been moved I also noticed
that two new, small light bulbs had been left on the side of the walk where a series of
small outdoor footlights had been located to illuminate the stairs. About six months prior
to finding the new bulbs I had replaced the footlights with a larger streetlight type fixture

DOING BUSINESS IN THE ADIRONDACKS by E. Macer-Story

at the end of the walk beside the driveway. It occurred to me that whoever moved the husks might also have placed the tiny light bulbs. This was of concern to me as I had recently in email correspondence made a joke to a friend about how I had not seen him around my place re3cently "screwing in the track lights". The track lights are high on the ceiling of the loft room and difficult to reach. But someone familiar with the small series of footlights once beside the steps might thick they were "track lights". How many alleged psychic detectives does it take to screw in a light bulb? One to open the computer email queue and one to place a miniature light bulb, which slides into the socket with a rectangular tab, upon the edge of the keyboard. For those unfamiliar with American slang, this is a familiar children's joke in the U.S.: How many "whatevers" does it take to screw in a light bulb? Answer: One to hold the bulb and three to turn the ladder. In other words, one would have to be dangerously stupid not to connect the small bulbs and transit of talismanic husks with email correspondence mentioning light bulbs for track lights.

Perhaps you recall the following paragraph of narration from earlier in this book. At about 3:30 in the afternoon on the day following, Easter Sunday, your present correspondent got a look at the license plate of a car seen before slowly circling the block in which her house is located in Woodstock. This was accomplished by pure luck--but various mystical philosophies and the modern theories of self-organization of natural systems would maintain that there are no real accidents. It was time for me to see an actual car with driver and realize that stray talismans left on my property were deliberate, and not all the poltergeist work of nature spirits, or my overactive imagination..

The plate was a deluxe issue from another state or perhaps another country. It read WOMBATZ. I web searched this and came up with a(a rock group from Australia doing quasi blood-occult stuff and b) the girlz web directory I had previously called to Dr. Jack' Sarfatti's attention when the web interference occurred whilst trying to access his book draft to proofread my "cat's cradle" addendum to that work . Recall, dear reader, that the quasi-porn personals entry "*Starslut*" showing a demure chick in sunglasses seemed a direct parody of his girlfriend's photo in the book draft of the book "*Destiny Matrix*", then on line, in combination with the URL "Stardrive.org" The '*Starslut*' paragraph about cosmic black holes, with its obvious sexual implications, next to a lady making a similar sunglasses glance downward seemed to me a superficial "take" on the Torah reference situated near his girlfriend's photo in the Sarfatti book draft. For the Torah is in Jewish mysticism the actual transcendent record of all material experiences and Sarfatti has written in his mystical-material physics of tiny "black holes" operating in non-local mind/matter effects. .

As disclosed to physicist Sarfatti by email at that time, result number b above, about the questionable sexual associations obtained by web search of a parody name which came to me wholly by esp when considering interference with the download of his book draft for proofreading check , was in my original notes after the incident but I did not transcribe it because I felt "ginger", as if a mention of this aspect of events might damage my credibility. I note here that this reluctance to mention uncomfortable, sexual details is not actually good journalism. But I have experienced in the past sexual hazing from psychical researchers and the editors of small journals on the occult which may have contributed to this omission. Early inclusion of sexual reference in my works was incorrectly taken to be evidence of a personal, sexual obsession or neurosis which does

DOING BUSINESS IN THE ADIRONDACKS by E. Macer-Story

not exist. It is necessary to discuss sexuality when discussing esp and spirit appearances not simply because of the emotional content of those experiences but because the "pranic" energy described by the yogis as operative in the living material body as a form of physical/mental consciousness patterning does activate the entire body of the experiencing individual, as when diving into a lake the private parts of an individual will feel the temperature of the water as well as the parts of the body seen outside the swimming suit.

The driver of this car with the WOMBATZ plate was bearded, in mid-forties approaching fifty, with receding brunette hair and a swarthy skin. He wore a multicolored sweater which looked to be designer quality, with blocks of color like stained glass or an abstract painting. There is no guarantee that he actually had anything at all to do with the Australian rock group by the same name. But there is also no guarantee that he did not have something to do with a milieu involving the presence of that particular rock group as a musical presentation on the dark side of occultism. It is possible that the license tag was a red herring, but out of context in upstate New York. A similar red herring in upstate New York might be a specialty tag reading *ICED TEA*, the name of a notorious rap music performer but also the name of a beverage which anyone might be entitled to have as a specialty license tag if they could afford the extra expense.

The wombat is a common wild marsupial somewhat like a large mole, found only in Australia, New Zealand and nearby islands.. Seeing wombats in your yard does not necessarily mean that the WOMTATZ surfer music group is playing with full rock amplification in your yard or even desires to play there. Yet on second web search there is a "girlz" logo associated with one wombatz retrieval which echoes the "girlz" or "gurlz" logo of the "starslut" location which perhaps attempted parody of the "Stardrive" personal history photos and/or coincidentally is the "Sitra Ahra" or reverse Kabbalistic echo of same. The actual "starslut" posting was not available to quick web search on April 17, 2002, four months after it had initially been detected. In general, it is not wise to play "hide n' seek" with such postings or to place much journalistic weight upon them in the sense of straightforward data. Obviously, a skilled cyber technician working on the "black hat"[16] side of the coin can place and replace falsely indicative websites like flipping on and off a light switch. One simply uploads "nothing" and/or " not nothing" to the invisible wombats frolicking in cyberland. Down this strange pest hole, dear reader, this particular narration is not going to wander.

It is completely possible that skilled "black hat" technicians are working for a variety of rogue warlords and drug lords who might not have the time to develop cyber and scientific skills themselves. If one goes beyond the image of "mad hacker" into the image of "unethical technician" with the memory in mind of the Nazi rocket technicians and intelligence operatives who were brought over by the U.S. government after World War Two to contribute their rare mental skills to Free World projects[17], one can then grasp the subtext of the deceptively "trivial" situation I have been indicating in these "web search" narrations.

Your present correspondent has previously intersected with a black magick group which is active in Australia. . Various associations with known and notorious cultist groups and belief systems were suggested by observers of this group's activities. None of these known categories has actually seemed to fit this group's activities. But it should be noted here that known harassment practices in Australia and elsewhere do seem to fit the wombatz web search conundrum.

As one example, a woman in Australia who had refused to "pay off" a cocaine dealer who had run up a tab on her teenaged son found out that she was being featured in international tabloids as a "Nazi" who "sacrificed children" It was very difficult for her to sue these tabloids as the lawyers kept suggesting that her concern about slander was trivial since movie stars and other celebrities are regularly slandered by tabloids, and take this as a form of backhand publicity.. So I am not going to zero in on nasty web sites in particular. I am simply going to suggest that in the case of the unfortunate Aussie woman a covert international Fascist organization was using the ancient martial arts trick of indicting the enemy for one's own strategy. As experienced occultist Anton Szandor LeVey of "Church of Satan" has stated in his writings[18], the "real witches" were most probably sleeping with the "witch inquisitors" during the notorious witch trials of the Seventeenth Century, hoping to obtain the real estate property of the deceased torture victims.

Therefore, since one URL in the wombatz web search was indicatively entitled "*Anarchy On Line*" I shall refrain from a detailed analysis of this reverse publicity situation. The technique is obvious. Such combative techniques are also used by secretaries who have covertly "slept with the boss" to keep a job and thus accuse the attractive investigative reporter (male or female) who is researching exploitation allegations at the firm of "being promiscuous" and "soliciting people". This strategy can work on any issue and we have all met this "reverse trick" in one form or another.

Skipping therefore to a clairvoyant assessment of the red sports car seen loitering at my front driveway on Easter Sunday 2002, it should be noted that when remote viewing this individual; from memory buildings looking like the adobe structures found in the Southwestern United States and South America came to mind. These were seen in the mind's eye as being on a steep hillside yet close together as in a city location. Wherever this individual's actual connections are located, the mystique did seem to be Native American and/or Hispanic. Yet buildings in older Mideastern locations also have this stucco arrangement of the edges of many buildings seen ascending a hillside in irregular fashion, as built gradually rather than designed as a unit.

Shortly after adding notes on this remote viewing session to this manuscript, I went to see a play at Theater For The New City, an off-off Broadway establishment which has produced a number of my plays. I had been given complimentary admission to a play set in a city slum. The stage set used in this play, which had many flats coming in from the side at oblique angles to represent small, close tenement houses, was painted in beige and brown tones. When I returned to my city "inner office" apartment, I glanced at the printout of the book draft simply to remind myself of where I was in re-drafting the manuscript. The similarity between the stage set I had just seen, which could be a slum or barrio in any city, and the mental image I had obtained by remote viewing weeks before was obvious.. The reason I could not geographically locate my earlier RV impression of a "stucco slum" was because I was not perceiving a literal city location. I was perceiving a stage set.

This is consistent with people who are associated with performance groups and/or masquerading as certain performance groups knowing where I might be living and driving by my house. For certain individuals associated with the Living Theater, a group which is also aware of sorcery and occult techniques, have been hostile to your present correspondent in the past because she did not endorse certain power-oriented uses of Kabbalist and other techniques of mental magick which involve use of naïve audience members as part of the performance. My view is that since the esp and spirit conjuration abilities are real in certain instances, this level of mental action should not be directly used as part of a dramatic performance lest susceptible members of the audience fall under the influence of actual spirits and/or telepathically altered states of consciousness endemic to the villain of the show. . Instead, interpersonal communication by telepathy and spirit effects is best represented using charismatic performance technique, which packs its own distinctive energy punch but does not violate the personal mental space of members of the audience..

Deliberate use of actual spirit conjuration onstage is like using live ammunition instead of stage prop explosives. Hypnotists are aware of this effect and professional hypnotists are not permitted to look directly into the camera when performing on television.

The Shiek Muburak Gilani of the Muslim faith warns also against the effects of naiveté about actual esp and conjuration practices in Americans (and certain educated global citizens) who may be induced by telepathy from discarnate spirits to do things they do not intend or cannot clearly remember. This type of effect must be why in the UK intoxicating beverages with a cheery social taste are called "spirits" on account of the observed similarity of behavior between those possessed by a demon and those who have had too much rum..

On March 13, 2002 , Dan Rather reported on CBS news that:

"Sheik Mubarek Gilani was the man Daniel Pearl was on the way to meet him when The "Wall Street Journal" reporter was kidnapped.
Gilani is a mysterious figure in the Islamic world. He is said to be a direct descendant of the Prophet Mohammed. But for Pearl two other things set him apart. First, Gilani along with his followers have appeared on the State Department's list of terrorist organizations. Second, and even more provocative, the sheik has thousands of disciples who live right here in the United States. "...
"Gilani says that he is used to being a suspect whenever there is a terrorist act against the U.S. He wanted to talk about what he sees as the most serious threat to the world, why bad things happen in America, including acts of terrorism. These bad things, he says, are caused by invisible forces.
"There are beings who are not visible to you," he says. "But they inhabit this earth. And they are damaging, causing psychotic diseases, fits, epilepsies. And controlling the agents, controlling the human beings."
Gilani says he can control those evil forces. He says that he is not a threat to the U.S., but could be its salvation.
To understand why, he points to an American television show "The X-Files." He says the mind control and evil influence that aliens wield over human beings in the program is much like the power of the invisible forces he believes in.
"What is an X-file? Most of things - could have happened or will happen," Gilani said. "Human beings can be made to do things against their will. They can be made to commit crimes. They can made to go and kill people. You know? And all your missiles, all your rockets, space ships go up. And electronics, they can be damaged, influenced, and misdirected through the agencies of gin beings." Muslims all over the world also believe in these invisible evil forces that are described in

DOING BUSINESS IN THE ADIRONDACKS by E. Macer-Story

the Koran. The sheik feels that these forces are a much bigger threat to the U.S. than terrorism. He says the United States should thank him for passing on his message about the invisible world instead of accusing him of terrorism.

Gilani says that his followers are not anti-American. "In America, the Muslims are better than any part of the world," he says. "They have more freedom. They are more facilities of life. Where will they go? OK, they do something wrong, where will they go? I don't want them. That's their country. The American Muslims are better off in America than anywhere else. And they will never do anything wrong against their country. That is my directive to you and to them."

TAKING SERIOUSLY THE JOKES OF THE DJINN

One day after adding this section about Shiek Gilani and the djinn to the draft of my manuscript, I had an unusual experience with a spirit light or small "ufo type" light which was so simple and strange that at first I thought only to joke about it with friends. But then subsequent events caused me to take this occurrence more seriously.

After working on some poems and various other odds and ends, I had turned out the light on the back porch and was sitting on a porch chair enjoying a glass of wine. I saw an oscillating light behind one of the trees, seeming to be at a distance in the sky. Clear as a bell in my mind was the telepathic warning: *You may spill your wine.* Instants later, there was a sound which startled me as I held the stemmed glass in my lap and I tilted it, spilling the wine onto the chair. As I mopped up this spill, which did not stain the fabric of the chair, I was inwardly quite irritated at the spirit light. Although I could not help laughing, I was also acutely aware that I might be meeting firsthand the notorious trickster djinn who have often plagued Sufi sorcerers.

Indeed just subsequent to the spill, whilst standing near the shower in the bathroom with a washrag and bleach in my hand I noticed that the faucet of the shower was in the opposite side of the stall from where it had been located prior to my returning from New York to my country house at noon . Initially, I pushed back this impression as being a delusion planted by the same weird entity which had accompanied the wine spill which caused me to get the bleach out of the laundry closet. But later I verified that the faucet was indeed in the opposite wall of the molded plastic shower stall.

I recalled then that Woodstock resident Tom Walker , bearer of the "gem magick" tale at the beginning and end of this particular book, had once told this reporter that he had been publicly derided for complaining that his shoes and clothes had been turned around backward while he was out of his house for the day working . Walker wanted to connect this situation with the existence of a "black magick" group which had eventually caused the death of his friend, the spiritualist who was working with gem magick.

If sorcerers were at work, were the objects in the house actually turned backward or did Walker—telepathically pressed—just think they had been reversed? If they were reversed, was this by an act of mind over matter as by a trickster djinn or was this a feat of stage prop magic engineered by people who had an extra key to the house?

It is a fact that a molded plastic shower stall is a prefabricated item which can easily be fully replaced with faucets on whatever side and the drain remaining the same. But this would be an expensive trick. However, the trunk switch magic of David Copperfield and other accomplished stage magicians is also expensive. There is not as much of a market for a touring side show these days as there used to be before satellite and cable communication. Might some of those adepts in the sleight of hand skills of the

DOING BUSINESS IN THE ADIRONDACKS by E. Macer-Story

inner cabal of tech magicians be otherwise unemployed? For hire as the innovators of nuisance phenomena? Why not?

Unfortunately for who or whatever tinkered with my pre-fab shower stall, I am left handed when reaching downward toward the sill on which I had set my shampoo and soap. As any observer of the shower could then witness, the soap—which had been carefully re-positioned as before—would be out of reach of my less capable right hand in the reverse arrangement. Whoever tinkered with the shower was right handed and did not notice that repositioning the soap exactly where it had been before the faucet was reversed would indicate to a left handed person that the reversal had indeed taken place and was not imaginary.

I tested this. I stood inside the stall, facing the faucets, and reached for the soap where it was resting on the sill. I could not reach it with my weak right arm. I recalled Walker's tale of being derided for claiming his clothes had been reversed in the closet and I decided not to check with the neighbors about whether or not they had noticed a plumber in the house. I also did not run around and check to see if other items had been disturbed. I decided simply to note the situation and leave it as an enigma.

There is one additional thread in this pattern. Had I not spilled the wine and gone into the small bathroom adjacent the laundry closet idly while deciding how much bleach to use on the stain I would not have noticed the shower anomaly until sometime the next day. This is not the main bathroom. So it is possible that a djinn had tricked me into perceiving a magic trick which otherwise might not have completely registered if sometime later myself and/or a guest had hurried into the shower, grabbing up the shampoo off the sill as we turned on the water.

What possible purpose could the covert re-orientation of a shower cubicle serve for anyone? There do exist certain schools of sorcery and geomancy which focus on the directional orientation of buildings, rooms and furniture. This, of course, is the Chinese discipline of Feng Shui. It had been rumored to me that there do exist "black hat" feng shui practitioners. I had also received on my office voice mail three odd calls which had only the sound of running water, and on one call the sound of a child's voice being prompted by a male voice to say something about "collect call" but the child voice did not follow this cue and the call disconnected. I had thought this to be a wrong number from someone's shower. But is it possible I am dealing with sophisticated sympathetic magick here?

If this is Advanced mental magick, perhaps involving remotely-activated hypnosis, could I have been telepathically persuaded to the fantastic scenario that my shower stall had been physically altered ? If so, this might be a tactic to make me seem crazed if I announced this alleged alteration or called a plumber about the situation. The stage mentalist Kreskin, in truth an adept sorcerer in his own right, has warned against the function of memory in advanced mental experimentation.[19] Memory can be altered by hypnosis. I may incorrectly "remember" the previous arrangement of the shower faucet as part of a telepathically-induced scenario. OR, and this remains a possibility transcending both "covert, human scenarios", the same type of "spirit light" or djinn which played mind games with me about accurately predicting a wine spill which it indeed may have caused can remold instantaneously a plastic shower stall including plumbing connections. Why not? There are several credible tales of a "ufo" teleporting an entire automobile over a distance of thousands of miles.[20]

DOING BUSINESS IN THE ADIRONDACKS by E. Macer-Story

This mind/matter molding ability would simply be an extension of the remote hypnotic healing and/or hexing ability known to be possessed by a variety of human beings. But before any discussion of "hex technique" takes place in this context, there should be some discussion of the "phantom phone" I heard ringing in my country house on the same day as I noticed the shower stall alteration conundrum. I was resting in the bedroom adjacent the shower-laundry bathroom when I heard a telephone ringing. Both of the lines in the house had a healthy dial tone as I checked them while still hearing the other telephone ring insistently in several sequences of rings, as if someone had tried a number, got no answer and then tried again several times.

In my city "inner office" apartment faint sounds of phones ringing in neighboring apartments are a regular fact of life. But not in the country house. It crossed my mind that cellular, cyber-activated surveillance might be active in both locations. My son and his wife were staying in the city apartment on the day I heard the "phantom phone" in the country house. Could electronic surveillance, filed in the mechanism under a linked code name, have malfunctioned? OR is this a co-presence of mind fields in timespace locations linked non-locally? Perhaps both.

Yet years ago I had detected a phone tap on my city phone line which I have regretted mis-handling. I had phoned Art Gatti, then writing articles on Soviet ufo research for a popular magazine, and a voice answered in what seemed to me to be an Eastern European language. I replied in English :"*Is Art Gatti there*?" There was a silence. Then a different voice came on the line in perfect English and said firmly: "*You have the wrong number. Hang up the phone.*"

I hung up the phone, dialed again and got Art Gatti directly. This was very inept investigative behavior. I should have stayed on the line long enough to record some portion of the call. A tap had obviously jumped out of perfect alignment with Gatti's number for a brief moment. I learned later that the Soviets in 1979 did have an antenna telephone tap system located on Long Island.

A cellular and/or antenna tap file triple code-labeled "a)Macer-Story city office//b)Macer-Story country house//c)Macer-Story city apartment" might also jump out of perfect alignment when two or more of these locations were manifesting sonic input at the same time.

By synchronicity, as I was sitting in my city "inner office" jotting notes for the foregoing speculations, the phone rang and a man claiming to be an insurance broker from an agency on Long Island asked for a certain person as regards a claim involving a BMW. The name was not familiar and I conversed briefly with the caller and then hung up the phone. However, with the thought of the telephone tap from 1979 fresh in my mind from the draft I was writing, I then dialed *69 to trace the insurance call. It had come from a town on Long Island named Melville and I did reach the automated answering system of an insurance franchise via the *69 referral

Yet I was nagged inwardly by the name of the claimant given to me by the alleged insurance agent. It seemed to me this was a name I had heard mentioned by the sister of "ufo contactee" Brian Lynch,[21] who was found dead of drug overdose in a warehouse on Long Island in 1989.. Or perhaps the name was not actually the same but some deep mechanism in my psyche was reminding me, in context of the anomalous insurance call, of the recent series of unsolved murders and disappearances among ufo contactees, psychical researchers and journalists of paranormal occurrences. Beginning in about

DOING BUSINESS IN THE ADIRONDACKS by E. Macer-Story

1979, there have been to date (Fall 2002) at least ten unexplained violent deaths or disappearances among people following the "Outer Limits" line of inquiry.

Very shortly after these thoughts entered my mind, I heard again of an upcoming meeting by the group on Long Island [22] which some "angelic" mechanism and/or deep subliminal perception had prevented me from attending a few months earlier in 2002. I wondered if there might be any connection between the "insurance" call and the activities of some member of this group.

There is no reason to suppose that supernatural manifestations and criminal chicanery are mutually exclusive. Yet sometimes unexplained phenomena which seem to violate known technical capacities are too easily dismissed as "supernatural" or "unexplained" when criminal activity using sophisticated technology may be the actual cause.

"During the last two weeks of April in 2002, strange lights appeared in the night skies over Saliquelló, Province of Buenos Aires, and in the morning cattle ranchers of the area found three mutilated bovines showing signs of having undergone a surgical intervention with unusual implements. A veterinarian told local media that the incisions "are strange ones in which some sort of heating element appears to have been used." The news was broadcast at the national level on Saturday through Cronica TV, which took images from the local cable access channel, showing images of the animals and a technician named Daniel, who analyzed one of the cases, providing details on the strange event. According to the televised report, the animals were found by the owners of rural premises near Salliquelo, a small city located some 80 miles east of the Pampan locality of Anchorena, after "strange lights" were reported in the sky. These bovine deaths were attested to by local police. A veterinarian inspected the abnormal carcasses, "They present strange cuts, as though resulting from an intense heat source. The skin is burned along the edges of the cuts, and the absence of blood in veins, muscles and ligaments is simply desiccated." He said, "It's as though you were cutting a piece of paper with a hot wire--the edges become dry, scorched and thinner. Furthermore, all traces of blood vanished. We only found some coagulated remains in the heart."

Daniel told the Saliquello TV that unusual cuts can be seen in the animals' bodies and heads. "One of them shows a perfectly straight cut on one mandible. Furthermore, its tongue is missing along with most of the alimentary tract, larynx, pharynx and saliva glands. The outer ear is completely missing. Another curious incision appears on the body (ribs and abdomen) which is teardrop-shaped through which genitalia was extracted," he explained. "It is a strange circumstance since there are no signs that the animal put up a fight, nor is their any evidence of scorched pastureland. I'm not saying that this is the handiwork of alien beings, but it's a strange circumstance nonetheless. Even the other animals refuse to come close to the dead ones, and curiosity is a characteristic element of bovines," he concluded. Intense bright lights were filmed over Argentina on April 18, 2002, by Ricardo e d'angelo. [23]

If "alien beings" of Advanced Intelligence and capabilities wanted to take flesh from cattle, why would they use a technique similar to a rudimentary laser scalpel? It does seem that in this instance we may have word of the covert plastic surgeons who are rumored to have changed the identity of wealthy international fugitives. Perhaps the unexplained aerial lights in the same time period only warn or comment upon the terrestrial bloodletting. Or do these lights attend upon the bizarre blood letting as accomplices to ritual activity? Possibly the ancient deities wish to "live again" in a

DOING BUSINESS IN THE ADIRONDACKS by E. Macer-Story

different form by gaining human attention in the context of bizarre surgery performed on rural livestock

In this desire to recreate archaic worship situations, powerful spirits may inspire and/or animate people to undertake some version of ritual activities which are anachronistic, seeming inexplicable because the original context within which the spirit manifested to human beings was lost as the host civilization advanced or deteriorated materially. This situation is not so different from the common situation of a place which is obviously "haunted" by a ghost which no one can exactly identify.

On April 30, 2002, the bus driver stopped the commuter bus enroute from the Catskills to New York City once again to ask the passenger who had given a ticket for the Rosendale stop to step forward and be identified. No one responded. After a few minutes of intense glaring at the bus full of passengers, the driver gave up trying to understand what was happening and the bus rolled onward toward its usual destinations.

Like the other passengers, your present correspondent remained silent. I am not sure whether other people experience the "missing passenger" at the Rosendale stop when I am not on the bus. I have a feeling that they do . Or may experience other phenomena in this place, which is a multiple crossroads beside a river.

At three in the afternoon on this same day, having reached my city "inner office" apartment, I found a subway token on the sidewalk outside the building as I was walking over to the Magick Mirror office This token would prove useful to me in a rainstorm a few days later, when the subway was crowded with people trying to purchase tokens and metrocards. I took it as an omen that the appointment that afternoon with a man from California who had claimed knowledge of Nordic "black magick" would benefit my business. This individual had exhibited suspicious behavior in correspondence, at first inviting me to speak to a group on the topic of far right "sorcery" groups imitating in the present day the Nazi ahnenerbe (occult research organization) and then listing my name on a "personals" form sent to me by the lecture organization with himself as "sponsor".

At the time of this initial contact, thoughts of a setup wherein I was represented as soliciting male companionship using my investigative work as an excuse for romantic contact flashed through my mind. So I immediately disconnected from this correspondence.

Several weeks later, the individual connected with the "magickal personals group" had once again contacted me and this time told me he would be visiting from California and asked for a psychic reading in my office. Fully aware that he would attempt some sort of "trick", I accepted his request and gave him an appointment time. I made no exact defensive preparations myself other than to be rested and alert. I am aware from my study of psychic defense and martial arts techniques that one of the prime objectives of a trained and/or instructed opponent may be to alter the behavior of the target according to the agenda of the "other". Sure enough: just three hours before the meeting was to occur, the "Personals Op" phoned my office to change the appointment from the scheduled 5:30 p.m. to an earlier time. I agreed to the change of time, fully aware that hypnotists will often make such trivial requests to test a target for "compliance". It did not occur to me at the time that an additional reason for the change of time might have been that the "Personals Op" knew that the lobby of the office building which housed the Magick Mirror office at that time was closed after 5;30 and he would have to ring the office suite bell. Of course, all after hours visitors who walk

DOING BUSINESS IN THE ADIRONDACKS by E. Macer-Story

through the lobby to the elevators are recorded on video by the building management for security purposes.

As it happened, this meeting was extremely lucky for my research into the existence of a "Thantatos" organization. For when I held his neck band in my hand and focused on a clairvoyant impression of his situation no conventional images appeared in my mind's eye. As recorded on a tape which he left with me after an irrational outburst about *not being able to listen* to the description, I saw in this individual's destiny pattern a completely empty room or lobby with several doorways. There was actually nothing behind those doorways and the prospect was difficult to describe and to counsel.

After I gave a bit of description indicating that one doorway led to several locations in Europe and another doorway led to South America, the querent filled in these situations a bit. But he was obviously expecting the "dial a psychic" sort of feedback involving recitations such as :"Soon it will be OK for you. Something exists around the corner." When I told him that he was indirectly involved with espionage activities in the Mideast involving the Arab/Israeli conflict, anti-Semitism and Afghanistan which he imperfectly understood and were not of benefit to him, he established direct eye contact and seemed affected by the news. He did not contradict me.

He also nodded his head when told that persons in his environment were following a spirit guide who manifested ability and power on the level of the popular "Seth" transmissions. The "Personals Op" was not fully aware that false projects and dead end cover facades had been told to him by the "channel" and others associated with a false. alternate universe inducted by recruiting, paying and then isolating individuals within the network of an "alternate universe" with a fictional history and objectives.

If a person truly believes in the false historical scenarios that "George Washington did not really lead troops of the U.S. revolutionary army" or "There were no concentration camps in Germany during World War Two" or that "William Shakespeare, a commoner, did not really write any distinguished plays" there is very little one can do as far as direct argument is concerned. As a professional playwright, I should comment that the reality of Wm. Shakespeare's achievement is documented by the elegy to him as "our beloved" by another playwright/poet, the Scottish Ben Jonson, who was his contemporary and obviously knew him well as a person.

A classic foible of the elitist attitude which undertakes to re-write history in retrospect is the underestimation of an opponent or advisor. In his haste to dismiss the ESP feedback about dead end and fictional projects, the "Personals Op" told me to keep the audio tape and listen to it so that I would understand my inaccuracies. He then offered to donate money to my Magick Mirror endeavor and had his wallet out in his lap when I refused the donation.

When he stood up from the chair, I noticed two pennies on the seat and—aware that witches and sorcerers often try to give their targets hex coins—scooped these coins off the seat and presented them to him as he left my office. He was startled that I had noticed the coins and was not pleased to receive them back into the palm of his hand. His reaction certainly was not in sync with the simple possibility that he had accidentally lost two cents from his pants pocket.. I noticed at that time, as I had previously, that he was wearing a red cord around his right wrist. There is a far right group which sends out email literature signed "Knights of the Scarlet Thread". Of course, many different sects might band themselves with read bracelets. But it was obvious that the two coins left by the

DOING BUSINESS IN THE ADIRONDACKS by E. Macer-Story

"Personals Op" were in fact emotionally significant to him and that he was very unhappy to have these coins detected and returned into the palm of his hand.

Moreover, in his haste to leave the Magick Mirror office with the coins in his hand this individual left me with the tape upon which he speaks and responds to questions, which is evidence of his presence and intentions. I had been wishing for years that I had some solid item to show to skeptics when I suggested the possibility of the "Thantatos" sorcerers.

It may be a mistake to assume that all such attempted "mind control" antics are perpetrated by government intelligence agencies. There are a number of private investigative firms and "think tanks" with demonstrated interest in ESP and occult topics, such as both the Rand Corporation and the LaRouche detective agency, as well as religious groups such as Church of Scientology and a variety of Fundamentalist sects of both the Christian and Muslim persuasion who might become obsessively interested in the business and/or personal behavior of anyone exhibiting "interdimensionalist" paintings and writing literature about the supernatural. The FBI and CIA have investigated at various time Arabic charities they felt might be implementing terrorist pursuits from a deeply felt religious rationale. This reporter has also heard from a hereditary Kabbalist who lives in the East Broadway area of lower Manhattan that there are also Fundamentalist mystic sects within the Hebrew community who might take such "mind control" actions if it was felt that the Jewish practitioner was diverging too far from standard practice.

Yet your present correspondent is neither Arabic nor Hebrew and has published to date only mild and various anecdotes having to do with these belief systems, as well as a general description of the Sepheroth on the Kabbalistic Tree of Life and a discussion of the belief in powerful "djinn" presences by the Sufi sect of Muslim practitioners. I have no strong emotional or religious attachment to these topics. My interest to date has been simply in the reality of effects possibly due to the actions of the living Sepheroth spirit entities and the djinn spirit entities.

Idealist practitioners and social activists are often used by criminal and/or political organizations who regard these individuals as useful fools. A cynically-conscious technique of love pats and modest financial reward is used to get the inductees into a "mellow mood". Then questionable ideas and projects are introduced in a way tangled with religious and/or social action precepts so that refusing to implement ethically questionable "projects" –which may include illegal entry into private premises and transport of contraband—is tantamount for the insecure or zealous person to terminating a deeply felt relationship or personal friendship.

As a matter of fact, certain of these endeavors use buzz words such as "friendship", "heart" and "lovey dovey" to include unqualified mutual ownership of individual property, by voluntary donation to he organization from the elderly, enraptured and immature, of course. There is also a commune in Chile yclept "Friendship", founded prior to World War Two, which features Nordic humanoid beings from outer space who claim to benefit and educate mankind—but only select and invited human beings, including Chilean neighbors who might provide practical services.[24]

This silly sort of stuff may be one of the reasons that Anton LeVey of the "Church of Satan", a theatrically-gifted pragmatist among mystics, was so firmly opposed to the "love generation" ideas of the expanded consciousness movement of the 1960's and 70's.

It is very likely that LeVey saw clearly with his famed yellowish & catlike clairvoyant eyes just where too much togetherness might be leading the gullible sucker. For LeVey, a musician whose early entertainment experience included playing the organ for carnivals, had a strong interest in the social hypocrisy he witnessed at these traveling events.

The average person, no matter how acute their intellect , is not ready for the chicanery of adept stage magicians used offstage in secular fashion. It seems the stage magician/stockbrokers mentioned at the beginning of this book had at one time gone beyond simply labeling this reporter's scripts on the supernatural "no". The artistic director of Theater For The New City, Crystal Field, was approached at one time by individuals identifying themselves as "financiers" interested in E.Macer-Story's work in the theater and on the Internet who were trying to persuade this producer that all witchcraft was "sex magick" and that her playwright friend E..Macer-Story had such secret spells and formulae in a record album entitled "Barbara, the Gray Witch" which they wished to buy for an astronomical amount of money. Crystal, of course, had probably been offered a cut of this money. But she is fortunately a wiser lady than to buy the line of these "financiers".

Anton LeVey, of the Church of Satan, from his experience in working for carnivals, grasped the scam potential in the property-sharing luv-org businesses immediately. For all his flaws and excesses, the Satanist LeVey should be commended in this instance for sounding a warning about the facades of the "togetherness" trend in his various books and interviews..

One Dr. Eric Ross Koss, working as a consultant in Virginia for the National Computer Security Center on government contract, could have used a bit of savvy advice on the Satanist potential of in-house tricksters. According to Virginia McCullough in her article *"Does Echelon Murder US Scientists Who Challenge The Special Collection Service?"* posted on the Sightings website in March 2000:

"Rosskoss had been a boyhood genius who earned his PhD from Vanderbilt and soon began working for the CIA, NSA, and the IDA [International Defense Agency]. The IDA was identified by an associate of Rosskoss's as a "spook agency".

Dr. Rosskoss had worked at the National Computer Security Center since 1988 on a three year program entitled "The Trusix Papers". This was a trusted computer system for UNIX designed to develop security systems for large companies, according to another employee of the Center. The Trusix Papers had been criticized by several large companies who publicly stated that the development was really a front for the NSA that would allow the agency to install a 'back door' or 'Trojan Horse' in order to monitor the 'companies' private product development.

In March or April of 1990, Eric told his parents that his employer or someone at the Center had injected errors into a paper he had written and was trying to get him to sign reaffirming his authorship of the paper. He sounded very upset.

The last time his parents heard from their son, Eric, was at 2:00 a.m. on June 27, 1990. He called his parents and said, "There are strange goings on and I am going to get to the bottom of it -- I know what I have to do".

On Saturday, June 30, 1990 at 11:00 a.m., Eric's parents received a call from law enforcement. They were told that Eric was dead. He had apparently been seen walking naked down the center divider of Highway I-95. Someone called police who said they arrived within 45 seconds but it was too late. A man who said that he had been driving all night had hit and killed Dr. Rosskoss at 3:30

a.m. the night of Friday, June 29, 1990. Of course, the determination was that Eric had committed suicide. "

It is probable that Dr. Ross Koss had been bolexed not by the mythic "*Echelon*" but actually by Foreign Intelligence, Corporate and/or Organized Crime operatives who were also employed by the Computer Security services and did not want to allow the creation of a U.S. "back door" monitoring system. But how did this young Ph.D. then find himself walking naked down a highway lane divider? Obviously, some form of hypnosis and/or consciousness-altering substance had been employed to enhance his already-stressed condition.

Or was a djinn or spirit hex used on this individual? Recall the warning of Shiek Muburak Gilani of the Muslim faith against the effects of naivite about actual esp and conjuration practices in Americans (and certain educated global citizens) who may be induced by telepathy from discarnate spirits to do things they do not intend or cannot clearly remember.

Aexus, the trickster personality associated with the 1970's Esalen, Rockefeller and alleged CIA undercover demimonde mentioned earlier in this book, recently sent out an Internet email notification implying that all persons reporting aggressive mental incursions by non-human intelligence were probably schizophrenic but that the mad persons might have "something to say" to the rest of us.. In this announcement, he included a quote from the book "*A Beautiful Mind*" by Sylvia Nasar, as follows:

Page 241(After disappearing suddenly from MIT campus in January of 1959...)
"A couple of weeks later Nash slouched into the common room. Nobody bothered to stop talking. Nash was holding a copy of The New York Times. Without addressing anyone in particular, he walked up to Hartley Rogers and some others and pointed to the story on the upper left-hand corner of the Times front page, the off-lead, as Times staffers call it. Nash said that abstract powers from outer space, or perhaps it was foreign governments, were communicating with him through The New York Times. The messages, which were meant only for him, were encrypted and required close analysis. Others couldn't decode the messages. He was being allowed to share the secrets of the world. Rogers and the others looked at each other. Was he joking?"

This book is the basis for the film by the same title, a true story about a Harvard mathematics professor who went off the deep end in claiming "ufo alien communications" about his work but then is said to have recovered the ability to function normally in the mundane world. Or did Dr. John Nash, in reality, simply learn not to mention his inspirations to skeptics? In typical trickster duality mode, Aexus ,after lambasting recent "ufo research" personalities, states:

" Is there really a kind of "communication" coming in to help advance our species, with its distortions and "over exposures" kicking many receivers into mental hospitals? I don't know, but it's a question that UFOlogy has been slow to ask, bristling as it is with its skeptics and "true believers," orthodox religionists and spiritual warriors, all eager to deflect any scientific analyses of a sociological or psychological kind. Even John Mack "missed" this element, which a lot of us once believed would be John's principal focus. Mack sold out his science. Should we "listen" to Nash? Why not?"

DOING BUSINESS IN THE ADIRONDACKS by E. Macer-Story

Why not, indeed? For in the book "Roosevelt's Secret War", espionage historian Joseph E. Persico reports that: *(page 139) "J.C. Masterman, who headed the British XX (Double Cross) Committee that handled double agents like Popov had also been given a copy of the questionnaire. Masterman concluded: "...[I] in the event of the United States being at war, Pearl Harbor would be the first point to be attacked...."However, he did not report this conclusion to U.S. authorities because*

Magnify or use reading glasses if text seems too small.

140 ★ ROOSEVELT'S SECRET WAR

because he did not want to appear to be another Briton nudging America toward war. The Americans, he believed, upon seeing this extraordinary document, would draw their own conclusion.

Just as extraordinary as Popov's instructions was the form in which they had been communicated. The entire questionnaire had been reduced four hundred times normal to the size of a period by the microdot process developed by a German professor, Arnold Zapp.

For awhile in the New Science and Conspiracy press there was a fad of claiming that the commercial bar codes on certain products contained hexes and spells.[25] This seems crazy. Yet, look at this small patch of text rendered about the size of a bar code sticker. The text letters seem to become solid lines. No more sophisticated method of decrypting a message sent this way is required than an ordinary, unobtrusive magnifying lens. It is well known that the ancient maps of Turkish admiral Piri Reis and others which show the American continental land mass much before it was officially "discovered" by the expeditions of Christopher Columbus were only able to be understood by modern historians when they were examined under a special lens. [26]

Modern adepts of offstage stage magic, as described in the opening sections of this book, may be very familiar with these traditional uses of "smoke & lenses" as well as more modern and computerized forms of obfuscation. However, conventional methods can be employed to trace the "smoke and lenses" crowd when they attempt certain forms of subtle chicanery which are designed either to cause psychological distress, as in the Eric RossKoss case, or to engineer what they might feel is a predictable, conditioned reaction.

On May 26, 2002 , I received an obviously suspicious email which was detected by my virus protection and annihilated. After destroying the virus-laden download—and before final annihilation--I copied the body of the email text. The title read "*Congratulations*" and the viral zip folder read "*Italian*". The rest of the email was blank,except for the Headers trace section provided by AOL server..

Of note is the fact that I had been discussing by email with several correspondents the survival by adept stealth of certain members of Hitler's elite

Ahnenerbe research organization after World War Two. These folk have managed to survive and reproduce themselves and there is now a new generation of hereditary "power magicians" and diabolic alchemists playing cyber and other neo-tech games internationally. "*Congratulations: The UFO Reality*", as previously mentioned,is the title of my first ufo book, which includes a section on the foibles of neo-Nazi ufo-model construction groups in Canada in 1977-79.

Crescent Press in L.A.--which published the original edition--was torched from four directions in 1982, as was the apartment building of the publisher. It seemed that persons with an elitist, swastika point of view might be upset with the off hand way in which their failure to make a sewing needle levitate on the surface of a glass of water was discussed in that book.

From my point of view, the present viral email (reproduced below) which mentions "*Congratulations*" is demonstration that these creators of the "*Dark Starlet*" type of nuisance communications are as stupid as they ever were in giving an overt example of the fact that my allegations of specific aggression against my research into "black magickal" practices by covert adepts are true and well-founded.

Subj: **Congratulations**
Date: 5/25/2002 8:10:23 PM Eastern Standard Time
From: *greatoffers@feedback.iwon.com (great offers)*
To: MagickMirr@aol.com

File: **Italian. zip** (59749 bytes) DL Time (53333 bps): < 1 minute

--------------------- Headers -------------------------------
Return-Path: <rioiab@fmsihop.com>
Received: from rly-xe03.mx.aol.com (rly-xe03.mail.aol.com [172.20.105.195]) by air-xe01.mail.aol.com (v86.11) with ESMTP id MAILINXE13-0525201022; Sat, 25 May 2002 20:10:22 -0400
Received: from smtp.fdn.com (smtp.fdn.com [216.199.46.19]) by rly-xe03.mx.aol.com (v86.11) with ESMTP id MAILRELAYINXE31-0525201016; Sat, 25 May 2002 20:10:16 -0400
Received: from Haioimr (216-199-59-162.ftl.fdn.com [216.199.59.162])
    by smtp.fdn.com (Postfix) with SMTP id 1D7AB5A6BD
    for <MagickMirr@aol.com>; Sat, 25 May 2002 20:10:18 -0400 (EDT)
From: great offers <greatoffers@feedback.iwon.com>
To: MagickMirr@aol.com
Subject: Congratulations
MIME-Version: 1.0
Content-Type: multipart/alternative;
    boundary=BNCa592U14
Message-Id: <20020526001018.1D7AB5A6BD@smtp.fdn.com>
Date: Sat, 25 May 2002 20:10:18 -0400 (EDT)

Anyone gazing at this brief communication in any detail can see the word "Haioimir" and a specific web location in the "Headers" section. This location is a site labeled 'Welcome to Cookware, Glassware, Porcelinware Industrial Spare Parts" and otherwise blank except for a gray oblong box at the upper left of the web page

:http://www.eternity-enamel.com/yan.html. I recalled that in a conjuration about ten days previously the word "faince" had been inspired and, realizing this was enamel and pottery work of some sort also web searched this word to refresh my memory. "Faience" is the correct spelling and, according to a reference site on talismanic arts and crafts: "Dynastic Egypt was famous for its faience (to be distinguished from the later European ceramics of that name). First made about 2000 BC, it is characterized by a dark green or blue glaze over a body high in powdered quartz, somewhat closer to glass than to true ceramics. Egyptian artisans made faience beads and jewelry, elegant cups, scarabs, and ushabti (small servant figures buried with the dead). "

Thus reinforced in my intuition, I looked up "eternity enamel" and found that this Turkish business would be exhibiting in fairs in 2002 in Turkey, Algeria, Morocco, Germany and Japan as well as Chicago in the USA. So somewhere in that mix there is a direct reference to areas of the world one might associate with covert & inspired mental activity which includes terrorism and the invocation of djinn to coerce the unwary as cited in the comments of Shiek Gilani and/or the canny planting of hoax material; to serve the same purpose and fire up the daring of would-be martyrs.

It is interesting that a link to these concepts should be so easily available in a simple web search from an email route trace but:why not? For although these cyber antics may inspire temporary, tinsel wonder in the circus rubes, deceit is not really sorcery. The actual sorcery in the situation was the inspiration to me of the word "Faince" during a conjuration ten days previous to the aggressive viral email. It seems that beneath the commercial "eternity enamel" site there is a secondary site—the one which first displayed—from which the "Congratulations!!Italian.zip" email was sent. Since by the time you read this, dear reader, the secondary site may have vanished from the web, take the tracing of this email as a prototype rather than an ultimate location of treachery.

The intended cyber trick in naming the viral zip file on the rogue email "Italian" was to tempt me toward the destruction of my installed computer software by flashing an adjective relevant to the fact that my artistic work had within the past few weeks received special recognition in Italy and that I had recently been participating in physics discussions on the Italian Physics Center group located at the Yahoo site.

So I went to the site "*The Great Trick*" a bibliographical reference site which is put together by a Romani scholar interested in the attempted extermination of the gypsies by the Axis forces during World War Two. At "The Great Trick" web page I searched for "Italian" and finding no "Italian" then searched for "Italy". I learned that during World War Two:

"Only in one occupied country were extreme measures not enforced: this was Denmark, where the problem lay once more in doubts over ethnic demarcations within the traveling population, simply classified as 'asocial' in its entirety. There was no room for such niceties in the German protectorate of Bohemia and Moravia, and events there far outstripped in ruthlessness those in nominally independent Slovakia, where the severe discrimination fell short of extermination but involved concentration-like work camps. Of 8,000 Gypsies in Bohemia and Moravia, only about 600 survived. It was, however, in Yugoslavia that the largest number of

DOING BUSINESS IN THE ADIRONDACKS by E. Macer-Story

Gypsies perished, after the young state had been dismembered among four Axis and pro-Axis powers (Germany, Italy, Hungary, Bulgaria) together with the collaborators in Croatia, which incorporated Bosnia-Herzegovina. Few Gypsies survived the terror in the north once the Croat separatist movement came to power and inaugurated a bloodbath against non-Catholic minorities. So ferocious in its atrocities was the Ustasha (fascist) militia that even the German military authorities were appalled"[27]

While gazing at the word "Italy" which occurs after mention of the Axis powers in this quote, I noticed the following quote about antiquities and ceramics:

"At the Hissarlik site of Troy [1871-1875], Schliemann had also found hundreds of objects ranging from pottery fragments and terra-cotta whorls to ornaments bearing the sign of the swastika. He immediately recognized this symbol from similar signs on pots found near Köningswalde on the river Oder in Germany and speculated that the swastika was a "significant religious symbol of our remote ancestors," which linked the ancient Teutons, the Homeric Greeks, and Vedic India. The extraordinary publicity surrounding Schliemann's finds at Troy guaranteed a wide European audience for his speculations about an ancient Aryan symbol bridging the mythological and religious traditions of East and West".[28]

So here it is interesting to locate reference to the Axis Inner Order's belief in the talismanic significance of ancient ceramic artifacts and the name "Hissarlik" which resembles the untraceable name "Haioimr" on the trace of the deliberate viral email which arrived onto my queue during Memorial Day weekend of May 2002. Memorial Day in the USA commemorates the soldiers in all Wars who fought for the Allied cause and for Free Enterprise.

In the same conjuration diagram which provided the word "Faince" the scribbled note "Strategy-Open Sesame-Boston-Sect-Tantra misunderstood" precedes that underlined word, which is prefaced by a lightning bolt leading into the F of "Faince". The double lightning bolt was of course the symbol of the elite Nazi SS. But this is a single lightning bolt, which is the symbol of the Nordic gods Zeus and Wotan, and of the Voodoo god Shango, entities cited earlier in this text who may be mighty angry at having been identified recently with the limited cause of National Socialism during a number of quaisi-antiquarian charades..

In "The Swastika and the Nazis" an essay found in May of 2002 on the "Friends of the Swastika" webring in a listing compiled by Servando González, the following assertions are made about the history of National Socialism in Germany:

"In Mein Kampf, Adolf Hitler claimed that the form in which the Nazis used the swastika was based on a design by Dr. Friedrich Krohn, a dentist who had belonged to several Völkisch groups, including the Germanen Order. Krohn, a dentist from Starnberg, submitted his design of a flag which had been used at the founding meeting of his own party local: a swastika against a black-white-red background. The swastika, for long time a symbol of the Teutonic Knights, had been in use by Lanz von Liebenfels the Thule Society and a number of Freikorps units.
Hitler gives his own account: "Actually, a dentist from Starnberg did deliver a design that was not bad after all, and, incidentally, was quite close to my own, having only the one fault that a swastika with curved legs was composed into a white disk." ...Krohn knew that the

DOING BUSINESS IN THE ADIRONDACKS by E. Macer-Story

Buddhist destroverse or clockwise swastika symbolized good fortune and well being, and made his design accordingly, with the swastika's legs pointing to the left. ..The majority of the Nazi leaders accepted Krohn's design, but Hitler insisted on a sinistroverse or anti-clockwise one and changed the design accordingly. Notwithstanding Adolf Hitler's claims on the contrary, some authors believe that it was Karl Haushofer, whom they see as Hitler's guiding brain, the one who suggested the Führer the adoption of the swastika as the Nazi symbol. This is, i. e., the opinion of Pauwels and Bergier in the influential book "Morning of the Magicians", which achieved international circulation during the late 1960's...Karl Haushofer was born in Bavaria in 1869...Haushofer is known to have had a reputation for precognition, which manifested when he was a young field artillery officer in the Bavarian army. In 1908 the army sent him to Tokyo to study the Japanese army and to advise it as an artillery instructor. .. Karl Haushofer had been a devout student of Schopenhauer, and during his stay in the Far East he was introduced to Oriental esoteric teachings. He became proficient enough to translate several Hindu and Buddhist texts, and became an authority in Oriental mysticism. Some authors even believe that he was the leader of a secret community of Initiates in a current of satanism through which he sought to raise Germany to world power, though these occult connections have been denied ....After Hitler came to power in 1933, Professor Haushofer was instrumental in developing Germany's alliance with Japan. Most of the meetings between high rank Japanese officials and Nazi leaders took place at his home near Munich. He saw Japan as the brother nation to Germany, the Herrenwolk of the Orient... Before the war Professor Haushofer and his son Albrecht maintained close contacts with British members of the Golden Dawn. When war between Germany and England broke out Haushofer tried to use his influence with Hess in trying to convince Hitler to make peace with the British...Due to these views, Karl and Albrecht Haushofer fell from grace and were denounced as mentally disturbed. Albrecht became involved in a failed coup d'etat against Hitler on July 20, 1941. Karl Haushofer was sent to the infamous Dachau concentration camp, and Albrecht to the Moabite prison in Berlin, where was later executed....Some authors claim that, while in Japan, Haushofer was active in the ultra-secret Green Dragon Society, whose members were under oath to commit ritual suicide if faced with dishonor. After the war Haushofer was among the Nazi members to be put to trial before the Nuremberg War Crimes Tribunal. But Professor Haushofer never went to trial. After killing his wife, Karl Haushofer committed suicide in the traditional Japanese way, cutting his intestines with a sharp samurai short sword, in a personal, formal ceremony called seppuku (commonly known as hara-kiri)."

In this context, it is worth noting that the word "Haioimir" from the "Headers" trace of the viral email sent to the Magick Mirror queue on Memorial Day 2002 and first identified with "eternity enamel" when separated into the words "Haioi" and "Mir" fetched a website located in Cambridge, Massachusetts which was featuring among other innovations a graphics display innovation by a Japanese company which instantly arranges frames of film on a contact sheet. This indicates not specifically that the Massachusetts site is part of a "conspiracy" but that the root name of the word "Haioimir" may be Japanese or Asian.

In historical context, the fact that key German officials of the Nazi regime during World War Two could have become dominated by fierce Japanese Shinto warrior deities or demons has not been adequately recognized by occult scholars.

Sometimes the exact identities of actual spirit guides or guardians can be obscure or puzzling whereas the effects are definite to the observer and can be documented. One of the significant incidents I recollect from my childhood--which may have been "spirit guardian-connected" --took place in a playground with a circular merry go round which the kids used to take turns spinning for each other. I have no memory of whether we spun this merry go round deosil or widershins but unlike water in drains fore and aft the equator, the direction of carousel spin would not have been governed by the rotation of the planetary area but by the way the mechanic had originally installed the central screw in the axle of the turning platform..

We would all get aboard and then someone would run, pushing the outer edge of the revolving platform, until it was spinning fast and then be pulled-jump aboard by the kids already on the moving platform.. On the day of this experience I was about 11-12 years old and was alone on the playground on a gray chilly day, standing about twelve feet from the deserted gym equipment. This playground was located in upstate New York on a former TB hospital grounds which had been converted for Federal V.A. use. My Dad was the director of the V.A. hospital and we lived in a spacious house on the grounds near houses occupied by the families of other V.A. personnel who were my playmates there. On this day, as I was standing in the playground with nothing particular in mind, a man in a business suit approached me and asked me some questions about who I was and why I was out in the playground. He then handed me his business card.

"I would like to do business with you." he told me, "Don't tell your parents you talked to me. I am not here to see your parents."

Then it hit me. I was a separate individual from my parents! Other people thought so too!! For years, as I was a precocious child and my parents did not actually understand the details of teachers' attention to my work, I had been annoyed at home and praised in public. The unidentified businessman then shook my hand and left the playground. I have no memory of seeing him walk away down the road or get into a car. This encounter was subtle. He changed my life in a positive, inner way which did not get me in Dutch with my neighbors, relatives and friends. It was a bit like changing one key bolt in the inner atomic mechanism without having to play games with the surrounding gravitational field structure. Of course, this is "behavior modification" such as a trained counselor might practice. But was this an ordinary human stranger or one of the fabled supernatural appearances common in Adirondack mountain lore? As in Washington Irving's story of the "Headless Horseman"there are many accounts in the New York State area of "phantom regiments", lone soldiers from the Revolutionary War, Dutch pirates, Native Amereican shamans, and so on.

This concept of a truly intelligent and strategic contact from Advanced Intelligence is an item to ponder for those who buy—literally or figuratively—the flashy exterior trappings of the "counter culture" gurus . These trappings may actually be damaging to the naïve "initiate" of these systems for practicing expanded modalities of consciousness if there are not within the natural, cultural context of the practitioner. Think now of the ill-fated Haushofer father & son and their desperate attempt to re-connect with Nordic ties among the Scots tribes in the UK prior to being arrested by a

DOING BUSINESS IN THE ADIRONDACKS by E. Macer-Story

Nazi government in disarray and heavily under the influence of foreign, Shinto "warrior" concepts..

Often the genuinely "paranormal" or "supernatural" events which interject themselves into the flow of routinely recorded history are completely unique and unexpected, unlike a failed parachute jump into a rugged country of individualists who had incorrectly been thought by an intellectual to hold standard beliefs on "Nordic" mythology and ancestry.

These truly unexplained events will frequently occur in the flow of the mundane hurly burly of life and only be fully realized as unusual later. Whilst I was drafting the previous section on "eternity enamel" as parsed from the printed trace of a nuisance email I was keeping appointments here and there and carrying my folder of manuscripts in process with me in a paper folder containing recent printed pages and a computer disk. A small black brochure with white type about two inches square was somehow inside this folder. I noticed it but did not read it immediately. When I finally read the small print, it startled me to see that it was a brochure for "Metal Effects" giving instructions on "patina finishing" conceptually similar to the "eternity enamel" process I had found by web-searching the Memorial Day viral email in late May 2002. But the web search had been a virtual information process. No actual solid 3-dimensional products were examined or included. I noticed that the return address for the "Metal Effects" product, evidently an enamel paint, was Hollywood, California.

Suddenly, prompted by the tiny black-covered brochure and the idea of "supernatural" guidance in finding the "fiaince" reference connected with the "eternity enamel" web search, I recalled an unusual incident which had occurred to myself and my college friend, actress Lucy Flippin, shortly after a tour of the Los Angeles area which had included a visit to the then "sorcerer's Shop" in Hollywood. This occurred in 1977, when Lucy was living in an apartment building in L.A. with her then husband Tom Tarpey. I was visiting from Boston and she had been driving me around L.A. in an improvised sight seeing tour. She had noticed the "Sorcerer's Shop" and thought I might enjoy a "Hollywood" take on Witchcraft, as I was just beginning to show public interest in this subject and had just finished my Bicentennial "happening" of the year long "Magik Mirror" installation in Salem, Massachusetts where the seventeenth century witch trials had taken place.(1975-76) . Enthusiasts of sorcery will notice that the "c" was not yet in the Magick Mirror logo at that time. I was a novice, and knew I was a novice. The event was a learning experience for me as well as an entertaining gathering place for those interested in witchcraft, ufos and the supernatural.

At any rate, when Lucy Flippin and I returned to her apartment building from a long, meandering drive through Los Angeles and Hollywood in 1977, we were startled to see a young man neatly dressed entirely in black and with a broad Scottish/Norse face, somewhat similar to the young Mick Jagger in appearance, inside the elevator with us. At this point in time, I cannot recall whether he entered the elevator on an intermediate floor or was already inside when the door opened on the ground floor. I do recall that he was happy to see us and was carrying a full paper bag of groceries. He rode up in the elevator with us. I was extremely nervous as I wanted to ask Lucy whether witches actually lived in the building or he was just visiting. But I had to wait until the elevator door closed behind us on Lucy's floor. She had never seen him before.

I thought he might have been associated with the "Sorcerer's Shop" and followed us but that was impossible because he was there when we got to the building. I had purchased a plastic bottle of rock salt at the shop and someone had consecrated it for me there. "Consecrated" means to pass a particular protective value into the talisman and does not refer to any specific ceremony. It is a mental action and a variety of material rituals might be used. I did not see the consecration. The bottle was taken into a cellar location for this and then handed to me afterward. Upon seeing the dashing young man in black business shirt and slacks in Lucy Flippin's elevator, my immediate reaction was a slight paranoia. Maybe they were "after" us. Maybe they had traced the plate of Lucy's car. But in retrospect, this seems impossible unless the "Sorcerer's Shop" had a direct line to the LAPD motor vehicle listings, which were not then on a computer network

I recalled this incident in a flash as I held the tiny black "Metal Effects" brochure marked "Hollywood". I feel I may have a "spirit guide" who presents the appearance of a British or Scottish rock musician. Recall now, dear reader, the "Break on through to the Other Side" incident at the Rosendale commuter bus stop where several other events including the verified appearance of the doppelganger of physicist Fred Allen Wolf as well as the spontaneous unlatching of my watchband as the bus pulled to a stop at the "Park N' Ride". A very savvy guide seems to be assisting me in the mundane sense by alerting me to "real" sorcery with power-oriented roots in the mundane life and social context of the magician who has cast the spell and/or transacted the chicanery with which I am intersecting.

Why would a black-garbed "rock band" type angel be the façade presented by anyone's "higher guidance"? Possibly this is because the negative "Thantatos" sorcerers attempting to subtly operate from behind the scenes with their rigidly atavistic male/female mythology of an elementary biological nature are being opposed by Forces of a greater mental sophistication. The rock musician image is clearly one with pan-sexual overtones.

In this context, it is worth noting that such a musician would probably been forced by the Axis regime during World War Two to wear a pink widershins swastika under suspicion of being a "soft man", and gay. During this period of time, women were supposed to be limited to sexual, domestic and clerical roles. However, according to the lore of occult historians [29] several women were used as spirit mediums by Hitler's Ahnenerbe research organization and produced telekinetic materializations and other esp/pk effects. However, these effects were directly linked to their sexual and emotional functioning. Other, male mediums were focused upon "spiritual" and/or intellectual esp/pk channeling as were the few, more sophisticated women who patronized such organizations as the Thule society.

It is interesting that though the research by the Axis into V-2 rockets and atomic weapons is often mentioned in historical summaries of the World War Two era, as is the cipher and espionage aspect of these campaigns, the concomitant research into the occult powers of the mind is not stressed except in specialty publications.. Is this simply because it is really not important or because certain adepts of these studies did escape the Axis countries just before the end of World War Two, taking with them research which has emerged as the "Thantatos" organization and the mysterious "ufo craft" which have been manifesting frequently in South America since the mid-twentieth century?

So that this narration does not become speculatively boring as are many of the "what if" adventure books, here follows the scenario of an "Anomaly News Minute" on this subject, originally commissioned by the ezine Elfis.com of Austin, Texas:

WHAT'S UP AT THE SOUTH TIP?
**UFOs, Espionage and Nuclear Power Installations in Tierra Del Fuego Archipeligo
Special to Anomaly TV by Eugenia Macer-Story   January 2002**

1. **Announcer:** What's up at the tip of South American among the islands of the archipelago shared by Chile and Argentina?
2. **Visual:** Map or aerial view of Tierra del Fuego Archipeligo.
3. **Announcer:** Since the mid-1980's residents of Chilean Patagonia have been reporting visits to them by blonde 'angels" from "The Friendship" subterranean installation located on a Chilean island in the archipelago which is accessible by ship from the port of Quenchi.
4. **Visual:** Illustration of so-called square-faced Nordic "angels" meeting local intellectuals.
5. **Announcer:** This might be taken as simply being more misguided "Chi Chi Chicotronics Charades" except that equipment used on "The Friendship's" island does have the practical effect of jamming normal electronic transmissions in the surrounding area. According to an article by Josep Guijarro in Issue #4 on Inexplicata Online Magazine…
6. **Visual:** View of Inexplicata Index Page Illustration with Soundtrack.
7. **Announcer:** …the subterranean installation sports modern electronic communications equipment installed within an Egyptian temple décor. Additionally, Guijarro reports that the name of Andrea Nisbeti, a former colleague of the young Werner Von Braun in Nazi Germany, has somehow surfaced in the conversation of local residents who have conversed with "Angels" from "The Friendship". Andrea Nisbeti was to have accompanied other scientists to the United States after World War Two to work on rocket projects but somehow slipped from between the pages of "Operation Paperclip" and was never seen again by U.S. scientists, at least overtly.
8. **Visual:** Archive photo of young W. Von Braun with other Nazi rocket scientists. Archive photo of Andrea Nisbeti as young man.
9. **Announcer:** A number of ufo sightings of various types were reported in Argentina and Chile in 2000 and early 2001.
10. **Visual:** View of article in Spanish showing "OVNI" title & photo.

DOING BUSINESS IN THE ADIRONDACKS by E. Macer-Story

11. Announcer: It has been claimed by residents of the areas where certain of these sightings occurred that "military authorities" were on hand shortly after certain of these sightings to collect debris. There may be a correlation between these sightings and the damage to jungle residents by ufo craft in Brazil in the early 1990's as reported by U.S. investigative journalist Bob Pratt.

12. Visual: Cover of Bob Pratt's book opening to show photo taken on site.

13. Announcer: On January 9, 2002 a letter was circulated by Guillermo Gimenez of CEUFO (Proyecto Condor) regarding the possible use of Argentina's Tierra del Fuego, the island at the tip of South America, for nuclear testing. Tierra del Fuego's governor, Carlos Manfredotti, signed decree No. 1369 on July 26, [2001], authorizing the installation of a base belonging to the "International Monitoring System for the Prevention and Prohibition of Nuclear Tests and Detonations" and invoking national law 25,022 of 1998.

The decree provides the members of this base with freedom of movement through the province if their studies so require it.

14. Visual: Archive photo of U.N. peacekeeping force at military attention or on parade.

15. Announcer: Residents of Tierra Del Fuego are currently protesting this installation of a nuclear test site on their island. They maintain that the installation will destroy traditional Fuegan culture.

16. Visual: Photo of shamans from Tierra del Fuego from the book "The Way of The Animal Powers" by Joseph Campbell.

17. Announcer: But will this nuclear testing installation also have the unexpected effect of placing a conventional, overt international military base in close proximity to the enigmatic and covert "Friendship"installation on a nearby island in Chilean Patagonia?

18. Visual: Comic illustration of Nordic blonde 'angels" meeting U.N. peacekeepers on the island beach road beside amazed Tierra del Fuego shamans.

19. Announcer: In research material recently issued by controversial U.S. ufologist Dr. Steven Greer there is one account by an ex-military enlisted man who claims he participated in a unique recovery of a crashed ufo craft while stationed in Peru to monitor air traffic for drug smuggling. By his own account, this man was threatened with retribution by covert U.S. military operatives if he came forward with his story.

20. Visual: Photo from Greer video of interview with informant.

21. Announcer: But can we trust this account? Might such descriptions draw attention from the truly unexplained aerial phenomena in South America which may come from "The Friendship" or some other non-governmental source with very real expertise in Advanced Interdimensional Communications? Stay tuned.

22. Visual: Credits over candid home videos of ufo sightings in South America give specific sources for previous visuals. Special Thanks to Scott Corrales, editor of Inexplicata Magazine

In a limited distribution video produced by Iciris Productions in 1993 there is an interview with Gunter Richter, a man who claims that he witnessed the flight of a "ufo" at Pennemunde research base in Germany when he was a child. In

DOING BUSINESS IN THE ADIRONDACKS by E. Macer-Story

this video, there are diagrams of theoretical ufos without the exact structural plans. These diagrams are marked with the double lightning bolt of the elite Nazi SS.

Peenemunde base, destroyed in 1943 by Allied bombers, was the location where the V-2 rockets, the first pilotless "guided missiles", were first developed by Nazi scientists during World War Two.

According to Richter, who appears in the I iris video with exact appearance disguised, his father worked as a scientist at Peenemunde and in 1943, when the family returned to Munich, was transferred from that vulnerable target location to a secret SS installation in the Hartz mountains. The family then lost touch with the scientist father. In 1960, according to Richter, his identity tags and a brief account of his death by heart attack were given by the German government to the family in Munich.

Where had the man who proudly showed his young son the flight of a V-2 rocket and a circular "ufo-like" craft in 1943 actually been located during the seventeen year interim between his reassignment to the Hartz mountain development facility and the return of his identity tag to his family?

According to historians of World War Two, there was a hollowed out mountain in the Hartz mountains of Germany where Top Secret research was conducted. Also according to known history, the elite SS identity medallion was a special alloy known only to certain metallurgists.

At the New Science Forum in Fort Collins, Colorado where the limited distribution video on Nazi ufo research was being sold in 1993, a woman who was vending this video wanted your present correspondent to see and handle a medallion and to give a psychometric opinion of this object. It was a plain metal disk on a sturdy chain, marked only with a number and no design. At that time, I had not been aware of the unique properties of the SS identity medallion.

When I held this metal disk on a chain, my mind went immediately toward the concept of an intelligent group of people, some in South America and some in Europe. I do not recall the entire session, which was improvised in the midst of a milling crowd at a convention display table. I do recall that the intent was to determine whether this group was still active and that it was my impression from holding the identity disk that they were still active. In retrospect. I realize that the persons vending the film may have been trying to determine whether the scientist who disappeared into the Hartz mountains in 1943 had escaped to South America or another location in Europe after the Axis powers were defeated in World War Two.

If this was his SS medallion I was holding, he did escape. For the rightful wearer of that identity tag had been in Europe and South America more recently than 1945.Here of course we enter an intermediate realm of strictly mental and "non-local" connections. But the Nazi scientists of World War Two were very familiar with this realm. One of the SS documents which shows a quadratic equation beside a mathematical matrix parenthesis also shows the radian of two concentric circles. Between these concentric circumferences is the symbol ♎ which could signify either the astrological sign Libra or the Greek letter Omega. Situated within the characteristic arc of a circular chart, it is probably Libra though no other astrological signs accompany it. Here there is evidence of sorcery and conjurations; not simply the few gathered fragments of an SS "ufo" archive.

In fact, as I was photographing documentation of the SS diagrams on video, a preternatural growling noise emerged from the VCR speakers. Although on one level I was aware that this could be due to the non-uniform reel speed of the amateur video, it did sound like a large and ferocious beast growling. I thought of "Fenris" the legendary Nordic wolf demon, said to have been invoked by a variety of German sorcerers, including members of the SS and also by contemporary motorcycle clubs, some with radical political affiliations in the U.S. and Europe.I wondered if a Fenris force was protecting the information on the video. Or perhaps "signaling from" somewhere within the non-local information threads attached to the images on the screen.

On the video, the narrator states at one point that the nominal "wolf packs" were used to conceal actual submarine research and that secret Nazi research was being conducted during World War Two at a secret underground facility below Anarctica at the South Pole. This is not far from the location of the Nordic "Friendship" commune on Tierra del Fuego in Chile, as described earlier in the Anomaly News Minute documentary..

On the face of the narration, such speculation seems like antiquated "science fiction" drawn from fantasy books of the 1950's which depicted "secret research" being conducted by weirdly uniformed personnel beneath the icy landscape of the Antarctic South Pole. But "truth" is stranger than "fiction" as the old saying goes. For on even such a popular and pre-adjusted U.S. news conduit as CNN cable television there is word in 2002 of a fantastic alliance between olde guarde Nazi die-hards and contemporary Fundamentalist Islamic terrorists. As interviewed in Berne, Switzerland by Nic Robertson in the Winter of 2001, the "Third Position" Swiss financier Ahmed Huber was surrounded in his office by memorabilia of both Adolf Hitler and Osima Bin Laden and declared his admiration for both terrorist leaders. Mr. Huber, involved at the time of the CNN interview in the Spring of 2002 with offshore banking in the area of the Bahama islands, which are between the independent Communist country of Cuba and the U.S. mainland peninsula of Florida, has been involved in the past with the Al Taqua management company, a financial group which included known terrorist investors.

The "Third Position" is a title used by a loosely knit trans-national terrorist alliance different from the familiar "National Socialist" organizations dating back into the early Twentieth Century. Described by the "*International Third Position*" website emanating from London in the UK in June of 2002 as "An alternative to both Socialism and Capitalism based on widespread diffusion of property" this viewpoint seems to be an updated Fascist belief system which includes as part of the revisionist menu an environmentalist and anti-materialist concern, which deplores even anarchism as a materialist philosophy. The "Third Position" system is Fascist because it implies that only "those who understand" beyond the mundane material world will be capable of governing, and thus attempts to create a trans-material "elite".

. Of interest to students of the medieval Catholic witch inquisitions and other righteous political purges throughout history should be the declaration of the "*upholding of the Moral Order within society*". Ahmed Huber, a Nordic Swiss citizen who converted to Islam, implied also in the CNN interview that he was representing a "high moral order" linked to the religious beliefs of extreme, Fundamentalist Islam

DOING BUSINESS IN THE ADIRONDACKS by E. Macer-Story

and mystical Nazi adulation of Adolf Hitler as an inspired leader.

In this context, an underground secret haven beneath the icy terrain of Anarctica or within a hollow mountain located in Europe or Afghanistan, and/or potentially anywhere on the planet where people tend to "live within their minds" only is not antiquated fantasy at all. If these people are actually more mentally-oriented than the average materialist citizen, they may in truth develop unusually acute mental abilities. Perhaps amid this speculation we should once again cite the opinion of Shiek Gilani about the activity of the djinn in these situations and be alert not only for material terrorist weapons but for the hypnotic and "wild card" conceptualist mental abilities of those individuals who do have powerful "spirit allies", whether or not the modern analyst regards these allies as part of the collective human superconscious mind.

One may, for example, rub the nose of a leprechaun curio under the impression that fairy forces are empowering some project, and have fantastic success. Maybe it IS the fairies. But maybe also the leprechaun talisman is a link to capacities of the human mind usually untapped in mundane activities. Whichever the elfin force may be, it is a reality which should be seriously reckoned with and brought into the scope of global business as it is conducted today. For business itself, as this manifests on both the stock market and in advanced electronic communications tools , is becoming increasingly a mental competition . This may be the meaning of the "business card" I received from a mysterious stranger as an adolescent in an upstate New York playground.

Why wouldn't certain individual stockbrokers and financial analysts also turn to the more mental occult systems as well as role-playing games designed to hone strategic ability? Beyond the attractions of "elite mystical conspiracy", might a certain class of power-oriented non-human Intelligences be attempting to forcibly activate or re-activate themselves in the status of "demi-gods and demons" by using the mystical terrorists as conduits for arbitrary actions which are not naturally on the shared human agenda? This tendency may be noted also in the fad for "extraterrestrial contact" claims since the end of World War Two in the mid-twentieth century. An expert on Kabbalist mysticism has stated in conversation that the Kelipoth, the powerful "angels of the reversed Tree of Life, may create pockets of time wherein the usual past/present/future sequence is blurred and the power-oriented adversary stands a chance of reactivating the defeated destiny pattern.

But if this is true of the negative adversaries attempting to dominate collective destiny, might such a concept also empower the positive, evolutionary force.? As the Catholic Jesuits state optimistically: "The devil has power over the past but not the future." It is possible to enter the temple of blurred time sequence and surprise the brilliant adversary in the act of destiny-tinkering.

Along this line of speculation, it is interesting to note that one of the Nazi-SS marked diagrams in the video by I iris productions containing anecdotal testimony by the alleged son of a former SS officer is the familiar domed shape with down-slanted skirt (the shape referred to as a "straw hat" in certain Chinese sightings) with three semi-circular, globe-like protrusions beneath the lower rim of the skirt. This shape is directly similar to the ufo craft described and photographed by controversial 1950's "ufo contactee" George Adamski,[30] who after pursuing Tibetan studies claimed he had been telepathically guided to a desert location in the Southwestern United States where he was

DOING BUSINESS IN THE ADIRONDACKS by E. Macer-Story

visited by a flying saucer containing a blonde, Nordic- appearing being from outer space. Adamski claimed to have ridden in this vehicle with the "Venusian"being.

Later, Adamski's photos and descriptions of this flying saucer vehicle were discredited because photos were shown of a light fixture with three bulbs installed within a metal shade with a domed top and slanted lower rim. It was said that Adamski photographed the light fixture and fraudulently claimed it was a flying saucer. But perhaps the vehicle actually resembled a light fixture. Stranger things have been documented in the history of anomalous and unexplained phenomena. If the vehicle actually was generating a field to interface with the Earth's electromagnetic & gravitational field for the purpose of propulsion and visibility, the device by which that unknown field might be generated would resemble in concept and shape a light bulb, searchlight or antenna apparatus rather than a rocket exhaust apparatus.

Furthermore: if such concepts of vehicle propulsion were known to an elite group of scientists who had fled to an undisclosed location before the Axis empire crumbled in 1945, this same clandestine group might wish to substitute for the original Adamski photos similar light fixture photos. Or the entire Adamski episode was engineered by this clandestine group, and the Nordic blonde Venusian was actually a "Thantatos group" cosmonaut. These polarities of light vs. dark and artificial vs. real are not completely satisfying theories.

Another possibility clearly exists and may unify the speculation about the Adamski adventures and other, similar encounters with "flying saucers" which seem partly evidential and/or are partly a clumsy charade. It may be that actual Advanced Intelligence of a form & capacity quite different from our preconceptions about stagecraft ET and "Star Wars" characters is inspiring a variety of people, for good or ill, to participate in such partly-realized "outer space" adventures.

Such "inspired" adventures push the capacity of the categorical envelope containing preconceptions about human knowledge without completely deluding the human players in the charade. Yes, there is genuine inspiration by Advanced Intelligence but the human understanding of this inspiration is partial. This situation of veiled knowledge and intent is different from a wholly human political group believing that they have received "superhuman" approval for every action from the sacred sword of their ancestors now resting in a museum case.

The "cattle mutilations" mentioned earlier in this book in both South American and Missouri Ozark context which are often attributed by traumatized livestock owners to "ufos" may actually fall into the category of human cultist activity, inspired and/or in the service of demi-gods with some elitist agenda. However, those motivated by this elitist agenda may in truth possess arcane knowledge which employs or is transmitted from some form of non-human Advanced Intelligence, not necessarily extraterrestrial. The intelligence behind the effects detailed in the following excerpts from an article published in *Diario La Arena (La Pampa, Argentina) on April 29, 2002* was perceived by local residents as "nocturnal lights".

"SALLIQUELO (Agencia Macachín) -- A few days ago strange lights appeared in the night skies over Saliquelló, Province of Buenos Aires, and in the morning cattle ranchers of the area found three mutilated bovines showing signs of having undergone a surgical intervention with unusual implements. A veterinarian told local media that the incisions "are strange ones in which some sort of heating element appears to have been used."

..."The veterinarian interviewed claimed that what he saw in his inspection of the carcasses was abnormal. "They present strange cuts, as though resulting from an intense heat source. The skin is burned along the edges of the cuts, and the absence of blood in veins, muscles and ligaments [...] it is simply desiccated," he said...." unusual cuts can be seen in the animals' bodies and heads. One of them shows a perfectly straight cut on one mandible. Furthermore, its tongue is missing along with most of the alimentary tract: larynx, pharynx and saliva glands. The outer ear is completely missing. Another curious incision appears on the body (ribs and abdomen) which is teardrop-shaped through which genitalia was extracted," he explained.

..."it's as though you were cutting a piece of paper with a hot wire--the edges become dry, scorched and thinner. Furthermore, all traces of blood had vanished. We only found some coagulated remains in the heart.. There are no signs that the animal put up a fight, nor is their any evidence of scorched pastureland. I'm not saying that this is the handiwork of alien beings, but it's a strange circumstance nonetheless. Even the other animals refuse to come close to the dead ones, and curiosity is a characteristic element of bovines," the veterinarian concluded."

Doctor Daniel Belot, the veterinarian who examined these animals, made this additional remark to *Diario "Nuevo Día" (Coronel Suárez, Prov. of Buenos Aires)*on June 15, 2002:

"I was confronted by an unnerving sight," the professional told NUEVO DIA, stressing that "those who haven't seen it cannot understand the magnitude of the situation." Belot explained that "the animal lay on the ground like a hare, and the entire left side of its face was skinned to the bone beneath the eye. All of its molars were visible. "When we performed the necropsy we found that it was missing its tongue, all of its vocal apparatus, which is to say the larynx and part of the pharynx, and something very odd: there was no blood inside or outside the animal. It was perfectly clean. That came as an enormous surprise for us."
He confirmed that there was no tearing [of flesh] of any kind on the animal, therefore discarding the likelihood that predators would have attacked it. "It is a deed that appears to have been carried out by humans, but even so it's something very hard to do." When asked if he was able to come up with any explanation whatsoever, Dr. Belot confessed that "my curiosity has not yet been sated, since I've sent samples to the University of Buenos Aires' School of Pathology and the only response I've received is that how the incisions were made cannot be determined."...
Two months after the first discovery, Belot pointed out that "after some time, the dead animals have already been attacked by predators. But until recently, they wouldn't come close." Regarding the behavior of the herd's other members, the veterinarian noted that "they appear indifferent, looking from a distance without coming close. What is commonly seen in the countryside is that the rest of the animals sort of "mourn" the deceased animal, and that has not occurred in this case."

During the interview, Dr. Belot further emphasized that *"the animals were killed elsewhere and dumped there, and that indication I'm inferring from the way in which the carcasses have been positioned."*
According to the news accounts, of June 24, 2002 (*Télam).*
" A pregnant sheep was found dead and "hollowed out" in Coronel Pringles, 120 km north of Bahia Blanca,Argentina, while new animal mutilation cases were reported in Cordoba and Entre Rios.

DOING BUSINESS IN THE ADIRONDACKS by E. Macer-Story

Meanwhile, two girls were hospitalized at Santiago del Estero due to the impact caused by their sighting of "multicolored lights" which were also reported by rural residents of the province of Buenos Aires
However, Bernardo Cané, the director of the Agroalimentary Health and Quality Service (SENASA) attributed the discovery of mutilated cows, sheep, deer and horses to the actions of "rogue surgeons" and dismissed the possibility that extraterrestrials or paranormal phenomena could be involved."[31]*"*

    This rigged veterinary surgery, whatever might be the motivation or rationale, may be the same type of inspired human-demi-god charade which serves to form the visible totems and rituals of so-called "primitive" belief systems which utilize masks, costumes and a variety of crafted talismans as part of ceremonies during which powerful entities with superhuman capacities are observed to descend briefly into human form within the temples and other ceremonial situations constructed for this purpose. (page 36) Santa Claus, of course, is also observed to descend onto street corners everywhere in the civilized Western world during Christmas shopping season.

    Yet, occasionally what seems to be communication from non-human Advanced Intelligence emerges as a matter of spontaneous interruption into the progress of ordinary human activities. and does seem to be genuinely "supernatural" in impact. Often, this upwelling of genuine anomaly will be in context of some mundanely-devised trickster event.

    On June 28, 2002, I received several obviously fraudulent email forms supposedly from the Internet service which hosts the Magick Mirror Communications domain. In the course of tracing these forms, which contained the year 1969 as one entry in the Headers section which records "send" transmissions, I both re-encountered the Australian punk rock WOMBATZ context discovered on web search when a "king snake" unexpectedly entered the rebus , as described earlier in this book, and discovered in present context that my site had been registered on the Melbourneit.com service as of November 14, 2000. This is an Australian service which, as I later found out, has a business connection with the U.S. Florida-based website company. A site can be arbitrarily assigned to this IT location. Initially, I did not recall registering with any service in Australia.

    Feeling odd about this date, as the obvious purpose of the fraudulent email forms had been to trick me into revealing the Magick Mirror website control password, I looked up the date in my journal for November 2000 to see if any interference had been noted on this date. There was nothing written for the exact date of November 14, 2000. But on November 8, 2000 there is the following entry:

    " While watching the Presidential election returns at about 2:30 a.m. I heard an animal ZZZZ-hissing sound which seemed to be in the living room near the TV. It was not an electronic glitch in the set. I looked in both the front and back yards and in the cellar right below the living room, but there was no such animal. I was viscerally afraid when I first heard the hiss, which did not repeat. Later, I learned that there is a problem with the election returns in Florida, which have to be re-counted."

    On one of the Wombatz websites I accessed from Melbourneit.com while probing the trick password collection form there is the color photograph of a large "milk snake" or "king snake" with bright red markings in the act of swallowing a live white mouse. A facile interpretation of this photo is simply that whoever has the site perversely enjoys

DOING BUSINESS IN THE ADIRONDACKS by E. Macer-Story

watching snakes eat rats. But your humble correspondent has learned to leave no stone unturned in these investigations of the anomalous. In a zoological description of the "milk snake" it is stated that the animal in non-venomous and has the capacity to absorb the venom of lesser reptiles it has swallowed. The author of one zoological description suggests that the milk snake is therefore useful in ridding buildings of vermin.

Perhaps the loud hissing from some invisible animal which I heard outside my Woodstock, N.Y. house on election evening 2000 was a version of the fierce transcendental guide which is rumored to protect the destiny of the United States from intrusive evil. As every U.S. school child is taught, one of the original designs for the U.S. flag was by the first Navy commander John Paul Jones. This design had a snake incorporated into horizontal red & white stripes, as well as the motto: *"Don't Tread On Me."* The implication is that, if provoked, the U.S. serpent power will strike back instantly. At the time it was proposed, this flag design was not universally adopted but remained the flag of the ships under the command of John Paul Jones.

It is quite likely that the more conservative Christian elements of the committee forming the U.S. government thought the serpent flag might suggest allegiance to the devil, who is termed the "Old Serpent" and who tempted Adam and Eve to eat of the apple of knowledge and thus become discontented. So be it.

For we know now that our conception of a Christian "devil" is a simple-minded notion, drawn from the anathematizing of beings worshiped in the Eastern world religions, which are often shown in reptilian form. Quetzecotl , the Mayan Plumed Serpent god, is only one of these positive serpent representations. This deity was seen in the heavens as the Morning Star, and the rays of light emanating from this star-like appearance were seen as feathers of plumes. This is similar to the description of "flying heads" by the Onteora Indians, who were the first residents of the Catskill mountains in New York.[32] These aerial beings, which would now be described by some as "ufo lights" were thought to have a ferocious power. Some were thought to be vampires. The Native Americans of the Catskills and Adirondacks warned of this power and were afraid to approach these beings at night in deserted wilderness areas.

In the flier I distributed on Halloween 2001 at Theater For The New City I included the reproduction of a length of twig naturally formed like a serpent with one wide open eye I had found in the mountains. I wanted those who received my "astral portrait" clairvoyant sketch as part of the festivities held so shortly after the 9/11 World Trade Disaster to remember that the power of this natural mountain guardian force is awesome. At that time, I commented below this photo of the serpent emblem*:" We here in the USA have our own ways & means of tapping interdimensional power. Sometimes we forget this. Remember your own power now."*

Here, in the following section of this book, I am taking my own advice. The temptation in the following commentary is to become too meticulous in documentation at the expense of coherence for the reader. Supernatural occurrences too numerous to detail accompanied in mid-June of 2002 the realization that double agents dating from the CIA experimentation with drugs, shamanism and esp/pk during the late 1950's and 1960's may have linked with contemporary pseudo-Shamanic personages from the Mideastern countries and Asia now using a variety of cultural exchange situations as a front for terrorist and black market activities.

DOING BUSINESS IN THE ADIRONDACKS by E. Macer-Story

Recall now the Sherlock Holmes story *Crucifer of Blood* originally named *The Sign of Four* in which Arthur Conan Doyle details a fictional involvement by British military and aristocratic characters in a long standing opium cult in 19th century East India which also conceals several colonial murders. It is possible that some of the tricks played on Dr. Conan Doyle in order to discredit his non-fictional investigations into spiritualism and a variety of supernatural events were engineered by an actual version of the type of clandestine cult he attempted to "expose" in the Sherlock Holmes short story. These situations of continual mystery have existed from antiquity, with adepts passing the "tricks of the trade" to youthful apprentices.

These would be unscrupulous people of whatever occupation with a working knowledge of the conjuror's art and the effects of a variety of narcotic and herbal substances. In this type of a demimonde there is a bridge between the raffish behavior of moneyed aristocrats and high rollers and the exploits of a more directly criminal street population of drug couriers, prostitutes, gigolos and the inventors of fabulous projects which exist only on paper.

Recall now also the claims of Dr. Jack Sarfatti in his dialogue with Aexus about the criminal political involvements of Esalen Institute personnel in the California "expanded consciousness" demimonde of the same 1950's and 1960's which contained questionable CIA experimentation with drugs and shamanism.[33] Many of the people involved in these very fluid social circles in the U.S. in the 1950's and 1960's were from Europe, Asia, South America and the UK. What prevents the "*Sign of Four*" demimonde of the late Nineteenth Century from being exactly the same demimonde as later manifested in the international activities of a variety of nominal "shamans" passing through the Esalen institute in California fifty years later?

Here enter the "*Temple of Blurred Time*", containing shamans, would-be shamans, fictional and non-fictional time travelers and those simply waiting for a bus or leafing through the evening news, a structure dedicated only unto the ineluctable nexus of fate shared alike by mortals, gods, demi-gods and demons. This is real time double exposure and not fictionally crafted speculation.

A few days after the sober investigations and professional opinions on the cattle mutilations in June 2002 in Argentina which were seeming to converge upon the finding that mutilations upon the livestock were artificial, using some sophisticated form of surgical cautery and/or portable laser scalpel , the formal opinion that the mutilations had been the work of many small carnivorous mice was solemnly rendered by an official investigative group yclept SENASA [34].

This opinion was debated by Jaime Polop, a specialist in rodents at the National University of Rio Cuarto in Argentina. According to the paper "*La Voz del Interior*" of Cordoba, Argentina According to Professor Polop, the "red-muzzled" variety of rodent blamed for the mutilations ingests barely 10 to 12 grams of nourishment per feeding and thus it would have been necessary to have hundreds of these tiny mice acting in concert in order to consume the mutilated cow tissue which had mysteriously vanished from the large, but locally isolated wounds upon these animals.[35]

Your present correspondent here once again recalls the "milk snake" swallowing the white mouse found on one of the WOMBATZ websites accessed by inspiration on June 28, 2002. The "king snake" was originally called "milk snake" in the Midwestern United States, according to a zoological reference, because it was thought the snakes

DOING BUSINESS IN THE ADIRONDACKS by E. Macer-Story

found in barns were taking milk from the cows. Upon more careful investigation, it was found that these snakes were actually eating the small nuisance animals in the barns, like mice and small venomous coral snakes.

Here's the question? Where did all those alleged carnivorous mice go after mutilating the livestock in Argentina? Were they then all eaten by busy clutches of milk snakes who then shed their skins and dived into the ocean, weaving together to become geodesically-inspired extraterrestrial submarines?

Fortunately, government authorities in Argentina had a similar, skeptical response to the SENASA "red-muzzled rodent" explanation and issued a follow-up report debunking this explanation. According to *El Diario de la Pampa* of: Tuesday, July 9, 2002:

"The provincial government dismissed yesterday the official report presented by the National Health and Agroalimentary Quality Service (SENASA) regarding the causes of death and mutilations of dozens of bovines, since the "red-muzzled mouse", the alleged perpetrator of dozens of bovine deaths and mutilations, is not found in La Pampa. This was made clear by the Minister of Production, Nestor Alcala, who pointed out that the rodents of this species "are unknown to me, nor do I believe they form part of the Pampan fauna.Veterinarians and agronomist engineers echoed this sentiment. Gustavo Siegenthaler, director of the National Museum of History of La Pampa, noted that "this species has not been found in the surveys we have conducted." From 1986 to 1992, Siegenthaler headed a multidisciplinary team which produced a report entitled "Survey of Vertebrates in the Province of La Pampa."

Where did the "rodent" idea originate? Certainly not with any qualified zoologist. Such fantasies may have arisen in the minds of people who customarily have the ability to arrange cruise and theme park environments, or to tailor somewhat the destinies of vulnerable individuals by exerting financial influence upon employers, friends and/or work associates. However, the actual "supernatural" is beyond the capacity of these individuals to completely engineer, even if they may be practicing "power magick" and spirit empowerment conjurations as in the "*Sometimes Disorder Is Good*" communications from the Church of Yahweh, which are self-interpreted as "divine".

As I was composing the following email about such topics, the computer suddenly disconnected from the Internet, calling my attention to the email itself, which I had been hurriedly jotting in an offhand manner:

"In a message dated 7/12/2002 1:06:14 AM Eastern Standard Time, RJM@earthlink.net writes:

I wanted to respond to this e-mail about the possibility that animal mutilation activity is some sort of diversion tactic employed by those smuggling drugs.

While the theory is an interesting one, it makes no sense for this to be a worldwide phenomena with so many instances of high strangeness or similarities in the events (i.e.: unknown aerial lights, changes in ground/vegetation, the same organs being targeted, et al) to distract law enforcement or other officials.

These animals have been found in remote areas..."

Greetings RJM:

So also have drug and contraband smugglers been found in remote locations world wide!! In fact, these clever folk have been found in these remote locations, surrounded by a variety of charades, for hundreds of years--a fact which is evident if one studies the history of colonialism and the drug trade since the expeditions of Marco Polo. Some would argue: even *before* the expeditions of Marco Polo.

I have interviewed several dedicated drug enthusiasts who claim that ALL ufos are caused by ingestion of "sacred substances". This is a very limited attitude but it sure can make you money if you're hustling. In my research and experience I have found that there are many "ufo" and "supernatural" incidents which cannot be explained as simple mental alteration by drugs and/or "tectonic stress".

But frequently the "sacred drug" enthusiasts will try to block the findings of myself and other straight investigators who just happen to be experiencing unexplained phenomena without a pre-arranged scenario. There will be more than a little bit on this topic in my upcoming new book: *Doing Business In The Adirondacks.*"

Upon investigation of the disconnection from the Internet whilst composing the controversial message preserved in the text above, your present correspondent discovered that a truck pulling out of a restaurant parking lot at the end of the lane had snapped an overhead telephone wire just at that moment. Is the timing significant or wholly accidental? If this was a significant co-incidence, why the truck? Why not a sudden line power flux or server malfunction?

Since the truck driver was a reputable delivery employee, he waited in the restaurant lot until highway authorities could secure the dangling power line. The vehicle was a large, high-cabbed white delivery truck, very new and shiny. It had never been used before in that lot and was simply too tall for the wires on the older telephone poles.

Oddly, this very large and real truck in 2002 matched the fantasy truck in my painting "*The Enchanted Truck*" which was completed in 1999, and was exhibited at the EUROART 1999 event at the Drassanes Museum in Barcelona. At the time the painting was executed, I was simply following a fictional theme of the supernatural I had first depicted in my one act play "*The Red Truck*", written in 1965 for a college seminar. But I thought the color of the truck should be white in the painting rather than red so that the viewer could identify the vehicle (tiny, in the painting) readily as a "ghost truck".

Perhaps this "truck" interruption in real time was an example of "sympathetic magick" as was used by shamans in antiquity who drew images of their intended hunting quarry on cave walls as part of a ceremony designed to obtain food for the tribe. My intent in making the "Enchanted Truck" painting, which has a large "pajaro", mystical bird image in the foreground, was to show how the "ghost truck" itself was only a tiny part of the larger spell or mental form, represented by the mystical bird. The truck in the painting is caught, so to speak, in the overwhelming pattern made by the bird spell.

One of the objectives always at the subconscious level of my work is to demonstrate a comprehensible example or explanation of the actual process of sorcery and esp/pk so that more people may come to an understanding of these possibilities. Here it seems I had inadvertently pre-anticipated in my painting the synchronous Internet disconnection by means of a new & shiny white truck driven by a jovial individual who could not explain how he had driven into the lot and turned around without tearing down

DOING BUSINESS IN THE ADIRONDACKS by E. Macer-Story

any wires but managed to rip away the cable connection to numerous phones when heading out of the lot toward the highway.

As the "ghost truck" is a tiny part of the larger painting, the driver on Internet cue with his large white van is a small but significant part of this narration.

The importance of flagging the casual email debate about "drug smugglers" is that "RJM", a well-intentioned correspondent, evidently has no direct experience with the bizarre twists and turns which may happen in the minds of people with a secretive practice of well-financed ritual combined with the use of illegal, consciousness-altering substances.

However, law enforcement authorities are professionally aware of the possibility of what they term "criminal insanity" or "abnormal psychology"and would be more apt to seriously credit the idea of a "cult of drug smugglers" as connected with the mysterious cattle mutilations occurring in Argentina and elsewhere. It is worth noting that in a summary of the wide variety of opinions on the Argentinian livestock mutilations of 2002 made by : *"El Diario de la Pampa"* on July 11, 2002 the police who actually investigated these occurrences first hand weighed in with the listed opinion: *"Cults: the theory originally proposed by the Buenos Aires police.'*

ENTERING THE TEMPLE OF BLURRED TIME

On July 3,2002 , the seven a.m. bus out of the Port Authority , bound for Albany, N.Y., blew a rear tire and the passengers wait for a new bus at Exit 17 near Newburgh, N.Y. Possibly, this was E-Z sabotage as the tire was to the outside left on a double-tired vehicle and would have been out of normal view of drivers and passengers during the boarding of the bus at the front right hand door.

Recently, I had been discussing by email the appearance of the year 1969 in a forgery of an email website form I had received which attempted to learn my Magick Mirror website password. In the year 1969, I had experienced a near-fatal car accident which also may have been due to sabotage as the steering column of the car shorted out for no explicable reason as I was driving on a rainy highway. I got full insurance value on the car.

Previous to the accident, I had been working as a newspaper reporter for the Fond du Lac Commonwealth Reporter in Wisconsin. The first apartment I had rented whilst at that job was a basement studio rental in a larger house. Shortly after I moved in to this furnished apartment, I was visited in broad daylight by a car containing several men in khaki uniform-like shirts and slacks who peered in the windows I was, of course, viscerally alarmed by this visit. I moved to the back of the bedsitter room, and sat on the bed near the kitchen area, pretending not to have noticed this car, which was a beige four door sedan about seven to ten years old at the time. It had a roof flasher which made the car look like a police or law enforcement vehicle. I recall the only comment I heard from these visitors, as it was completely off target emotionally in the situation:

"O: it's all right," said one of the men, "She's just making love to her pillow." Sometimes the very absurdity of an event or comment will impress itself in the memory forcefully when other, more rational details, phone numbers and so on are lost in antiquity. The fact was that these folks were "checking" on my activity within the apartment by driving up with roof flasher militantly blipping and thought themselves quite entitled to decide whether my private conduct was OK. Who were these people? I

DOING BUSINESS IN THE ADIRONDACKS by E. Macer-Story

had remained with my hand on the phone to dial the operator for help, and as soon as they left the driveway called the Fond du Lac police. These folk were NOT the police and the officer who answered the phone had no reports of similar incidents.

It was obvious that I did not privately manifest whatever they were seeking. The intruder looking in through the open venetian blind slats probably saw inside the apartment the dim figure of a woman sitting on a fold-out couch bed holding a pillow against her lap and chest. He did not see the woman's hand on the small phone beside the bed nor did he read her thoughts about pretending to be concerned with the bed linen. I was, at that time, twenty-four years old, temporarily working as a reporter in an unfamiliar environment and very frightened by this intrusion. Shortly afterward, I moved to another apartment which was on the second floor of a divided frame house, and less vulnerable. As it turned out, there were poltergeist events in the apartment where I had sought refuge which seemed to involve a remnance from several murders which had been committed by tenants of the second floor apartment. On July 4, 1969 my house key became soft and bent in the lock like putty or bread dough. I had to call the local police to let me in the premises as my landlady and the other tenants were away for the weekend. When the officer arrived, he explained to me that he was relieved since on the previous July fourth he had been called to deal with the suicide of the upstairs tenant, then living in the apartment I had rented, who had committed suicide at the kitchen table. The officer also described a previous murder-suicide in the same apartment a few years previous to the July 4th event, during which a man had shot his wife and then had driven around the town in his car, finally committing suicide.

Obviously, the sensational nature of these murder narrations eclipsed in my mind the previous khaki posse incident which had no actual resonance with the police department. Nut in context of current "cult" inquiries, attention now returns to the unexplained visit by human beings seeming to impersonate military or law enforcement personnel.

Frequently, it will happen that the genuine supernatural and/or haunting incidents—such as the key turning soft in the lock of the "murder house" on July 4th,-- actually occur within circumstances which also contain impostors or self-appointed "high priests/esses" of cult situations. Thus "investigations of the paranormal" can become quite complex. If one is going to delineate the "para-normal" then one should already have some grasp of "normal" expectations. But, as we are now beginning to acutely realize, in the global cultural perspective, one person's "normal" routine can look forebodingly "weird" from another, local standpoint. People do therefore sometimes confuse abnormal behavior with the manifestation of extraordinary mental and/or physical aptitudes. There are no absolute rules in this area. Sometimes gifted people are quite shy or conservative and sometimes they are to be found dancing on the café tables. So it behooves anyone interested in anomalies to consider each case individually.

According to the book, *The Trickster and The Paranormal* by George Hansen,[36] the author Carlos Casteneda , who was a graduate student in anthropology at one of the California state universities, drew most of his inferences about "Don Juan Tenorio" , the sorcerer- protagonist of his best-selling series of books about Mexican sorcery and marijuana, from scholarly references he had studied in the university library.

But how does Hansen know this is absolutely true? How can we be sure that Castaneda was not simply following up hints and brief references about sorcery practices which he had obtained from living practitioners and/or by direct spirit guidance from an actual "Don Juan" inspirational figure? A record of library access to reference materials, if this is the method by which this observation was obtained, will never specifically tell the querent what was being done with those research materials Perhaps Castaneda was simply trying to see where his direct and on site research fit with anthropological accounts of shamanic practices..

Your present correspondent has made similar inquiries in the library, at one point obtaining an original Nineteenth century copy of George Jean Holman's *Pow Wow's Or The Long Lost Friend* from the 42nd Street Public Library reference service in New York.[37] As it turned out, the original edition of this book—which well may be talismanic as well as verbally informative—was available for examination within the watchful realm of the reference librarians. But glancing through this small booklet did not invalidate my direct experience of finding talismanic wand-like worked sticks on my upstate property.[38] In fact, the use of these talismans had caused me to research several traditions of sorcery & hexing.

I was never sure what I wanted to assert individually amid these fluctuating "systems" of framing reality outside established norms. Possibly it was this uncertainty which saved my life under a variety of unique circumstances. For I have never completely entered any of these reality systems, including the canonical system taught in the globally-linked intellectual establishment of colleges and universities. Therefore, I use the words "unusual" or "anomalous" to mean "unique" rather than "deviant". For the idea that "different is deviant" implies a comparison of individual events with shared norms which I am unable to accept as absolute strictures.

Though the uninformed individual whose practical occupation and intentions focus elsewhere than upon mathematical diagrams may dismiss speculations about the fine details of atomic structure as mumbo jumbo, airy fairy nonsense, this absolute dismissal is unwise. One invokes "common sense" in dismissing debates about abstruse models of atomic structure at the risk of waking up one morning in an environment which has been substantially altered by the impact of technology based on micro-structuring.

In the former Soviet Union, there was extensive research on the nature of time and molecular density as this relates in a practical way to the possible speed of the photon within varying areas of molecular structure. Since the breakup of this Communist system in Eastern Europe, those who knew this research have resettled in enclaves around the world in a diaspora of unemployed avante guarde technicians. Some, of course, retain positions in modern Russia and the Eastern bloc countries.[39]

The United States and other globally-oriented economies also have their Internet avante guarde physics representatives. Such U.S. theorists as Hal Puthoff, Jack Sarfatti and Tony Smith and other luminaries gifted with conventional Ph.D.'s regularly venture beyond the canonical norm on private lists and as part of the Yahoo groups postings. A language barrier sometimes separates these English-speaking mental divas from their Asian and Mid-eastern counterparts.

ATLANTEAN SPECULATIONS OUTSIDE TIME

Dr. Jack Sarfatti's work[40] is a noble effort which points in the right direction but is conceptually flawed, in the opinion of your present correspondent, by the concept of "superluminal" or "non local" signal as occurring entirely within electromagnetic

DOING BUSINESS IN THE ADIRONDACKS by E. Macer-Story

context. Such non-sequential transfer of signal cannot occur inside a linked, coherent macrostructure tuned to "speed of light" as the defining, photonic limit. But if inside the atomic nucleus there is an access to a non-electromagnetic matrix of energy which shrinks//expands coherently-linked mass structure, then there are two basic possibilities for superluminal signal transfer:

    A) Signal transduction by means of the atomic shift itself which occurs within a limited four-dimensional area of timespace , and

    B) Signal transduction by means of the additional "fluidice matrix"[41] which is a configurational energy substance touching the atomic, nuclear density to accomplish the insertion of non-local atomic shifts resulting in neural signaling as well as spontaneous alteration of mass structure.

Unexplained green lights seen at the Los Alamos experimental laboratories in the United States after the initial testing there and subsequent use of the atomic bomb at the sites of Nagasaki and Hiroshima, Japan[42] may indicate either some unknown component of matter or an intelligence and/or logos attempting to "warn" or "transmit the idea" that all is not neatly known about the cosmos or atomic structure. Unknown aspects of nuclear structure may involve a non-local memory component which attaches both to the fusion//fission process and to the original mental/emotional circumstances of the use of uranium to design the first atomic bombs.

    In 1991, your present correspondent was shown a fragment of metal which had been found deep within a coal mine in the Ukraine and was asked by retired Col.Kolman Von Kivitsky, now deceased, to psychometrize this item.

    The process of psychometry is an accessing of the spacetime structure of an object by melding the subtle mental energies of the querent with the subtle mental/material mass structure of the object.[43]

    Of course, I was skeptical when Mike Luckman,--a New York City entrepreneur then associated with Col. Von Kivitsky—got in touch with me through a mutual friend, artist George Rauchus, about the artifact. But out of friendship I consented to try psychometry with this Ukrainian metal fragment.

    I was surprised that when I closed my eyes and held the small piece of metal I had the definite inner image of an explosion and that the fragment had once been part of a doorframe in some "Atlantean"[44] circumstance preceding our known pre-historical records. I felt that energies manipulating the inner atomic structure had been used in the original timespace situation of the fragment. In considering this object, I was overwhelmed by an alarming possibility. If technicians had perpetrated such time manipulations in the remote historical past, might the esp querent also have touched a timeline connected to these machinations which actively extends into the modern future as well as the far distant, "Atlantean" past? This is a bit more subtle than the "time travel" play previously offered as educational entertainment.

    Then, might the Thantatos sorcerers also have made a similar connection with "Atlantean" technical ambition plotting for re-entry into the known historical records of this present civilization? Might there be much more on the line here than simply a cult of elitists who can afford renegade tech and medical services?

    Behold the following dialogue between Aexus and Dr. Jack Sarfatti which appeared on the Internet in a list post on May 26, 2002: Recall here, dear reader, that Aexus is the suspected mercenary operative whose reaction to an email alias used by this

DOING BUSINESS IN THE ADIRONDACKS by E. Macer-Story

reporter was accompanied by a viral bombardment of the Yankee Oracle Press web address then featuring photos of actors who might have been the "Shakespearian" critic of the alias identity.. It is typical of Aexus that gratuitous sexual inquiries and images may be introduced into dialog or inquiry, as well as deliberately false or misleading suppositions, as in a detective's interrogation designed to provoke incriminating statements. This individual is either simply mentally disturbed and being monitored by disruptive gurilla adepts or is himself a rogue mercenary operative:

[Aexus]
You harbor considerable ill-disguised resentment of (ex-Army Major Gary) Zukav, a seeming ex-military New Ager who's made megabucks stroking Oprah's "id" and generally humping the Transcendental Cosmic Ego Masturbatory circuit.

[Jack Sarfatti]
Yes, that is also in my book. Gary made it to fame on my back then betrayed me. The facts are there in my book with accounts from several first hand witnesses.
Without me, Gary would have probably been dead by suicide years ago. He had a lot of post-traumatic stress Vietnam syndrome. I stopped him from a suicide threat once when we were room mates. Others did at other times. His former girlfriend at the time is in touch with me today BTW with many corroborating details.

[Aexus]
But we no doubt all would be transfixed by a more detailed description of your New Age spy adventures, especially given your more recent flummoxing of Gorbachev via his World Forum high-dollar street theater presentations, of which you were architect?

[Sarfatti]
Read my book Dude, soon. I will send you a free copy.

[Aexus]
Details please, Dr. S. What was your role? Was it for Office of Naval Intelligence? Was Ed Mitchell directly involved in your aspect, as you've previous asserted was Brendan O'Reagan's (for CIA),

[Sarfatti]
No, I did not say that exactly. Brendan would joke that people thought he was CIA. If he was anything I suspect it was for the Brits not the Americans.
I was on Navy War Ships as a PACE instructor several times, once under condition Zebra near Iran in 1987 - so draw your own conclusions.

[Aexus]
Whose (Brenden O'Reagan's) last position before his untimely death was at Ed Mitchell's (and Willis Harman's) "Institute of Noetic Sciences," which spun out of SRI International after CIA's research contract with that organization (then Stanford Research Inst.) to study "Remote Viewing" and other psi-spy potentialities .(Puthoff, Targ, et al.)?

[Sarfatti]
Yes, so what do you think? ;

DOING BUSINESS IN THE ADIRONDACKS by E. Macer-Story

[Aexus]
In what way did the Esalen-New Age, funded to a degree by Laurance Rockefeller ?

[Sarfatti]
All I know directly from Laurance was he would telephone Jean Lanier at my place on Nob Hill across from Grace Cathedral when Jean was funding us at PCRG via Michael Murphy. There is an article about this in SF Chronicle ~ 1976 re: Nobel Laureate Brian Josephson's stay with me and Jean Lanier for over a weekend his visit to SRI Puthoff & Targ. Do your homework. Investigate! Jean was widow of Chairman of Stone-Webster Construction Corporation and a long time friend of Laurance's. See also http://stardrive.org/chip/[45]

[Aexus]
And reportedly some other big oil money (Pew of Sun Oil, et al.) continue in the"consciousness research" initiated by CIA using LSD in the Sixties, a project which spun Jerry Garcia from being a bluegrass banjo picking Army guy into what Grateful Dead folks continue to mourn, and John Lilly from a Navy-NIH neuro-sci researcher into being Ambassador of the Dolphins to the Center of the Cyclone; and the whole host of "ET" stuff that Mitchell and his Navy intell cadre did after his Apollo flight?Or will all of that, or at least your "spin".

[Sarfatti]
That's your spin not mine. Remember I was an idiot back then, a useful idiot, a Parsifal.
I was not as stupid as Joe Genius is today, but close! ;-)

[Aexus]
And compartmentalized awareness of it, be in your next book also? Given how important your "Space, Time and Beyond" was as a foundation to subsequent "New Age / New Science" best-selling authors like Capra, Zukav and Chopra, can you delineate when, why and how you departed what you term a Cold War undercover operation?

[Sarfatti]
This has to do with an incident at Esalen with George Koopman that Saul-Paul can explain. Basically, I could not dissemble, I could not hide my true feelings of contempt for New Age idiocy and I went on a rant to these New Age Idiots at Esalen on how stupid they were. I was like Sean Connery in ZARDOZ and George Koopman got upset. He was the local intell spook there who was controlling the money. So George had me replaced by Nick Herbert who now defends David Irving. Of course I was high on an illegal drug George provided right before the seminar where I lambasted the fools, so what was really going on is hard to say. Basically, I was in their eyes a "loose cannon" too unpredictable, uncontrollable, would not follow Party Line. Like Patrick Mc Goohan in The Prisoner I was put on ice in North Beach for 20 + years where I got involved with the Hollywood Billionaire at Enrico's and Trieste who made the Sean Connery James Bond movies with Al Brocoli and people very very close to Reagan.

[Aexus]]
Did these other authors "stay in" it? It is apparent that you continue to resent, or otherwise be bothered (ignored?), how the guys you helped to launch went on to public success and acclaim,if dishonestly (as you have repeatedly suggested).

DOING BUSINESS IN THE ADIRONDACKS by E. Macer-Story

[Sarfatti]
Yes, that is correct.

[Aexus]
Capsulize why the "global mind change" was put into play, who paid for it, and how its bigwig patrons envisioned it being a success.

[Sarfatti]
This is your spin not mine. Schwartz[46] knows why. Ask him. Gorbachev played a big role in all this don't forget.

Here during the course of this intense dialogue the focus shifted from a double cross in New Age philosophical politics into a heated exchange about the function of esp/ufo research in world politics as a form or espionage or espionage cover operation. Yet does this typical bounce in anger move too quickly? Is there "another" interest group operating covertly outside standard, known political interests and using occult techniques and sorcery which "work"?

Did analyst George Hansen also move too quickly when in a general way he attributed Carlos Casteneda's works on sorcery to pirated academic research? Perhaps the simple fact is that these previous anthropological monographs were accurate studies and therefore agreed with Casteneda's authentic practice of a certain, specialized form of sorcery.

University of California anthropologist Scott Littleton, who knew the controversial Carlos Casteneda , is convinced that the access to "other dimensional" realities and powerful. Spirit guides was absolutely real for this person in a way which transcends the rivalries of strictly human politics. According to anthropologist Littleton:

"Re Carlos, as you can imagine, he was an extremely complicated guy, despite his naïveté in certain areas. In his later years, he came to conceive of himself as a something of a trickster. Indeed, there was a puckish quality about him that was at once endearing and exasperating. Yes, there are some discrepancies that that asshole Richard De Mille gleefully points out in his highly critical *The Don Juan Papers* (I'm in there, too, as a loopy "new anthropologist"; see below), and there were times when I'm not sure he (Carlos) was fully able to distinguish reality from fantasy, not because of any drug problem (see my previous message), but because he became so enmeshed in the "Way of the Warrior" business that he some times had trouble telling up from down.

"But, at bottom, I'm convinced he was almost certainly *NOT* a fraud. I'm sure that a prototype of "don Juan" really existed (the name, of course, is a pseudonym; "Matus" is apparently the equivalent of "Smith" or "Jones" among the Yaqui) and that Castaneda became his apprentice in much the way he says he did. (Disguising the names of one's informants is part of the ethics of the profession, so you can't fault him here!) Did he actually have all of the experiences he claims to have had, both before and after his mentor's physical death in 1973? Perhaps not, but he was convinced that these experiences were somehow real, if perhaps in some alternate realm that don Juan showed him how to tap into these.

DOING BUSINESS IN THE ADIRONDACKS by E. Macer-Story

"Perhaps the most startling of these experiences was what happened after his initiatory leap, in the company of Pablito & Nestor, from a three-hundred-foot cliff somewhere in central Mexico. His account of this experience in the "Preface" to *The Second Ring Of Power* is perfunctory. His simply mentions that he bounced seventeen times between Nagual (chaos) and Tonal (order, or "cosmos," a la Eliade). But what he didn't put into the book is that he was convinced that the final bounce took him to the corner of Wilshire and Glendon in Westwood, in front of the now defunct Ship's, a coffee shop where a lot of us off-beat UCLA types used to hang out, and only a few block from his apartment. Moreover, given the time difference between Mexico City and L.A., his jump occurred less than a hour before he got "home"! No commercial airliner could have made the trip that fast ! (Yes, someone returned his rented van to the agency in México City, but it's not clear who did so.). But what's even more interesting—if that's possible!—is that the most vivid of his intermediate "bounces" took him to a not-quite-Earth-like planet illuminated by TWO SUNS, one large and relatively dull, the other small and extremely bright! The color of the sky was pink, and there were small, humanoid in evidence, most of whom barely acknowledged his presence. How long he was there was an open question as far he was concerned; it could have been a few seconds, or, subjectively, it could have been a lifetime. Despite my urging, he never published this aspect, as he felt that it was simply too weird even for his fans, and that his skeptical detractors (like Richard de Mille), who were already on his case, would have a field day—which probably would have been the case. However, this and several others of his experiences led me early on to believe that there was a strong UFO element here. Indeed, it's not impossible that "don Juan" himself was an alien in drag, as it were. I raised this question with him several times in the late '80s, and he was open to the possibility. Indeed, I urged him to read some of the serious UFO literature of the era, which I think he did, at least to some extent. (I might add here that it was yours truly, together with Kees Bolle, a now-retired UCLA historian of religion, who also knew Carlos in the 60s & 70s, who urged him to read the Tibetan Book of the Dean and Blavatsky's works. This we all know he did, as they turn up in the later books. But trust me, he was *NOT* familiar with this stuff when he published *The Teachings Of Don Juan* in 1968.

"In any case, I could go on for hours with Castaneda anecdotes, as could any of those who knew him in those days. I published an article on him in the '70s that you might want to look at as you assemble your bibliography. The reference is : *"An Emic Account of Sorcery: Carlos Castaneda and the Rise of a New Anthropology,"* Journal of Latin American Lore 2:145-155 (1976)."

If, as this reporter has observed in documented circumstances,[47] there does exist a variety of creatures which can appear on film as if formed like human beings made of a more subtle energy, are these appearances simply spirits of deceased human beings or is there another species, another life form composed of an organic energy coherent at a slightly different electromagnetic frequency, alive on this planet today? Was this same species of Intelligent life alive also millennia ago, when the "Atlantean" civilization flourished?

Are these beings, in fact, Atlantean in origin? If, as Australian scientists have speculated,[48] the speed of light was slightly different millennia ago and will be similarly different millennia in the future (rendering the signal from distant quasars slightly different in frequency index from the coherent electromagnetic frequencies within the human body) the electrochemical systems of living beings in those eras past and future

DOING BUSINESS IN THE ADIRONDACKS by E. Macer-Story

would by heredity be different from the electrochemical systems of living beings in this era of timespace, if no interbreeding had occurred with other biological humanoid species. The "fairy folk" of the British Isles were in legend said to be of the size of regular human beings but inhabiting a mythic land adjacent to ordinary Earth landscapes.

Taking this legend literally, this effect would be due to the fact that the organic sensory system is for the purpose of relaying environmental information to the intellective identity piloting the organic vehicle. If the environment had once been at a different coherent electromagnetic frequency, the natural sensory system of the inhabitants would also resonate to this frequency. Likewise, certain troll-like intelligences would be bound to and/or control certain definite terrestrial regions which have a slightly different gravitational and/or electromagnetic index.

It may be a flaw in some modern attempts at sorcery that would-be mental operators ignore this necessity to establish and/or utilize a *material anchor* within the usual environment such as the "*troll anchor*" which acknowledges that a certain area is haunted or owned by a nature spirit and/or is a location where the ordinary terrestrial gravitational index is different. A tip of the hat to the troll is quite different from a separation of the environment into "material mansions" and "astral" or "spiritual mansions". For the troll exists in both material and spiritual worlds and is the gatekeeper between worlds within the "devil's croft"[49] or troll territory.

One flaw in the objection by Dr. Jack Sarfatti to the activities at the Esalen Institute during the 1960's and 70's,as previously cited in this book, may be the mental narrative level upon which this debate is continuously conducted. A repeating Round Robin which, as University of Arizona theorist Dr. Stuart Hammeroff has commented on numerous occasions,[50]has continued relatively unchanged for a number of years.

As one participant has commented, the discussion concerns the relationship of "non-physical entities to the physical world." But, except for the work of strangely-fated researcher Dr. Andrija Puharich, there is little "hands on" experimentation which might change or modify the thrust and primary topics of this ongoing discussion

When your present correspondent attempted to interject new material into this repeating intellectual flow of Internet discussion about the theoretical physics of "microtubules" in the brain and nervous system, this innovation was ultimately not able to enter the Round Robin mechanism of the discourse. Yet the terminology and numbering of "microtubules" in the debate is largely hypothetical. In this way, the debate between Sarfatti and Hameroff is like a scholastic debate on the numbering of the Kabbalistic Worlds which is cut off from material effect except at moments of active inspiration when the realization according to number "crosses the abyss" from the numbered body of Adam Kaedmon into the material-mental sphere of some actual person whose experience can be discussed or recorded.

A question occurs here: Is this lapse of gifted minds into strictly mental/theoretical realms which are materially impotent being cynically encouraged by

DOING BUSINESS IN THE ADIRONDACKS by E. Macer-Story

the equally gifted intellects who have been enlisted into the "Thantatos" operation? Since, as this present correspondent has observed ,the adepts of this covert organization seem versed in the material operations and contingencies of sorcery as well and such mental/emotional activities as spirit conjuration and the construction of mathematical and flow chart diagrams, it is entirely possible that the wish to mislead their rivals into the area of theoretical speculation rather than material construction and observation.

Recall, dear reader, the Tim Mathews "black aircraft" article quoted previously in this book. Subsequent to including mention of this article in the text, your present correspondent discovered that reporter Matthews, identifying himself at the time of the "*triangular ufos are really U.S. military aircraft*" article in 1998 by the logo of "Black Dawn Military Research" is a former member of the British National Party and presented a talk on "Nazi UFO" research at a conference sponsored by the BNP in 2002 in the UK. Though Matthews claims no longer to be a member of this neo-Nazi group, the group attempted to charge a large fee for a video copy of Matthews talk to be sent from the UK. After a short but fierce correspondence with the organizer of the conference during which this reporter bargained down the price of the Matthews lecture tape, your present correspondent declined to send any fee for this talk, suspecting a double cross from the same people who originally wished to charge over one thousand US dollars for this media item but then rapidly came down to the sum of one hundred dollars.

Now, I do not gamble except with my cousins on the town riverboat in Evansville, Indiana,USA; but I will bet that the actual "ufo research in Nazi Germany" tape I might have received from the UK would have been worth less than ten US cents in terms of actual material on the tape itself. The important investigative item is the financial game which was played when this reporter attempted simply to get a copy of a talk she could not attend for reasons of geographical distance . If the situation had been straight, the tape would simply have been supplied for an ordinary lecture tape fee.

In August of 2002, a reporter named Nick Cook, formerly on the staff of *Jane's Defence Weekly,* wrote a free lance article for that publication entitled, "The Hunt For Zero Point: Inside the Classified World of Anti-Gravity Technology" which promoted his book of the same name. This article was hotly disputed in Internet correspondence between professional physicists. One of author Cook's claims is that U.S. covert military programs took information on "zero point" energy from Nazi scientists and military records directly subsequent to World War Two.

However, *Jane's Defence Weekly,* the English-language publication which had employed Nick Cook as a staff reporter and had run the advance article promoting his book, has a rather elusive Internet listing of editorial offices said now to be in the UK. Here common sense recalls the Swiss financier Ahmed Huber with neo-Nazi and Al Quaida sympathies and Gunter Richter, the man linked to alleged "ufo plan" documents with an SS logo who claims that his father had participated in building a ufo-like aircraft for the Nazi research center in Pennemunde, Germany and was moved to a secret project in the Hartz mountains of Germany toward the end of World War Two.

DOING BUSINESS IN THE ADIRONDACKS by E. Macer-Story

It is possible that reporter Nick Cook, whose initial information rapidly evaporated from intense Internet discussion subsequent to the public debate on his "zero point" by professional physicists, was given the impetus for his claims by an Al Quaida or New Axis-related disinformation informant who used the term "zero point energy", a term not in use in the 1940's among cutting-edge physicists and not used in context of the alleged SS ufo plan documents passed to this reporter on video in Colorado in 1993. It is doubtful whether Neils Bohr, a prominent Quantum theory physicist during World War Two, would have used the "zero point" ideas at all. Bohr's theories do not postulate a simple electromagnetic universe which would contain the mater/ anti-matter diagrams used to simply illustrate "zero point" energy for the public. Rather, Neil's Bohr, whether or not he was mistaken in his politics and physics formulations, invented and used a system of quantized atomic orbital correspondences which include sophisticated contingencies not accounted for in the "zero point" mythology. Thus, one can conclude that the idea of "zero point" technology passed to U.S. military researchers subsequent to World War Two is false or deluded as an absolute historical fact. Who else wants to tell the public that unexplained "ufo" manifestations are due to technology obtained from refugee German scientists after World War Two? This is also the theme of UK reporter Tim Matthews, who was once a member of the British National Party, and spoke on "Nazi ufos" for a conference organized in England by the BNP in 2002. It should not be surprising that reporter Nick Cook's work on "electrogravetics" quoted earlier in this book is also mentioned in the 1998 Tim Matthews article describing "ufos" sighted over the UK as secret U.S.. aircraft.

Here the theme is basically that anything technically advanced had originally to come from Fascist technicians who were forced to go underground when the Axis was defeated in World War Two. This reminds me of the book *UFO's:Nazi Secret Weapon* by Frederich Mattern which may have occasioned the dramatic arson response at Cresent Press in 1980 in Los Angeles.

Why arson a small publisher whose books are not widely distributed anyway, and in a ritual manner of four directions? Several explanations arise. The most probable is a genuine interest in the details and practice of sorcery by those involved with the book carried in the E. Macer-Story volume *Congratulations: The UFO Reality*. This practice of sorcery would of course be directed toward the infiltration of Allied military and governmental organizations by the Axis-oriented "second generation" of Fascists , as described in the book *UFOs: Nazi Secret Weapon.*

It is far more likely that Axis scientists, following the actual theoretical writings of Bohr, a philosophically-oriented theorist who ultimately renounced Fascist views, became involved with experiments into sorcery, esp and mind control techniques in the same sense that present "Quantum Mind" physicists are interested in these topics. In fact, physicist Nick Herbert, well known for his writings on quantum theory, also purports to "channel" the spirit of Max Weiss, a deceased Nazi military official with anti-Semitic views. Though his colleagues often dismiss physicist Herbert as crazed by drug use, it is possible that he actually is replicating some form or sorcery channeling work similar to work actually done by the Axis ahnenerbe during World War Two. Thus, the very issue of "circular Axis aircraft" may be a red herring. The actual "top secret Axis discovery" during World War Two may lie in the area of the powers of the mind, and such faculties as sorcery by spirit conjuration, hypnosis and telepathy. Recall here the initial discussion in this book of the words of Shiek Gilani and the sad fate of N.Y. Times reporter Daniel Pearl.

This reporter recently gave a lecture for an invited group at the *Jeckyl & Hyde restaurant* function room in Greenwich village. There was a large crowd of people in attendance, dressed in the costumes of the "Goth" underground and sporting artificial vampire canine teeth. At the end of this event, one member of the audience presented this reporter with a bumper sticker, decal and poster for a website entitled "Corporate Goth" but when this fascinated but wary reporter accessed the site there was only a blank web page with that name, an info@corporategoth.com email contact address and one sentence warning interested parties to " *beware the twilight*". OK. Was this warning about the "Twilight of the Gods", the Gotterdamerung of the German legends? Or was this simply another witch trick related to a gathering which "does not exist" if questioned by conservative critics? I think the former explanation is more likely. If the group had been hostile, they could have kidnapped your present correspondent. For I went to lecture the group alone, assuming that sophisticated people playing with concepts of vampirism and power magick were interested in my ideas. I won that gamble or I would not we writing this passage now.

So, what might be one of these sophisticated "vampire game" persons fear? That's simple. Adepts of equal or greater aptitude who are practicing a mentally-advanced from of Axis power magick from whose gatherings and/or surveillance projects persons designated as dangerous to the "cause" or as sacrifice material do NOT return alive or uninjured.

Though *Jane's Defence Weekly* reporter Nick Cook may have been deceived in the particulars, perhaps by disinformation experts aiming to make his report ultimately unbelievable in the larger arena, reporter Cook may be on the right track in beginning to take tales of a "Nazi Secret Weapon" seriously as the source of certain inexplicable aerial manifestations and other instances of evidently non-local signal transfer which can affect both Internet and mental functioning. . But in the area of neo-Nazi activity, there is also the Charles Manson variety of criminal neo-Nazi individual who is tapping a source of diabolic "power" very real to him/herself and assorted followers and who may have linked with Al Quaida and/or other terrorist organizations through the mercenary manipulation of U.S. street gang and prison subculture communication networks. This is also true, of course, in the street gang situation internationally.

On Thursday August 29, 2002, your present correspondent received on the Magick Mirror Communications cell phone voice mail a message about "insurance" and the "Lee Spahn" property. This message was left on a service seldom used for incoming messages and was delivered in a rural Southern accent. At one point, the voice said an appointment was urgent because the inquiring individual was "seldom down here". But the area code of the number left on the service was for Syracuse, N.Y. and not for a

DOING BUSINESS IN THE ADIRONDACKS by E. Macer-Story

Southern location. Therefore, the call was not returned. "Spahn Ranch" was the location of Charles Manson's 1960's sleaze gang and "Lee" is the first name of my ex-husband. I figured I was asking for trouble if I actually returned any call to Syracuse, which is within close driving distance of Woodstock and New York City.

Was this call a co-incidence? This is not likely. Within the last year I have received a number of odd calls on the Magick Mirror line business phone in Manhattan. Usually, these calls will be vocal imitations which cite names and places which might be construed to have emotional impact. For example: a few days after the remains of missing Washington, D.C. Criminal Justice intern Chandra Levy had been found in a D.C. park with jogging attire nearby I received a Sunday morning "Hey, Babe" message on my business voice mail which invited me to go jogging. The vocal imitation was remarkably like the voice of a man I had dated years ago when I was a graduate student at Columbia University . At that time, we used to jog in Riverside Park uptown.

But who would know of this relationship thirty years later? Who would actually know the vocal patterns of this man well enough to imitate them? A number of possibilities occurred to this reporter. For the young man at that time had written a play critical of the Vietnam War effort which was not accepted by the graduate department of playwriting at Columbia University. His landlady at the time was a Cuban refugee who had fled the Castro regime with several crates of valuables and his two roommates were East Indian graduate students. I do not recall the area of study of these East Indian men. Was this "voice" a ghost? Or was this "out of frame" communication a material clue? What obscure causality might link events of thirty years previous to the mysterious death of a graduate student now about the same age as the caller had been thirty years ago?

At first, a speculative scenario about radical political activists of 1968 "Weatherman" vintage hidden in the hills somewhere seemed possible. Crazed, suspended mentally in time, a person resentful at not receiving thesis credit for a play on the Vietnam War might also be resentful for thirty years against a person whose thesis play entitled *The Children's Crusade* was accepted for MFA credit. For the theme of this reporter's thesis play had been the immaturity of the "student radicals" at that time.

Yet how could this vocal imitation be possible? I had also received during the preceding weeks several calls from voices imitating children which seemed to be in the shower or beside running water. I had thought these crank calls humorously referred to an Internet discussion about the water molecule and related topics. So the "Hey Babe" call might be part of that other crank sequence, and not related to Vietnam War or other political issues except by co-incidence. Yet the vocal similarity was provocative.

I web searched the name of my previous companion and found nothing. Likewise, his name was not included in mational 2002 telephone information. Could he be dead? Or could some other ghostly force be trying to pull my reportorial wire on issues related to the death of D.C. Criminal Justice intern Chandra Levy, who disappeared on Walpurgisnacht (April 30) 2001 just four months previous to the September 11 World Trade Center-Pentagon terrorist attacks by Al Quaida operatives.

At the time of Ms. Levy's disappearance, I had sent a post to CNN news, directed to the mailbox of anchor Bill Hemmer, which suggested a link between the disappearance of this intern and Senator Gary Condit's involvement with the motorcycle club "Hell's Angels" in California. According to my research,[51] "neo-Nazis" connected with a motorcycle club in New York City had harassed an attractive blonde woman living in the East Village section of the city, roughing her up and threatening to kill her.. Finally, she had to move to a town upstate, where she lived anonymously in fear they would find her.

I am not suggesting that the Hell's Angels as an organization regularly celebrate the German Walpurgisnacht, similar to Celtic Halloween, when spirits are free to wander through the mountain ranges of Europe. I am suggesting that rogue bikers, members of an occult club which does celebrate Walpurgisnacht and other Axis rituals, were familiar with Chandra Levy through her association with Senator Gary Condit and lured her into a sacrifice gang bang situation. It may be significant in this context that though standard jogging accessories were found with Ms. Levy's skeleton in a D.C. park, the parents and friends of Ms. Levy assert that she did not jog outdoors regularly.

Perhaps we have in this situation a possible link between Al Quaida interests and U,S. street terrorism. For Ms. Levy was working as an intern on the Oklahoma Federal Building bombing and the Tim McVeigh records as well as being an associate of Senator Condit, then on the Senate Intelligence Committee. She may have sensed and commented upon casual material and/or co-incidences which link the McVeigh situation to prompting by foreign operatives. Since the terrorist attack against the WTC-Pentagom locations was then in the final stages of planning, this insight would not have been welcome among street gang connectives wise to the strategy.

One detail of the "Hey Babe" crank call received by this reporter on May 27, 2002 does harmonize with this interpretation. The caller gives his name as "Simon". The author of an occult grimoire entitled the "Necrnomicon" uses the pseudonym "Simon". I met this person on several occasions in the 1980's at the former Magickal Childe bookstore when we were both lecturers in a series of workshops sponsored by the proprietor, Herman Slater. I have not seen him recently. Perhaps the caller was attempting to provoke a reaction which caused me to re-contact "Simon". Or to attribute the call to members of the local witchcraft and sorcery demimonde.

If so, this strategy was not successful. For I had recently learned that another of the Magickal Childe regulars from the 1980's , now using the name Peter Levenda, had published a book on the magickal roots of Nazism[52] and was thus being reviewed and featured on the dark occult ezine *Dagobert's Revenge.* I had commented on my whimsical memory of Levenda, as a young man using an occult pseudonym, in public email list correspondence. But I was also aware that back in his "Magickal Childe" days Mr. Levenda had left New York suddenly to seek his fortune in the Southwest U.S. and had at that time been vending magickal amulets engraved with angel sigils and designed traditionally for various purposes. I had purchased one of these items by mail order, which I still own. So I am aware that the interest in occult topics displayed by Mr. Levenda is genuinely long term and specifically informed .

Recall here, dear reader, the "twilight" warning on the enigmatic 2002 "Corporate Goth" web page, posted with no other overt comment.. I had purchased the amulet from young Levenda years ago because I felt he was in flight from something 'evil" or dark he had encountered on the path in NYC and I wished to be supportive of his relocation. I do not think magickal protection can be purchased as the attachment of thought to an object is subtle and not always congruent with the visible and/or auditory symbols. As the old saying goes: :"*The devil can quote scripture.*" The reverse can also be true. Those seeming to wear the cloak of darkness may actually be concealing their inner light from predatory vandals.

For example, in Europe in the '30s[53]." Nazism had all the features of an apocalyptic religious movement: a zealous leader, an ideology of good and evil, a program of action to expunge the evil elements in order to establish the pure Aryan community, and it had sacred texts. Apart from Hitler's testament, *Mein Kampf,* one of the most influential was the *Protocols of the Elders of Zion*, an anti-Semitic document produced by the Tzarist Police in Russia at the end of the 19th century. Identical in substance to diatribes now being circulated by "Church of Yahweh" in the United States, *Protocols of the Elders of Zion* purports to be an account of how some powerful Jews expected to orchestrate the collapse of the western world. It was discussed in Nazi circles in Berlin and this is an account by a Jewish observer who attended gatherings of Berliners discussing the *Protocols of the Elders of Zion*) in the 1930's. incognito, unrecognized as Semitic by the crowd

"In Berlin, I attended several meetings which were entirely devoted to the Protocols. The speaker was usually a professor, a teacher, an editor, lawyer, or someone of that kind. The audience consisted of members of the educated class: civil servants, tradesmen, former officers, ladies, above all, students, students of all faculties and years of seniority. Passions were whipped up to boiling point.

Sometimes a speech from the floor was permitted. Whoever dared to express a slight doubt was shouted down, often insulted and threatened. If I had been recognized as a Jew, I doubt whether I would have got away without physical injury, but German scholarship allowed belief in the genuineness of the Protocols and the existence of a Jewish world conspiracy to penetrate ever more deeply into the educated sections of the German population. So that now, it is simply ineradicable. Here and there a serious Christian newspaper expressed slight doubts, raised mild and timid objections, but that was all. None of the great German scholars rose to unmask the forgery."

So let us now consider the "Twilight of the Gods" from an immediate and modern viewpoint rather than solely from historical perspective.. Recall now, dear reader, the writings of Church of Yahweh on the topic of "*Operation Vampire Killer*" which attempts to like ancient quasi-Biblical superstitions with modern politics..The author of these diatribes assumes a conspiracy of wealthy Jews who are attempting to control World politics, as did the established Nazi apologists during the mid-twentieth century.

Suppose there was a conspiracy of this sort but that it was not actually a Semitic conspiracy. Suppose this is actually a "syndicate" of some sort using elitist technical and mind-control techniques and employing a variety of individuals of diverse racial and cultural backgrounds. What might unite these individuals? Could strictly mercenary tactics actually hold such a covert syndicate in place?

Here we must diverge to one of the original themes of this book. Recall, dear reader, the power of certain areas in the Catskill Mountains of New York State to bring to the individual exactly what is actually desired and/or needed, in every sense of the

DOING BUSINESS IN THE ADIRONDACKS by E. Macer-Story

word., a materialization boomerang function . Shortly after hastily printing out the above paragraph before rushing to catch a taxi to the 12:30 noon commuter bus in Kingston, N.Y. on Monday September 9, 2002 , I found upon the last vacant seat in that bus a N.Y. Times special section from the day before captioned: *"Unseen: A Special Section On Intelligence"*.[54] In an article entitled *"Learning To Spy With Allies"* , Douglas Franti writes:

"The spy agencies are a throwback to the days when nations fought each other, rather than an amorphous international web of nihilists with no national interests or political program to slow them down."

Though Franti's article refers specifically only to the Al Qaeda terrorist network, this observation provides a necessary transition into the following citation of quotes from individuals identifying themselves in internet exchanges as being some type of black magick syndicate.

"Now I'm no economist, But it seems to me that there is a very different sort of system for dealing with supply and demand in the Mage world. My mage could offer you money for something but if you've got enough Matter magick you could make it yourself. Ditto for gold and gems and other forms of monetary standard in the sleeper world. Syndicate mages are really the only ones who fool with that stuff and only to purchase power...

"Favors: One of the more common forms of barter among mages who know one another only casually. Favor brokering can be very useful when powerful enemies come looking for you and discover that an entire contingent of mages has turned out to protect you, either because they owe you or you owe THEM.

As a game master it also behooves you to put Players in debt to other mages with the old "favor to named later" trick if they want certain things from N.P.C.'s. The formality of the favor trading depends on the people involved. Hermetics and syndicate mages tend to be very formal as do Progenitors and Iterators. Virtuals do favors very easily for one another but are very costly to others. Verbena will do favors but often expect a threefold return on their investment....

Books:What does one do with their copy of Unausprechlichen Kulten when one has read it a few times? To me tend to be a finite resource and when exhausted are useful for barter. A few hermetics and virtuals in my campaigns have taken to collecting hard to find books of the Art and translating them into C.D.rom or optical disk format (complete with a graphics package for pictures and diagrams.) They do a brisk business in books on all kinds of matters and can translate these works into all sorts of different languages.

Some books of course are too dangerous to fall into the wrong hands and thus are not widely available...

Euthanatoi often enjoy a wide panoply of skills that make for great services. They are second only to the Ecstatics when dealing with divinations. They know the Shadow-lands like the Dreamspeakers know

DOING BUSINESS IN THE ADIRONDACKS by E. Macer-Story

the rest of the umbra,and they have extensive knowledge of martial arts,weapons of all types,poisons,and explosives. It is however a good idea NOT to assume that all Euthanatos perform Assasinations for hire. Some like it, some don't care...but some consider it the ultimate form of blasphemy..."

The pseudonym employed by the writer of the above material, which is more lengthy than the significant sections here quoted, is "Reverend X.S. Kinesys." (excess physical energy). The email trace on this posting from 1997 contains the tantalizing element: "mail.nada.kth.se" , a web address in Sweden. Shades of the idea of nihilist terrorists suggested by N.Y. Times reporter Douglas Franti!

However, one item this reporter has learned in tracing these enigmatic communications is that standard logic must be employed only provisionally, as it often leads nowhere. Rather, it is noteworthy that in the midst of a rambling essay of instruction in magickal bartering, making of talismans, assassinations and so on there is sudden and brief citation of a book entitled "*Unausprechlichen Kulten*", a German title.

Upon researching this title, it is discovered that this reference is part of a "game" entitled "Delta Green". Sections from a scenario by one Delta Green game player are given below. If this stuff bores you, simply surf this necessary example for references involving the history of European Fascism as revealed in a dream and thus hop and skip three and one half pages forward where an analysis awaits your contemplation. However, it is recommended that the following example of "role playing" game material be read carefully for "real time" implications.It is reproduced verbatim, without alteration.

Section 1.01   UNAUSPRECHLICHEN KULTEN

Tome:	**Unausprechlichen Kulten** and associated papers - Friedrich Wilhelm von Junst 1839 printing
Language:	German
Mythos:	+15%
SAN:	-1d8/2d8
Spell Mult:	x4
Study Time:	
Spells:	
Condition:	
References:	Encyclopedia Cthulhiana 2nd edition, pg.309, Daniel M. Harms

Section 1.02   HISTORY LESSON

Date: Tue, 15 Dec 1998 18:54:45 +0100
From: anon
Subject: EH - Italian Chapter - A Bit of History

DOING BUSINESS IN THE ADIRONDACKS by E. Macer-Story

Hi!

I've been instructed to send the stuff I dream up to you directly, and here I go.

For starters, I have some general Historical background to the events that will be the subject of the scenario proper.
I'm also outlining the contenders in this match, but I'll post them in a separate message.

So, from the beginning (sort of):

The Unaussprechliken Kulten has been wrapped in an old army jacket this last 50 years.

April 27 1945, Musso (northern Italy)
A group of Italian partisans stops and inspects a German convoy en route to the Swiss border. One of the "German soldiers" dozing in the back of one of the trucks attracts the men's attention as he is carrying a suitcase. Positively identified as Benito Mussolini, fugitive former Head of the Fascist State, the man is arrested and, the following day, in nearby hamlet of Dingo, summarily executed on orders from the CLN (National Liberation Committee), together with his lover Clara Peace.
This act, later variously disavowed by political factions, causes Italy to lose the occasion to openly and democratically process the man for war crimes.

A dark shadow is cast on the newborn Italian democracy.

The first of many.

Apart from some idle talk about "The Gold of Dingo", nothing is known about the fateful suitcase and its contents, that are never seen again.

Until now.

Section 1.03   Unaussprechliken Kulten : Some Historical Background on the Gatto-Borghi Copy.

1839   Mulder German edition of the Von Junst classic printed.

1843   French Sansrire translation Published in St.Malo

Summer Cardinal Livio Gatto-Borghi - in France for "personal affairs" -acquires the
1848   German copy on which the Abbe Sansrire based his translation, together with
        the man's notes and support texts, with the intention of adding it to his collection
        of esotherical works. The Sansrire papers will be later erroneously reported lost.
        While (hopefully unrelated) chaos erupts in Europe, Gatto-Borghi decides

DOING BUSINESS IN THE ADIRONDACKS by E. Macer-Story

nonetheless to get back to Italy, and take the book and the papers to Rome but, after an unprecised "incident" while crossing the Alps, he detours toward the town of Pavia, where he deposits the book in the vault of his family's private summer residence.

1848 - 1938	The Gatto-Borghi Book is an unconfirmed rumour among occultists, none of which has a detailed knowledge of its whereabouts nor of the wealth of support material it includes. The Von Junst is sometimes imprecisely referred to as "The Gatto-Borghi Manuscript".
June 1939	soon after the "Steel Pact", German "operatives" start sniffing around on the trail of the book, focusing primarily on Rome. The Gatto-Borghi villa in Rome is sacked without results; the German Consul in Rome tries to convince Pope Pius XII that handing over the Gatto-Borghi papers and diaries, now part of the Vatican Collections could be a relevant step in the fight against Bolshevism - some of the pontifex special advisors are dead against it, and the talks come to nothing. OVRA (the Fascist Secret Service) keeps an eye on the "allies" activities, and later (winter '39-'40) hands the file over to La Cricca" (lit. "The Clique") an independent mixed unit that already handled esoteric emergencies on behalf of the Regime in the previous decade.
June 1940	Italy declares war on France. La Cricca beats the German agents to the Gatto-Borghi Book, and adds it to its library of occult tomes in the Turin base. When German diplomatic pressure about the whole matter becomes suspect, OVRA steps in and asks to be handed the book. La Cricca is disbanded, its army members sent to the front, the civilians exiled.
Autumn 1943	Mussolini - under arrest in the Gran Sasso area - uses the Gatto-Borghi Book to force the German Ally to act on his behalf. Otto Skorzeny is sent with a team to rescue the man - despite the fact that by now Mussolini is politically dead. Mussolini is brought to Berlin, and then back to Italy.
April 1945	after the crash of the Gothic Line, Mussolini tries to join the German fugitives. The Gatto-Borghi book, wrapped in an old army jacket in his suitcase, is going to buy him a ticket to Argentina...

On the trail of the book in the chilly april of 1945 are

- Count Ottolengo Starnazza di Vicolungo
  occultist and former member of La Cricca, acting "for the sake of humanity" and meaning to dump the book in a dark, secure place as far away as possible.
- Don Alfonso "Fofo" Caribiddi
  Sicilian landowner and a friend of friends, acting on orders from the Nicosia-Maranzano clan and their American contacts.
- Captain Emil Kricheldorff
  a man "just executing orders from his Furher".

DOING BUSINESS IN THE ADIRONDACKS by E. Macer-Story

- Father Jean-Paul Theiller
  Jesuit priest and St.Jerome operative, seeking the book for the Vatican Library Z
  collection

And the winner is...
Alberto Fagotti [who?!] - paper-chase outsider, opportunist, part-time partisan and free
enterprise upholder, that set his eyes on the suitcase no matter what it could contain - it
would be sellable anyway. He gets it soon after the execution - thanks to the
disorganization of the irregular unit - and dumps it in the woods for later.

Only in 1949, Fagotti - now mayor in a small town near Como, goes back to the suitcase
burial ground, digs it up and finally opens it

The suitcase contains:

- various personal effects of purely emotional value (photos, letters)
- gold and jewelry for about 200.000 lire
- some spare clothes
- some food (bread, cheese) that's long gone for the worst
- a lot of old papers wrapped in a dirty old army jacket.

So much for the fabled "Mussolini's treasure"
[the numbers and details of his five separate Geneva bank accounts were actually sewn
inside the jacket the Duce was wearing when captured, and have long been redirected to
another seat altogether - but more on this later]

Fagotti cashes in the jewelry - having disassembled it so that no connection can be made -
and burns the clothes. The rest he places in his attic, awaiting the right moment for selling
it as collector's items.

Senator Alberto Fagotti (respected member of the Socialist Party) dies peacefully in his
Rome house in April 1969 - mourned by many, missed by few

The Mussolini letters and photos surface discreetly in the mid 80s, courtesy of the
enterprising Eleonora Sabatini, social climber and fiance of Fagotti's second son, socialite
Luigi.
The Hitler Diaries scandal causes the bidders - national magazines Panorama and
L'Espresso among them - to withdraw.

In 1990 pretty Eleonora dumps Luigi and leaves, taking the letters, the photos and the
books with her as a parting gift. A few weeks later, she shacks up with a noted fashion
designer, the first of a string of opportunely placed "friends".

In autumn 1993, the OVRA archives are declassified, and they are opened to foreign

DOING BUSINESS IN THE ADIRONDACKS by E. Macer-Story

nationals in 1995.

The Gatto-Borghi Book is once again out of the sack.

And this is it for the time being.
The resurfacing of the book should set in motion the three main factions in the Italian game: DG, Karotekia (through the "Propaganda" entity and its minions), Vatican (through a St. Jerome recon unit).
These three players are already well rounded.
I hope to put together the Bischofe by tomorrow morning - as soon as I have something definitive I will send it along.
Other players are possible but I'll leave that open.

More news as soon as possible.
Let me know what you think of all the thing.
Cheers!

Davide M. Anon.

What fun!!!! A game!!! Yet when accessing the "Delta Green" site, the brief cover description is:

"Deception is a right. Truth is a privilege, Innocence is a luxury. Born of the Federal Governments 1928 raid on the coastal town of Innsmouth, Massachusetts, the covert agency known as Delta Green spent four decades opposing the forces of darkness with honor but without glory. Stripped of sanction after a disastrous 1969 operation in Cambodia, Delta Green's leaders made a secret pact to continue their work without authority, without support, and without fear.Delta Green agents slip through the system, manipulating the federal bureaucracy while pushing the darkness back for another day—but often at a shattering personal cost."

Yet, does this role-playing game cleverly mask the intent, as cited in the book *"UFO: Nazi Secret Weapon"* by Frederich Mattern, of covert post World War Two Axis operatives to infiltrate Allied governmental institutions? The whereabouts of certain elite SS scientists were secret even from their closest relatives, as alleged in the Iciris "Nazi UFO" video described earlier in this book. The 1969 action in Cambodia referred to in the Delta Green introduction may have been the busting of the "Golden Triangle" opium trade by U.S. Green Beret forces.

This game playing strategy appears to refer to the U.S. Special Forces Operative Bo Gritz and his undercover drug investigation in the "Golden Triangle" area of Burma which in 1986 resulted in the information that "high level U.S. Executive Branch officials involved in illegal drug trafficking"[56] were implicated in the Asian black market situation. According to his Internet-posted biography, Colonel Gritz served as a Green Beret commander in Southeast Asia from 1964-69,and was the Intelligence Officer and Reconnaissance Chief for Delta Force, commanding the first guerrilla forces which expanded into a Mobile Strike Command of 3,000 mercenary and free-world special operations forces.

Here in the "Delta Green" game situation we have clever rogue disinformation which muddles the actual undercover Intelligence operation with narrations of free lance, "fictional" covert activity directed toward "*slipping through the system, manipulating the federal bureaucracy*" to oppose "*powers of darkness*" . Recall in this context the Arthur Conan Doyle story "*Sign of Four*" which became the feature film "*Crucifer of Blood*" as processed through mid-twentieth century popular media mechanisms.

It seems possible that the original title of the Conan Doyle story may refer to some actual occult symbol used in the opium trade. For this reason, pressure may have been subtly brought upon establishment publishers to change the name and/or omit that particular tale from Sherlock Holmes anthologies. Arthur Conan Doyle, as well as being a medical doctor, was a spiritualist with extensive experience in actual aspects of occult practice. Actually, the word "four" in Chinese (Ssu) sounds similar to the Chinese word for "death". It is thought to be bad luck to say the word "four" at Chinese New Year. Here, in the possibility that Conan-Doyle may have known the pun between "four" and "death" when titling his "*Sign of Four*" tale, we have another parallel with U.S. Colonel (James) Bo Gritz who, in his role as military Intelligence officer in Asia, became fluent in the Chinese language and well-versed in the traditional Oriental martial arts practice as well as hypnotherapy.

In fact, Gritz describes himself as an "eternal warrior" in the religious, martial arts sense of the word. Is it possible that the "Thantatos" Organization of black magick adepts is attempting to block public knowledge of the Bo Gritz Asian black market investigations in the Burma "Golden Triangle" area in the same subtle way this network managed to block the "tip off" story about East Indian sorcery and opium by Dr. Arthur Conan Doyle a century ago? Gritz, though he has served law enforcement in mediation capacity during armed standoffs with far right extremists, is often portrayed by the media as a member of the lunatic fringe, or not portrayed at all.

If so, how do we go about untangling this present obfuscation ? For, if Colonel Bo Gritz is correct, the Axis sorcerers have co-opted key executive, media and publishing channels internationally. Blockage of relevant information on the expansion of the ancient "Silk Route" into an international "Silken Web" of rogue intelligentsia might typically occur subtly, along the route of intelligence which leads to the CEO of whatever organization is convenient to the covert network of mercenary sorcerers. True rogue wisdom in this situation might lie in changing the "root web" of a corporate entity rather than in simply "changing the opinion" of the most visible executive or critic. Certain news items simply never reach the public.

For example, were you aware, dear reader, that there exists in the United States a "*United Fascist Union*" based in Wilmington, Delaware? In the U.S., the state of Delaware is a hub of corporate licensing and legal activity because the laws of that state are designed to facilitate corporate transactions. Recall here the fellow with the

DOING BUSINESS IN THE ADIRONDACKS by E. Macer-Story

"corporate Goth" bumper stickers who seemed uneasy about "twilight" activities. (page 152).

In the Manifesto of the *"United Fascist Union"* it is stated that the U.F.U. *" has to be the gray area in the political arena. ...The U.F.U's functions are to create an authoritarian, centralized government that will have unilateral control over all of the political instruments of a united earth".*[57] Crackpot stuff, eh? Do not make this judgment so quickly. The Manifesto, which was sent to this reporter unsolicited and with a proper cover letter, advocates the use of "logic" by an elite who will ensure the coming of a "new age" of freedom of speech and racial equality. Of course, the document itself, which uses some standard occult lingo in places, is quite Fascist in the sense of freedoms "managed" by an elite. Who typically manages affairs "for" people? Corporate organizations and their representatives. The U.F.U. Manifesto states that in the coming new age *"mere mortals will be transformed into gods"* as people become more psychic in orientation.

That's exactly what "Barbara the Grey Witch" states on her record album about a variety of witchcraft practices.[58] But in a certain type of witchcraft practice the Initiates are called *"Immortals"* and those unaware of their enhanced level of activity are termed merely *"Mortals"*. So we may have on hand here in the State of Delaware less of a *"United Fascist Union"* than a *"United Faustian Union"*. Recall, dear reader, that in the year 2000 there was an attempt by self-identified "stockbrokers" to buy information on the "Barbara the Grey Witch" record album and actually whatever else these folks could dig up on the occult activities of your present correspondent from Crystal Field, CEO of Theater For The New City in New York.

In a recent book about Yale University's "secret Skull & Bones Society", journalist Alexandra Robbins writes:

"THE LEGEND OF SKULL AND BONES

Sometime in the early 1830s, a Yale student named William H. Russell—the future valedictorian of the class of 1833- traveled to Germany to study for a year. Russell came from an inordinately wealthy family that ran one of America's most despicable business organizations of the nineteenth century: Russell and Company, an opium empire. Russell would later become a member of the Connecticut state legislature, a general in the Connecticut National Guard, and the founder of the Collegiate and Commercial Institute in New Haven. While in Germany, Russell befriended the leader of an insidious German secret society that hailed the death's head as its logo. Russell soon became caught up in this group, itself a sinister outgrowth of the notorious eighteenth-century society the Illuminati. When Russell returned to the United States, he found an atmosphere so Anti-Masonic that even his beloved Phi Beta Kappa, the honor society, had been unceremoniously stripped of its secrecy. Incensed, Russell rounded up a group of the most promising students in his class-including Alphorns Taft, the future secretary of war, attorney general, minister to Austria, ambassador to Russia, and father of future president William Howard Taft-and out of vengeance constructed the most powerful secret society the United States has ever known."

According to publicity blurbs, Ms. Robbins is herself supposed to be a member of one of Yale's "other" secret societies and got all her gruesome information about Skull & Bones from an undisclosed informant. There are several conspicuous problems with this situation although the book might make interesting reading for a person interested in

DOING BUSINESS IN THE ADIRONDACKS by E. Macer-Story

Gothic literature. First off, if "Skull & Bones" is actually a secret society, why does everyone know about it? Secondly, how do we know that Ms. Robbins' undisclosed informant is telling the truth or even if she does have an undisclosed informant other than the "Bones Whore" mentioned in the book's publicity . After all, Alexandra Robbins claims to be a member of yet another "secret society" at Yale.

Years ago, when your present correspondent departed from Yale School of Drama, where she was enrolled as a candidate for the MFA in playwriting in 1966, and went to New York City to seek her fortune, ending up as a Schubert Fellow at Columbia University, where she did receive an Ivy League MFA in 1968 after all, incredulous bystanders often asked: "Why on earth did you leave Yale?" Well, the fact is that though no one came forward and announced that "secret societies" were on campus I did have a weird feeling about several graduate school events I attended there.

At one reading of the poetry of William Blake, I sensed birdlike "presences" in the lecture hall and became extremely uneasy. This was six years prior to my becoming aware of any enhanced clairvoyant sensitivity in myself. I speculate now that someone in the audience or actually presenting the reading had a greater knowledge of "spirit channeling" than I did at that time and had made a deliberate link with certain of the spirit entities, personae and/or idea forms which poet William Blake (1757-1827) perceived and memorialized in his poetry.

Is Yale benefactor William H. Russell's fascination with an "insidious German secret society" using opium in the early Nineteenth century, as alleged by Alexandra Robbins, the same perhaps as the colonial opium gang involving British aristocrats fictionally represented by Sir Arthur Conan Doyle in his original Sherlock Holmes story *"The Sign of Four"*? Could it be this same group which arranged to fool Conan Doyle in some of his spiritualist pursuits, and also to change the name and thus the impact of his opium den tale to *"Crucifer of Blood"*? For the Nazi swastika is a four-armed sigil and the hierarchy of the German third Reich did use opium and heroin, as well as experimenting with varieties of sorcery which employ these consciousness-altering substances.

In a quote from her book *"Secrets of the Tomb"* released as publicity, Alexandra Robbins does specifically make the claim that the "Skull & Bones" society attempts to control the communications media:

"Fast-forward 170 years. Skull and Bones has curled its tentacles into every corner of American society. This tiny club has set up networks that have thrust three members into the most powerful political position in the world. And the group's influence is only increasing-the 2004 presidential election might showcase the first time each ticket has been led by a Bonesman. The secret society is now, as one historian admonishes, " 'an international mafia'. . . unregulated and all but unknown." In its quest to create a New World Order that restricts individual freedoms and places ultimate power solely in the hands of a small cult of wealthy, prominent families, Skull and Bones has already succeeded in infiltrating nearly every major research, policy, financial, media, and government institution in the country. Skull and Bones, in fact, has been running the United States for years."

Not so fast. One does not "run the United States" by scaring the pants off college sophomores. These allegations appear to be a red herring masking what may be

DOING BUSINESS IN THE ADIRONDACKS by E. Macer-Story

actual, international conspiracy to control the mass media and perhaps lines of communication within U.S. intelligence agencies by use of the mirror-image accusation technique. This strategy is thousands of years old. *"It must be understood that deceptive actions are significant in war."*[59] Strategy 6 of the classic Zen text *The 36 Strategies* [60] whose actual author is lost in antiquity is simply:

"Feint East, Strike west: You spread misleading information about your intentions, or make false suggestions, in order to induce the opponent to concentrate his defenses on one front and thereby leave another front vulnerable to attack."

It is significant that the book *"Secrets of the Tomb"* by Alexandra Robbins came to the attention of your present correspondent on an Internet list post from a "UFO Disclosure Group" demanding that the United States disclose secret information about flying saucers. Dr. Carol Rosin, a former assistant to rocket expert Dr. Werner Von Braun, is a prime organizer of this group. Of course, Dr. Von Braun assisted in developing the Nazi V-2 rocket technology during World War Two and was brought to the United States after the war to assist in developing the United States guided missile program during the cold war with the USSR in the 1950's. This rapid but expedient transformation of Dr. Von Braun from a Nazi rocket scientist to a U.S. rocket scientist is worth noting in the context of reporter Nick Cook's allegations in his 2002 book *"Hunt For Zero Point"* that Axis scientists had designed "electrogravetics" devices which were secretly assimilated by U.S. black ops projects.

Alexandra Robbins also alleges a Nazi and neo-Nazi connection within the "Skull & Bones Society" at Yale University. Can the World War Two Nazi's have done so much "secretly" which is now well-known in the U.S. and UK, and yet actually have been strategically ineffective? What's happening here?

Recall now, dear reader, the strategy of infiltration of Allied institutions described by Frederich Mattern in his book *"UFO: Nazi Secret Weapon"* and the peculiar resonance between the "Delta Green" role-playing game and the actual activities of U.S. Special Operative Bo Gritz in the "Golden Triangle" area of Burma during the mid-1980's. Instead of a "ufo-based" strategy of infiltration, could this actually be a narcotics-based strategy partly derivative of the already-existing colonial drug trade cited by Conan Doyle in his short story, originally titled *"The Sign of Four"*?

By now, the actual identity, military role and accomplishments of Colonel Gritz have been significantly obscured by a variety of assertions about the "Golden Triangle" investigation of drug smuggling. As one correspondent on this issue posted on the Internet:

"You don't know the Gritz story... In Burma there was only opium. Bo did not bust anyone in the 60's, but stumbled into the U.S. involvement in the drug trade when he was informed wrongly that General Kuhn Sa of Burma had MIA's in the Eighties. Bo, financed by Ross Perot took 3 of his ex- Green Berets friends on a private mission to Burma to see if in fact Kuhn Sa had MIA's To Bo's disappointment he found no MIA's but was told of Kuhn's drug dealings with Ted Shackley, Richard Armitrage and others. This is all documented on film.

Kuhn Sa gave Bo a message to take back to the U.S. Govt. asking for financial assistance for crop substitution.. Bo in his naiveté when to the NSA and told them of the good news in eradicating the drug trade... As, Bo excitedly told an NSA official, the response was... Bo, "There is

DOING BUSINESS IN THE ADIRONDACKS by E. Macer-Story

no interest here" Further, this was all way after the end of the Vietnam war, probably around 1985. You completely are off target as the U.S. govt. railroaded Bo for exposing its role in the drug trade. He was not awarded any medals for being a Narc.. He was actually indicted for traveling on a false passport(issued and approved by Military intelligence,."NSA, CIA, etc.) imprisoned and faced 5 years in jail. Scott Weekly his co-hort was sentenced to 5 years in prison... What you are missing here is that the U.S. Govt. got "hooked" on the drug trade to finance the secret war in Laos and Cambodia because Congress would not approve funding. The Yanks learned from the Brits about using Drugs for mind control and financing wars. "

There is only one problem with this narration. The author of these words is the same "Thantatos Org" pawn recorded for posterity on a tape he left behind in frenzy after this reporter refused to accept "marked money" as a donation during his visit to the Magick Mirror office in the Spring of 2002 when he was asking for advice on "theatrical" projects in Germany and elsewhere which did not exist as stated. During this same email correspondence the "Thantatos"-linked individual also claimed to have planned to produce a film about Bo Gritz which never happened. It is thus quite probable that the U.S. government was never "hooked" on opium in Southeast Asia. Possibly Gritz was a bit green in the area of espionage intrigue and simply had met an undercover agent who had infiltrated the Cambodian drug trade in order to provide information covertly to U.S. authorities.

But the idea of "Yanks learning from Brits" about the drug trade is congruent with the tale told about opium trade by Sir Arthur Conan Doyle in *The Crucifer of Blood* and somewhat like the tale in *Secrets of the Tomb* of Ivy League graduate students picking up opium in Germany from a secret society in 1833 and then plotting to control World politics. In both of these tales, the colonial operatives learn opium from established, foreign sources.

Is the "Thantatos" organization of sorcerers detected and described earlier in this book the same as these exotic drug conspiracies cited in contemporary urban folk tales? Notice that the bearers of these various tales are not drug-addicted and do not overtly claim to have exact knowledge of the inner workings of the conspiracies they cite.

The spinners of yarns also claim that the operatives of some "black world" intelligence agency have infiltrated the media and control news and public entertainment broadcasts to the extent that no actual information about potential "media control" ever reaches the public in a convincing way.

The image of covert "media control" as previously cited may be the exact red herring which the Thantatos organization wishes to keep in place. The actual, adept media control may come by more subtle infiltration. In April of 2002, an activist in the area of Afro-American studies wrote the following comments after massive interference with his computer system, then using the Earthlink server:

"Your suggestions that I discuss mobile van "Nazi" technology with the Earthlink Technical Support Team, or its Supervisory Command Group, is pushing a point considerably. Additionally, the man on the phone with me already expressed his agreement, and that of his superior, that there may in fact be terrorist activity by Earthlink-employed infiltrators. Notably—it has been my experience that this kind of thing can confront people like us on levels that appear to be ideological",

DOING BUSINESS IN THE ADIRONDACKS by E. Macer-Story

This individual, whom I will call "the Black Kabbalist" certainly has direct experience in the magical action of ideology. For it was about 48 hours after he attempted to duplicate a web search on a U.S. government employee, a second generation German-American who had bragged of his Nazi heritage, that the onslaught of computer interference began to occur.

Your present correspondent had asked "the Black Kabbalist" to perform this search from his computer as she had noticed an effect to the search engine shortly after searching the name of this individual for the first time on the Internet from old printed files. The first search yielded a mix of U.S. government and neo-Nazi links, both types including the name of this individual. In the second search, a day later, the neo-Nazi material was not present, as if some auto-detect function had reported the origin of the search request. This was frustrating as your humble correspondent intended to print the mixed results as evidence. "The Black Kabbalist" was able to print a less mixed version of the original search from his computer, and sent it by postal mail. Note that even from a different address on a different server the search results then did not show as radical a neo-Nazi mix. Shortly after printing this information, his computer was sabotaged from the server by a "virus" and became inoperable.

It is worth noting in this context that during the Bo Gritz email correspondences cited previously there was a mild sort of cyber interference which blended some of my short messages with the CC list in a hologramatic way so that it was not possible to copy the text without also copying a link to the entire list of email addresses.

"The Black Kabbalist" claims this interference is not Al Quaida or terrorist-linked but is CIA monitoring of persons such as Afro-Judaic activists who might have radical associations. However, why would the CIA fall upon and rend someone's computer software whilst monitoring activities? One needs the software in order to make the surveillance connection. Likewise, why would CIA turn the CC list into a hologramatic tracer pattern when a known CIA employee, Ron Pandolfi, is on this and other lists generated by the same clique?

One of the strangely interesting aspects of the follow up web searches on the elusive identity of the German-American with the dual U.S. gov't employee/ neo-Nazi identity profile was that the name by which I had met this individual, when he bragged of his father's role as one of Hitler's elite sharpshooters, was also listed as the name of a character in a James Bond film. What's happening? Are the neo-Fascists stacking the media cast lists?

Or are the "powers that be" active here to signal attention toward the possibility of impersonations and chicanery involving the media? The classic Chinese text "*The Art of War*" by Sun Tzu admonishes the combatant to make no absolutely specific plans since the actions of the gods and fate are continually altering the territory . Here the territory has been altered considerably by discovering that the sought after name is also listed as the name of a character in a spy film.

This is like the "Delta Green" role-playing game in the "Golden Triangle"/ Green Beret controversy. One suspects that behind the surface of the search engine index listings there is a tangled morass of connectives which lead nowhere in specific, except to similar ATM cash machines. Patronizing those rogue accounts may be the RV and Van computer experts which "the Black Kabbalist" was too ginger to mention directly to Earthlink server customer service.

DOING BUSINESS IN THE ADIRONDACKS by E. Macer-Story

Yet this intelligent, mobile subculture exists and some cabal is financing their vehicles and equipment. The FBI investigated one particular segment of this role-playing population during the 1980's and several articles [61] on the mobile, computer-equipped vans of the KKK and similar neo-Nazi groups were published in the New York Times and other major newspapers . Of course, not all the mobile cyber-equipped buccaneers are actually enrolled KKK and/or National Socialist members.

In an article by Jean-Pierre Cloutier which appeared in *The Haitian Files* newspaper in 1987, pay to mobile mercenaries is described directly:

"On Monday, August 3, reports from Jeremie indicated a group of armed men led by Bernard Sansaricq had encountered the Armed Forces in a gunfight. Rumours of the group offering $1,000 to anyone who joined their cause in overthrowing the government prompted a justice of the peace into probing into the matter. Accompanied by an escort from the police, he tried to search the hotel where the Sansaricq group was staying, but was met with gunfire and grenades according to a government statement. Representatives from the authorities fled the scene, leaving behind a vehicle which was used by Sansaricq to leave the city. On its way out, the group would have set fire to one of the military posts of the city. Sansaricq, leader of the Parti Populaire National Haitien-PPNH (National People's Party of Haiti), is a long time opponent of the Duvalierist regime."

By an interesting co-incidence of names, the CEO of America West publications is named Dr. Pierre Cloutier. Recall here, dear reader, the odd co-incidence of discovering that fictional "James Bond" characters had been drawn into real life situations of possible espionage, and that a U.S. government employee with neo-Nazi background not only came up with a duplicate "James Bond" film identity in a web search but that a printout of these search results led directly to the tangle of the "Black Kabbalist's" account of disruption on Earthlink server.

As previously described in the section on 'Delta Green" media game playing Bo Gritz worked on special assignment within the narcotics scene in the "Golden Triangle" of S.E. Asia for U.S. Intelligence agencies. This trade included opium, cocaine and heroin. This was my only knowledge of his identity when I saw his name in the 1991 *America West* newspaper--which had been sent to me from their regional office, then located in Plattsburgh, N.Y. along with a tape recording of a female spirit medium channeling "Commander Hataan". The content of both the newspaper and the channeling was anti-Semitic, anti-U.N. and hinted at a mysterious mideast connection between "Commander Hataan" and ancient Roman Legions which were going to save the United States by the use of ancient Egyptian military and religious practices connected with the deity Aton My immediate response was to assume that consciousness was being altered in some unusual fashion by the editors of these publications, and I wondered if Gritz was a narc in the situation. I then wrote a play entitled *Commander Galacticon* about a group of anarchist revolutionaries masquerading as streetfront Santoria witches who encounter the actual supernatural in the form of a mysterious green fog which ends their operations by exterminating them. I will spare the reader any direct dialogue quotation from this play but the playscript remains available for future production.

DOING BUSINESS IN THE ADIRONDACKS by E. Macer-Story

In the Fall of 1996, while visiting Oklahoma City. , your present correspondent was presented with several books which mix spirit channeling with revolutionary politics. One of these books, entitled *"The Garden of Aton"* was financed by Dr. Pierre Cloutier of *America West* publications , the same publisher as the newsletter sent from Plattsburgh, N.Y. in 1991. In the "Phoenix Journals Bonus Selection" offer of new books and reprints at the back of this volume are the topics: "High Freemasonry-New York Trade Center", and "Wacko Waco, a Who's Who of American business and politics" along with other references to war and police state topics. One major problem in this assemblage is that whereas the Branch-Davidian siege at Waco had occurred previous to the book's publication in 1993, neither of the WTC disasters had yet happened.

In a taped lecture which was given to me with these books, and which occurred in 1996, a speaker mentions "money from the mideast" being provided to fund the "Commander Hatonn" sessions. All this is quite vague and associative. The book at one point re-prints abolitionist documents from the mid 19th Century and at another point discusses the "white race" as falsely claiming Aryan identity during World War Two in Nazi, Germany. The *"Garden of Aton"* seems to assert that the actual Aryans were of Indo-European, Egyptian and Arabic origin but this is hard to parse as the narration is confused, perhaps deliberately contradictory. At one point the word "Nasi" is used ti identity an Ashkanazi "Prince" in Semitic antiquity and it is soberly explained that the word "Nazi" (National Socialism in Germany) and the word "Nasi"(ancient Hebrew prince) are by co-incidence similar.

Recall, dear reader, the other droll co-incidences of names of actual operatives with "James Bond" characters turned up in research and web search whilst tracing rogue operatives. It does seem that "Commander Hataan" may be a Luciferian intellect channeling through these publications. Perhaps this evaluation of the Commander Hataan literature brings this commentary back around to consideration of the supernatural and esp/pk perceptions as recommended by Islamic Fundamentalist Shiek Gilani in his admonition that severe action by negative forces employing the djinn and superconscious mental capacities should alert the individual to more positive action using these same Intelligences and capacities. It should be mentioned in this context also that the "black kabbalist" who performed the web search on a suspicious name which resulted somehow in the demolition of his computer system is also a spirit medium, intellectually interested in the Kabbalah and related systems of mysticism. His pseudonym in this book is practical rather than evaluative since his genetic identity is actually mixed Hebrew and Afro-American and he does assert that certain nominally Afro-American organizations in the United States with international connections are actually rogue cover operations, and not actually humanitarian as they claim..

Another person of mixed genetic identity who has written a significant memoir on the neo-Nazi use of occult systems in contemporary context is Andre VandenBroeck, a person of Hebrew and Dutch ancestry. Initially, his Jewish heritage was not perceived by R.A. Schwaller de Lubicz, a practitioner of *"Al-Kemi"* , who shared with young VandenBroeck a variety of occult theories related to the link between molecular chemistry and architecture. Certain of these theories of Gnostic practice, as repugnant as

DOING BUSINESS IN THE ADIRONDACKS by E. Macer-Story

their elitism is to civilized consideration, may be valid as "mind control" techniques. Therefore, the possibility of neo-Fascist action according to these theories must be seriously considered.

"*Al Kemi*", according to the system of de Lubicz, means "Black Land", the Nile valley, and signifies Pharaonic Egypt. "Les Veilleurs", the group of elite sorcerers founded in 1919 in France and Germany, are those focused solely on the aptitude of the individual in gnosis, mathematics and the abstract rather than the mundane, concrete aspects of reality. Under his original name of Rene Schwaller, the occultist "de Lubicz" known primarily for his "Temple Of Man" books about mathematical coding in the architecture of Egypt, originally wrote racist and elitist tracts for "Les Veilleurs".

The Nazi warlord Rudolf Hess was a member of this original "Thule Society", according to VandenBroeck, and this was the first Germanic group of any significance to sport the swastika emblem in direct modern context. Here we consider a group of wealthy individuals and/or those under such patronage, with the means to act out abstract fantasies, implemented by mercenary employees. R.A. Schwaller de Lubicz lived in Switzerland after World War Two, where he died in 1960.. Photos of terrorist warlord Osima Bin Laden as a schoolboy in Switserland have been posted prominently in biographical data on the Internet. As a youth, Bin Laden dressed in European clothes and was familiar with persons of diverse backgrounds in the jet set circulating between the Mideast, Switzerland and the UK, as well as France and Germany.

The identity of this individual, therefore, is not wholly formed by the Fundimentalist Muslim beliefs he nominally espouses. Jet set social circumstances have influenced in the organization of Al Quaida the situation of elitist mental development as advocated by the power oriented neo-Axis magicians actively implemented in skill-oriented strategic planning via the modern communications mythology of cellular telephone transmission and the Internet as religious and mystical tools..

Recall here the Swiss resident Ahmed Huber , interviewed on CNN cable television in 2001, who is engaged in offshore banking and has in his office photos of both Adolf Hitler and Osima Bin Laden. Mr.Huber's original name for his offshore banking enterprises, which have connections in Germany, Switzerland and the Mideast, was Ataqua, later changed to "Nada". Nada of course may be similar to "Dada", the international surrealist movement begun by artist Andre Breton (1896-1966), who linked his artistic activities with revolutionary political activities. Later in this book, dear Reader, you will find a reference to the beliefs of Andre Breton in a passage describing the terrorist writings of Internet surrealist "Indrid Cold".

At one point in the CNN documentary interview of Swiss financier Ahmed Huber by Mideast correspondent Nic Robertson the Egyptian ankh symbol is clearly seen amid the Nazi and Bin Laden memorabilia. It is significant that the public now is familiar with the terrorist name "Al Quaida" and the name chosen by R.A. Schwaller de Lubicz for his neo-Egyptian mathematical interpretations is "*Al Kemi*".The standard word for transmutation of lead into gold in ancient European scholasticism is "alchemy", with later

DOING BUSINESS IN THE ADIRONDACKS by E. Macer-Story

reference to chemistry. This has been the spelling of the word in Europe since the Middle Ages. In the neo-fascist use of the word "Al Kemi" we have the fantasy of an elite pursuit of "mental power" such as was researched by the Nazi adept Karl Haushofer.This is not, of course, the only meaning or use of the ankh, which is an ancient symbol with potential also for powerful, positive sorcery. Sometimes the symbol itself will upset the nefarious designs of someone trying to use it for negative plans. According to popular history:

" A frequent visitor to landsberg prison where hitler was writing mein kampf with the help of rudolf hess, was general karl haushofer, a university professor and director of the munich institute of geopolitics. haushofer, hitler, and hess had long conversations together. hess also kept records of these conversations. hitler's demands for german "living space" in the east at the expense of the slavic nations were based on the geopolitical theories of the learned professor. haushofer was also inclined toward the esoteric. as military attache in japan, he had studied zen-buddhism. he had also gone through initiations at the hands of tibetan lamas. he became hitler's second "esoteric mentor", replacing dietrich eckart. in berlin, haushofer had founded the luminous lodge or the vril society. the lodge's objective was to explore the origins of the aryan race and to perform exercises in concentration to awaken the forces of "vril". haushofer was a student of the russian magician and metaphysician gregor ivanovich gurdyev (george gurdjieff). both gurdjieff and haushofer maintained that they had contacts with secret tibetan lodges that possessed the secret of the "superman". the lodge included hitler, alfred rosenberg, himmler, goring, and hitler's subsequent personal physician dr. morell. it is also known that aleister crowley and gurdjieff sought contact with hitler. hitler's unusual powers of suggestion become more understandable if one keeps in mind that he had access to the "secret" psychological techniques of the esoteric lodges."

Recall here the alleged escape of S.S. scientists to a secret location in the Hartz mountains after the Allied destruction of the military research facility at Peenemunde, Germany at the end of World War Two which is represented in the Iciris productions video.. It is quite possible that certain of the tactics now in use by Al Quaida trained personnel involve derivatives of physics and Zen theories which can be implemented by pawns unaware of exact action until orders arrive from a commander who has thrown lots or otherwise used divination techniques to choose an exact target, unanticipated by the enemy. For example: a male or female pawn such as the individual lacking exact references for action who raced inappropriately out of the Magick Mirror office in 2002, leaving a tape of his conversation behind, could be instructed to visit a reporter and make some sort of confusing sexual advance or conflictive assertion of "facts" which interjects a previously non-existent annoyance..

A strategy of this sort would accord with the physics theories of Werner Hiesenberg, and of Neils Bohr, who maintained that no actual future timeline exists with certainty until the moment of observation and/or decision by a witness. This view, which

DOING BUSINESS IN THE ADIRONDACKS by E. Macer-Story

is now seriously questioned by physicists interested in the self-organization and synergy of the cosmos, fits easily with elitist theories of mind over matter.

Crudely expressed, a Fascist physics would then be formulated so that the witness with the strongest mental ability would in effect control the direction of events simply by making decisions about these events. One can understand how such a belief might animate anarchist and/or terrorist actions which seek to re-configure the destiny of nations. However, there are other persuasive theories along this line. One of the traditional Kabbalist teachings holds that the "next" event is more powerful than the one preceding. The year 862, for example, is more powerful than the year 861—no matter which events transpired in each year. Another way of expressing this insight is: "He who laughs last, laughs best". However, in a non-linear context it might be possible to jump from 862 to 870 and attempt to remedy 863-869. Facile notions that "checkmate" has ended the eternal contest between good and evil are always wrong, or an illusion planted by a "trickster" Intelligence.

In a pre-publication version of his autobiographical book "*Destiny Matrix*", controversial California physicist and commentator Dr. Jack Sarfatti relates his encounter with Nazi refugees Egon and Ernst "Putzi" Hanfstaengl At the time young Sarfatti encountered these folks in 1978, he was an impressionable free lance beatnik fresh from a number of establishment physics awards and "special programs" for gifted youth and was releasing pent up energy into the Jet Set demimonde in California.

Sarfatti's description of nineteen year old Egon in lederhosen folk dancing at parties and of his father "Putzi", a Nazi operative paperclipped to U.S. operations at the end of World War Two, as "Hitler's Private Buffoon" has the antic stamp of genuine description. The significance of this description, which matches a more sober account of these personalities in *"Roosevelt's Secret War"*,[62] resonates with Sarfatti's account in his writings of the questionable nature of the "Esalen Institute" activities during the 1970's and 1980's when international celebrities regularly passed through the sessions there, rubbing shoulders with such as. EST entrepreneur Werner Ehrhard, who worked also for the KGB in Soviet countries. (page 18)

"Putzi" Hanfstaengl , as documented by historian Persico, had been a close associate of Adolph Hitler and Rudolf Hess during the Third Reich in Germany. He was also a Harvard graduate who was rescued from internment in the UK near the end of World War Two by fellow Harvard alumnus Franklin D. Roosevelt, who used "Putzi"'s services as a privileged informant to U.S. intelligence operations.

Joseph Persico is an interesting source on this situation. For he makes the point that "Putzi" Hanfstaengl was not happy in U.S. service, where he maintained an abrasive, elitist attitude, and that Hanfstaengl was also notably prescient, actually gifted perhaps with some version of the mental abilities so prized by the "Thule" and "Al Kemi" crowd.

The claims made by Dr. Jack Sarfatti and others of the "Esalen Institute" and other similar "consciousness" groups of the 1980's in California that the situation was

DOING BUSINESS IN THE ADIRONDACKS by E. Macer-Story

being used by foreign intelligence and/or a murderous "black magick" cult should be taken seriously in light of the synergy via use of the "*Protocols of Zion*" and other quaisi-Biblical "teachings"between neo-Nazi belief systems and political charades such as "*Operation Vampire Killer*". In both the Sarfatti and the Persico writings, a firm emphasis is placed upon the link of Hanfstaengl with Ivy League and East Coast socialite families. "Putzi" was indeed by blood a member of the prominent Massachusetts Sedgewick family and this actual kinship did make him marginally acceptable to the circle of people surrounding U.S. President Franklin D. Roosevelt in 1944 . Lest we forget, dear reader, that the nominal theme of this book is "*Doing Business in the Adirondacks*", it should be mentioned here that Roosevelt was a native of New York and had a country home in the Adirondack mountains not far from the site of "flying head" appearances in the Saranac Lake area. If it is true that elitist adepts are employing "black hat" sorcerers and technicians to serve their nefarious purposes, then it should be remarked that the "flying heads" of the Adirondacks and the "foo fighters" following Allied aircraft during World War Two date from antiquity and also have an agenda specifically related to human limitations and capacities as a terrestrial eco-species.

In the hyper-citation of the "Skull and Bones" club at Yale University by persons "outside the loop" of the Ivy League, is this generic "Ivy League" connection to Occult Fascism actually a red herring? What's missing? Perhaps a clue to the missing link in this attempt to make sense of what seems an endless chain of half-correspondences regarding collusion and conspiracy simply lies in the area of the supernatural, telepathy and "mind over matter".

Recall here, dear reader, the preternatural interference with the original download of the book "*Destiny Matrix*", which contains the reference to "Putzi" Hanfstaengl just cited in this discussion Likewise also recall the preternatural promptings, such as pieces of fan blade literally falling from the ceiling fixture, which caused this reporter to add a citation in this book of oracular pronouncements previously made in poetic and dramatic works.. It had seemed at the time that there was an esoteric cyber interference on my usual email address which made the download easier on an alias address. I had not been sure whether this was cyber, spirit telekinesis or a combination of both types of interference. But, after a deliberate mental focus to repel negative spirit influence, I was able to finish the download task.

Recall also the preternatural growling sound which emerged from the speaker of the VCR as I was photographing alleged SS blueprints of circular aircraft from a paused videotape. This may have been due to a "Fenris" protection placed upon the original documents by an Inner Order adept and/or there may have been some type of spirit attachment to the video itself, which also shows documentary footage of Hitler and an interview with a man who claims his scientist father took him to view the flight of a circular aircraft at Pennemunde in 1944.

These manifestations experienced on electronic equipment during the composition of this book were not figurative. The effects were quite real, stressful and interruptive.

But these incidents, whatever might have been the talismanic trigger, were between the researcher and the equipment.

On October 5,2002 a different level of occult interaction became manifest in the form of a handprint in oil on the outside of a glass-sided porch. As I wrote in an email discussion on shamanism with a correspondent in Capetown, South Africa:

" Hi Mike-- Definitely. Understood. The "researcher" IS the magic walrus. I have been trying to get folks to understand this for quite some time. But most psi researchers have a frightened, Cartesian mind-split and retreat behind the facade of "Statistical studies" etc Since ancient times, the basic advice to the would-be mental magician is "as above//So below". Personal development & transformations. Total alchemical practice. I was writing on this topic in the draft of my new book last night. This morning I discovered, in the rays of the morning sun, a handprint in oil made through the outside screen onto the glass of my back porch. I photographed this and it disappears under natural light through the window but is very visible in the flash photo because it is in oil of some sort...here's the rub: to all those who doubt that another sorcerer (not myself) is placing talismanic stuff on my property[63]...what about this hand print, an ancient symbol in all cultures, the shaman's own print, left OUTSIDE my window at night? Eh???? Phantom, maybe...but actual."

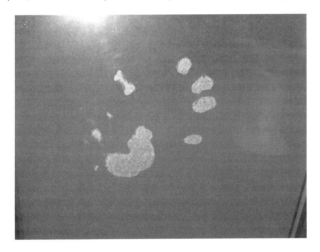

There exists here the extraordinary possibility that Andre VandenBroeck in his probings of Fascist "Al-Kemi" and Shiek Gilani in advocating practical awareness of Fundamentalist djinn are exactly correct in their warnings not to underestimate the powers of the mind and of rogue spirit entites conjured by rogue sorcerers. A society of people with rogue but extraordinary abilities , perhaps a rogue version of the Hindu/Aryan practitioners studied by the Nazi Ahnenerbe, may have found the link to "Atlantean" skills and perceptions also demonstrated by positive practitioners such as the Tibetan lama "Sharmar"... These individuals, as specified by R.A. Schwaller de Lubicz, must exist outside of ordinary social contact because their use of enhanced mental power is hyper-individualistic and elitist in orientation.

DOING BUSINESS IN THE ADIRONDACKS by E. Macer-Story

Recall here the Internet web search for "Sharmar", the incarnate Tibetan lama who has allegedly had many lifetimes as the same person, as described earlier in this book, and the discovery that there was an incomprehensible but somehow cyber-related site posted by another individual, and showing talismanic emblems of an unfamiliar ritual practice. As well as people like Sharmar, who practice esoteric skills within established religious context, there are "lone witches and wizards" who may also develop awesome mental skills.

The "Black Kabbalist"of the American Afro-Judaic tradition has a touch of this power in his ability to spontaneously, for example, print out a web search format "forbidden" to other querents by a cyber-rigging of the search engine. Notice now that actually it was the "Black Kabbalist" who forced attention toward the fact of cyber sabotage with his communications to this reporter about web "viral" difficulties assaulting his computer system on cue, as described earlier in this text. It seems that those intent on acting straightforwardly may underestimate their game-playing opponents. The "Black Kabbalist" has consistently also attempted to identify individuals posing as Afro-American activists who do not have proper credentials and are not actually known to the grassroots black community. Certain of these individuals have, for example, falsely claimed to have traveled to the Mideast region or Africa, and returned from nowhere with actual money in hand.

There are two potentially dangerous groups, as it seems, who want to derive power from ancient Egypt without actually ever consulting Egyptian archeologists about this type of project: Al Kemi and Al Quaida.. Yet who is behind the hidden death mask of the Atlantean pharaoh? Who are the actual "Thantatos" sorcerers whom I had glimpsed shadowing me in the Albany,N.Y. airport upon my arrival from a Midwest location? As I had occasion to write to my correspondent upon topics of expanded consciousness and perception, then located in Capetown, South Africa:

"Greetings from scenic upstate N.Y.: When I checked the backyard this afternoon after running a number of errands prior to my trip to Germany on Monday I found that below the steps near the mostly evaporated hand print on the porch sliding window there was a growth of chartreuse mushrooms.:-) Very yellow-green items similar to the small white capped standard mushroom. So I checked the rest of the yard. Beneath the cellar window--where I previously had found plastic cross talismans several years ago--there was a growth of tanish, white capped mushrooms and also dislocated tall white mushrooms lying plucked about the back yard.:-) I am momentarily without comment. I know nothing about mushrooms or how fast they grow. A few years ago a tall white mushroom had been artificially embedded at the side of the lane near my driveway.[64] Whatever this all means, let me assure you I had eaten no mushrooms last night.:-)

At the time I had found the tall white mushroom embedded artificially in the earth in 1999, I had the sense of a positive "wolf" spirit attempting to warn me of the reality of negative activities in my near environment.[65] When I reached the Frankfurt Book Fair in Germany on October 9, 2002, there was a small item on the front page of "*The Bookseller*" daily newsletter being distributed at the fair. This following news item serves to support the speculations advanced earlier in this book that a network of negative

DOING BUSINESS IN THE ADIRONDACKS by E. Macer-Story

sorcerers may be working their wiles cleverly through publications and the media, rather than by direct confrontation and conflict.

" A report on Berttelsmann's past links with the German Nazi Party has cast a shadow over this week's Frankfurt Book Fair, where it is one of the largest exhibitors. Bertelsmann's publishing empire includes Random House US and UK , exhibiting in Hall 8, Random House Deutchland in Hall 3.0 and BertelsmannSpringer in Hall 4.. In stark contrast to the company's official biography, the report by a group of scholars says that Bertelsmann did not resist the Nazis and made direct use of Jewish slave labourers during World War Two. It also used its ties with the Nazis to transform itself from a provincial Lutheran printing company into a mass market publisher which was the largest supplier of books to the German Army. Bertelsmann's new chief executive Gunter Thielen acknowledged the conclusions of the report, which was initiated by his predecessor Thomas Middlehoff in 1998".[66]

The point here is not to whip a major publisher around the block for past offenses committed sixty years ago by individuals no longer in charge of the firm. This forum is not a law court. The intent, dear reader, is simply to assert that practical control of the minds of the populace does not always arise through direct censorship , insult or confrontation. Sometimes, as in simply changing the name of a short story to eliminate the idea of "secret signs" connected with the colonial opium trade, this same effect can be achieved by alteration and subtraction, clever editing which either eliminates trigger concepts or neutralizes the impact into a children's story or romance fiction. Perhaps this might extend to detective and science fiction, as in the discovery that the name of a person who had bragged of Nazi ancestry was also twenty years later the name of a character in a James Bond film.

In fact, the clever opponent will use such tactics because seemingly benign alteration is difficult to trace or confront. One suspects that, as in the early Alfred Hitchcock film *"Remains To Be Seen"* wherein the holiday buffet counter is actually a tablecloth-draped casket, the "Thantatos" sorcerers are operating not in the closet using peculiar code symbols[67]but out in the open, by means of sophisticated and cynical deception, non-locally mobile in work vans and using obvious symbols of an occult triggering nature as a code transmission within ordinary video or audio products. Here this reporter is referring not to electromagnetic subtlety, but to overt presentations understood only by the initiated. As one example, a red Stetson could indicate a drug courier if that person is also working a crossword puzzle.

IDENTITY OF THE COVERT "THANTATOS" SORCERERS

One returns finally to the question of the identity of the "Thantatos" sorcerers, those who seem mysteriously to be attempting to bolex and/or control events, but are nowhere to be seen directly. Perhaps these individuals are the SSI (Solid State Intelligence) described by Dr. John Lilly as being hostile to human life. According to Dr. Lilly, these are intelligent micro-organisms , virus-like in size and structure, and hostile to human life. It is possible that such lifeforms have the ability to project the façade of human form and/or the illusion in the mind of the percipient that a human being

DOING BUSINESS IN THE ADIRONDACKS by E. Macer-Story

has taken action. Recall in this context the diabolic impersonations of "Cytron", the materially-damaging entity claiming to be a "cyber" persona but having a name curiously close to the ancient name of "shaitan".[68] It is possible that such lifeforms have the ability to project the facades of human form and/or the illusion in the mind of the percipient that a human being has taken action.

Or, and this is where the Fascist use of "Egyptology" in the deep structure of cyber-cuing via "Al-Kemi" may enter the enigmatic picture, the "Thantatos" power may be truly "Atlantean", coming forward in this electronic age from a time in our own present "prehistory" when electronics was also known in some form, as well as the accompanying "cyberspace" associated, for example, with the worked metal fragment of Kolman Von Kivitsky described earlier in this text with reference to a possible "Atlantian" explosion. Sometimes artifacts and/or illustrations are discovered which indicate sophisticated "technical" knowledge by some human civilization existing prior to the dawn of our presently known "prehistory". Usually these are shelved as unidentified or end up in the pocket of some zealous independent investigator like Von Kivitsky.

Remember also the jump from 862 to 870 possibly made by the mentally-alert adept who wishes to correct a situation which happened at 867. If, in the Atlantean situation, adepts are able to use the knowledge of atomic flux which we term "quantum" structure to cantilever "time" in the electromagnetic, structural sense , then some residue of the power-driven intellects and/or idea forms of the "Atlantean" power sorcerers may yet be attempting to set a foothold within the present material continuum in order to live again in full dimensional form. Recall here the inexplicable metal alloy found embedded deep in a coal mine in Eastern Europe which sparked Atlantean speculations.. It is worth noting that very few known artifacts from this pre-historical civilization have been catalogued in public museums. Perhaps this is because these significant artifacts reside in private collections, as relics which have been quietly handed down for many generations.

For such an Intelligence outside of four dimensional manifestations is always latent and somewhat ineffective materially, though ideas and motivations may be transmitted by an organism living outside the electromagnetic continuum through an electromagnetically-living organism as a form of surrogate action. Vampire appearances such as the bookstore "Highgate Vampire" matrix which resonated in the UK, Greenwich Village, New York and San Francisco, California in simultaneous timespace via linked (though chronologically separate) incidents relating the supernatural to concepts of espionage may sometimes actually be these disembodied "Thantatos" adepts rather than simply the survival of bloodthirsty tyrants known to folk traditions such as the Romanian "Lad the Impale", said to be the original model for Bram Stoker's famous vampire novel "Dracula". These grimly flamboyant appearances may transfer "meaning" into the linked situations by interrupting accustomed thought process to introduce the stereotypical idea of "weird" or "danger" which serves to transform an ordinary flow of events into a special. limited and limiting circumstance.

In this context, it is worth noting that as I began to copy the "vampire page numbers" above from my notes, the computer turned itself off spontaneously and it was

DOING BUSINESS IN THE ADIRONDACKS by E. Macer-Story

necessary to go through a "rescue" process in order to save the draft copy containing the new section on Atlantean vampires. The event reminded me that I had forgotten to stress that the vampire intelligence may also work through the corpus of computers and other electronic devices, as Dr. John Lilly theorized.

It is possible that Hitler's "Third Reich" belief in the national superiority of Germany, as this coupled oddly with the Shinto beliefs of national superiority in World War Two Japan, was actually a brief attempt by these discarnate Atlantean forces to re-establish connection with some pre-historical and power-oriented "Empire of Elite Intellect", and to re-seed these concepts and practices into present day civilization.

It was only the out-maneuvering of this Axis alliance of "Elite National Superiorities" by the counter-move of the atomic bomb which thwarted in a practical sense any successful re-kindling of the Atlantean attitude . In essence, the Allied use of the atomic bomb to end World War Two by forcing Axis surrender was the hyper-material blockage of aggression by the patterning power of the non-substantial elitist intellect. This was the physical arrest of the mad genius then channeling directly into World events through use of the counterclockwise swastika.

Yet atomic fusion/fission had from the outset inexplicable side effects such as the green aerial fireballs sighted at the Los Alamos labs, and other facilities which had developed and/or implemented the original use of atomic energy derived from dislocating the nuclear structure of the atom. [69] These side effects clearly indicated that the strictly material manipulation of inner mass structure as a weapon involves a partial control of the mass fabric, and not a completely-understood and total control of the mass structure. So unexpected and/or uncontrolled effects would be seen in the non-electromagnetic and non-local patterning energy which is not strictly sequential, in the sense of electromagnetic time.

It is well-known that "flying saucers" and "ufo"s became more of a regularly-experienced type of phenomenon just subsequent to the end of World War Two, although reports of such phenomena can be found off and on throughout the known, recorded history of this planet. Rather than trying to define "ufo"s, let us simply say that historically it is a fact that such things are mentioned more frequently in written and pictorial accounts since 1945 than in previous historical records. Whether this is a literal, material situation only or a matter of disruption and changes in the collective human consciousness is not possible to exactly discern.

However, since disruptions and changes in the collective human psyche may be induced from outside socially-linked human organisms, either by environmental circumstances or by the intervention of non-human intelligence, there is no reason to assume that the observation of "ufo"s and the sense of "alien intelligence operating" is not provoked by unknown stimuli exterior to the human organism.

Here we return again to the original subject of this book, the evidently anomalous effects in certain areas of New York State upon business and behavior and the seeming

DOING BUSINESS IN THE ADIRONDACKS by E. Macer-Story

presence of an environmental condition or "intelligence" which enhances ordinary human mental/emotional functioning. This native presence may unexpectedly reveal and/or compete with "Atlantean"-style attempts orchestrated from the shadows to hijack the identity and projects of the more "naïve" members of society.. For example, the furnace breakdowns associated with the considerations of the Tobyhanna, Pennsylvania "ufo" material first discussed in the book:"*Dr. Fu Man Chu Meets The Lonesome Cowboy: Sorcery and the UFO Experience"* were shared by two researchers at a distance, were mundanely unusual but without ritual pomp and circumstance.

The odd but determined scenarios of the "Thantatos" organization may have been more obvious to your present correspondent on several occasions-- such as the ritualized crossing and re-crossing of my path by persons dressed as businessmen in the baggage claim area of the Albany, N.Y. airport on June 18, 2001 -- simply because the upstate Catskill-Adirondack mountain area of New York State itself enhances the subtle level of mental dynamics.

One is, perhaps, not supposed to notice the subtle intrigues of this "Thantatos" organization , which are different from the hired guerrilla activities of their expendable pawns. The hired activities seem much like a movie extravaganza with an ongoing plot which leads nowhere, acted by grade B level soap opera performers who prefer the absurdist guerrilla role to the equally absurd role of selling popcorn at intermission in order to be creatively employed somewhere in the professional arts scene. In the airport scenario, stockbroker-Goth adepts may have known about the family inheritance business transactions in the Midwest from which this reporter was returning at the time. If there is a link here with the "neo-Nazi" political Confederacy in the United States, occultly odd financial considerations might have been the esoteric reason for this discernable criss-cross in the baggage area.

One notices when three airplanes hijacked by mercenary dupes suicide dive into public buildings such as the U.S. Pentagon and World Trade Center, as they did on September 11, 2001. But is this flamboyant absurdity merely the smoke and mirrors of a more subtle attempt at power-manipulation by a covert group of death merchants and power brokers, who envision themselves as "elite" and in contact with superhuman force and intelligence either because they are channeling voodoo or royal shamanic deities or because, on the dark side, as one Cambodian rogue leader once stated: *"Kill me, and Opium will continue."* In one CNN video clip of the collapsing twin World Trade Center Towers, a clearly defined "demonic" face is formed in the swirling smoke which surrounds the falling structures.[70] This may represent the diabolic intelligence which inspires the adepts of the Thantatos organization, fueled to manifest by both the deaths of the thousands of employees inside the collapsing buildings and the deaths of the pawns who had been told that by following this surrealist blueprint for architectural destruction they would ascend into legendary heaven worlds where 72 virgins would attend to their carnal and spiritual needs forever. Of course, this idea of waking up in a sensual paradise sounds like the feverish delusions of opium, delium or mental illness.

DOING BUSINESS IN THE ADIRONDACKS by E. Macer-Story

Your present correspondent has noticed that sometimes in the presence of events which seem enacted by the victim of a "vampiric" intelligence, minor infections will occur on the body. These will typically be small, feverish, encysted pockets of puss. When lanced, these pustules are filled with a foul, rotten-smelling liquid. Possibly the SSI of Dr. John Lilly , those intelligences defined as being like cyber or crystalline viruses, &/or the 'Atlantean" virus acting by micro-timer shift can actually act as a cause of local infection in organic bodies as well as computers. A number of physicists worldwide are working on the ramifications of micro-time shift, which in organic bodies might sometimes cause weird or harmful effects, as well as hopefully healing and transformative effects.

However, the rogue intelligence attempting to exert covert control over World events in the "Atlantean" mode may have competition in the form of regular use of standard corporate outlets for the same purpose by opportunist intellects seeking to implement limited psychological and/or sociological agendas. It is known, for example, that computer consultants working for IBM and other large corporations during World War Two devised the accounting method for the numbers tattooed on concentration camp inmates in Germany and Eastern Europe.[71]

The iron "masks of shame" and "iron maiden" devices of legal discipline from the Middle Ages of Europe circa 900 until 1300 A.D., as displayed in the Kriminal Museum in Rothenburg ob der Tauber, Germany, are attempts by a ruling technical elite of that era, the skilled smithys and architects within a Guild organization, to contain and standardize the spontaneous and creative expressions of the populace. Those who strayed beyond the rigid system of "morals" enforced by the elite were forced to wear iron masks and body suits which were sculpted in a clownish caricature of the behavior being disciplined. Some of these "masks of shame" are actually well-crafted works of art complete with bells which ring each time the victim changes position. But these devices also contain subtle details which are designed to inflict pain on the person sentenced by the medieval court to wear them.

The use of tattooed computer tabulation to number concentration camp victims by the Axis technical elite during World War Two is much like the encasing of village wits and successful lovers in the regularized iron strictures of the medieval legal system. For the skilled craftsmen who built the torture and community discipline devices were employed by the hereditary Lords and Ladies of the feudal Manor system just as the "black hat" technicians can be employed by wealthy criminals and/or criminal organizations to create covert communications networks and disinformation quagmires.

Certain of the medieval iron "masks of shame" are forged with a leering mouth, backed by s a tongue clamp and topped with a belled frame shaped like the horned foolscaps of the Tuscan commedia. Oddly, the construction of rigid masks with fixed, morality play expressions is also literally like the modern day "psychiatric elite" attempting to force unique human behaviors into Procrustian motifs which they have pre-ordained in a "one size fits all" manner.

Destructive to the iron "masks of shame" medieval behavior modification scenario is the sense of humor exhibited by the alleged moralists whose torture devices, including an iron flute with small stock imprisonment holes for the fingers of a "bad musician" and a neck cuff to hold his head continually near to the mouthpiece, are weirdly amusing.

Recall here the weird sense of humor also operating in certain of the "crank calls" and odd talismanic gifting experienced by this writer during 1998-2002 in New York, far from the location of medieval Bavaria. The prophylactic glove found beside this reporter's upstate New York country house in occult context, the "Spahn Ranch" insurance phone call and tall quasi-phallic mushrooms found strewn in the back yard and/or embedded beside the country house lane are clever erotic symbols or talismans, deliberately planted. But the psychology behind this stuff is profoundly twisted and abstract or self-referent to the perpetrator(s). Thus, no real interpretive context can be found for these odd "talismanic" offerings and none will be offered here. This guerilla talismancing is done in somewhat the same wickedly droll modality as advocated by surrealist artist Andre Breton during the early 20th Century. In fact, an individual spamming the web with inflammatory neo-Fascist compendiums under the pseudonym of "Indrid Cold" actually cites Breton in the following excerpt from a rogue email sent on October 16, 2002.

"The Dadaists produced accidental art by combining elements at random; Tristan Tzara even produced "poems" by picking words out of a hat while blindfolded. This is non-Aristotelian, certainly, and therefore, like modernism in general, un-American. Picasso was an openly avowed Communist and, although there is no clear evidence of overt membership in the BILDERBERGERS, the number of his mistresses and concubines undoubtedly surpasses that of King Solomon, Aleister Crowley or even George Washington. Like Van Gogh, Gaugin and the whole "modernist" movement, and like Jazz and Rock, Picasso's art definitely "plays on the interface between noise and information." He actually painted a Jazz band once, and he said, in defense of decadence, "One must run faster than beauty, even if it appears one is running away from it." He even deliberately imitated the primitive art of Africa instead of the art of nice white people, and if Mr. Tame looks closely I am sure he will see Voodoo symbolism in some of Pablo's Cubist renditions of tortured bulls and sexually frenzied women. Evil is everywhere, for those whose eyes are open and ready to see it.

Jean Cocteau, 23rd Grand Master of the ill-famed Priory of Sion, was homosexual and his paintings, poetry and films are as non-linear, non-Aristotelian and therefore barbaric as the works of his friend Picasso. Cocteau said specifically that "To be an artist is to be a suspicious character" and

DOING BUSINESS IN THE ADIRONDACKS by E. Macer-Story

"The true artist is always a revolutionary." He helped
launch Surrealism, with all its barefaced celebration of
erotic, African, primitive, irrational and overtly Communist
elements. Andre Breton revealed the anarchistic and
sociopathic impulses behind Surrealism blatantly, hanging a
lurid sign in the gallery that inflicted the first exhibit
of Surrealist art on the unsuspecting and previously sane
and decent public; the sign, seemingly humorous, gave a
clear warning of what was to come. It said:

DADA IS NOT DEAD!

WATCH YOUR OVERCOAT!

Salvador Dali differed from the other Surrealists only in
preferring Hitler to Communism, and once offered the
typically Surrealist rationalization, "Hitler has three
balls and four foreskins." Dali also said, "The only
difference between me and a madman is that I am not mad" and
insulted us with such degenerate un-American paintings as
the Cthulhoid, monstrous, unspeakable _Debris of an
Automobile Giving Birth to a Blind Horse Biting a Telephone_
and the vile, vulgar, lewd and infamous _Great Masturbator_.
(Although not a lifelong bachelor like Beethoven, Dali has
lived in so-called "celibacy" since the death of his wife.)
Worse yet: he once gave a lecture inside a diving suit,
making it impossible for the audience to hear him."
Art as Black Magick and Moral Subversion
by Heinrich von Hankopf

This entire rogue email quotation by "Indrid Cold" is by its very nature surreal whilst at the same time purporting to deride the surrealists. For the sudden introduction of such content into the flow of an ordinary email list correspondence stops the rational progress of the discussion, exactly as the original surrealists such as Andre Breton intended when they advocated such political acts as assassination as an art form.

Part of the pre-supposition of the assignment of rigidly forger "masks of shame" and tattooed computer ID numbers by the elitist jokester is that this structuring of events and behavior in actually correct and appropriate action taken to contain criminal and roguish improvisation.. Note the "moral" tone in the rogue email quote from "Art as Black Magick". Yet "Indrid Cold" has been labeled as a "cyber terrorist" by those receiving these provocative spam notes.

As Sophia Mappa points out in her book "*Planetary Democracy: A Western Dream*"[72], the democratic idea of the importance of the individual is actually not shared by all societies on this planet. She points out in a publication originally issued in France that the French Revolution was immediately followed not by individualist anarchy but by a hierarchical re-ordering of authority. All governments require some type of hierarchy in order to be efficient. According to Ms. Mappa, the rationale for this hierarchy may be

DOING BUSINESS IN THE ADIRONDACKS by E. Macer-Story

"occult" as well as overtly democratic or tyrannical by Fascist mandate. There is actually some justification for the idea that certain technological and scientific techniques should be restricted to certified experts lest the democratic idea that "anybody can perform surgery" or competently assemble an electrical machine be abused to the detriment of persons injured by incorrect procedures.

One cause of the perplexity in U.S. and European psychical research is similar to this basic political problem involving democracy and individualism. It is thought by the Western analysts studying esp/pk functioning that (in the democratic sense of all humans having identical abilities) a statistical profile using random subjects and repeatable protocol will scientifically "prove" or "disprove" aspects of mental abilities linked to non-local, extrasensory perception.

Yet common sense will tell us that certain individuals have a stronger psychic "eye" than others in the same sense that certain individuals have a more exact musical ear or mathematical sense than others. Some individuals are tone deaf, color blind or unable to read sequential language (dyslexic). One of the reasons ordinary investigation has not documented and/or perceived the "Thantatos" organization is that such an alliance of individuals with extraordinary abilities and/or resources is not thought to be possible.

Consider the possibility that the "random selection" of the surrealists may not be as random as these artists might have originally intended and does not actually challenge cosmic coherence and linear logic.. If the person selecting lots out of a drum to construct a poem is individually gifted at the fingertips, as in the "Al Kemi" of R.A. Schwaller de Lubicz, then the lottery may yield exactly what that individual may desire or fear.

But this is not a book on political theory or sociology. Rather, this is a book about the actual seeds, teleologically intelligent and multi-dimensional, of ideas and data which may provide the stimulus for events and decisions which otherwise might justly be regarded as "inexplicable".

Sometimes a "seed" might at first seem to be a "cyst" created by negative viral action since the eruption of inexplicable negative stimuli is also a cause for curative and/or agenda changing positive action. A venerable Jesuit belief is simply that this generation of a "cause for correction" is actually the positive function of "evil" or the "diabolic" within the cosmic fabric. British author Colin Wilson, in his book "*A Criminal History of Mankind*", echoes this historical interpretation in non-religious fashion, theorizing that the criminal action of hyper-intelligent rogues actually raises the evolutionary level of the collective human species by calling forth clever innovations of an advanced nature to block this criminal aggression and/or trickery.

This philosophy is also similar to the Kabbalist belief that event 14 overcomes event 13, and so on. This may not be exactly true if the individual is active in configurational time and thinking to plan non-locally and non-sequentially. In the materially-limited dimensions, 14 does overcome 13 and is then overcome by 15 but in the absolute situation, upsets in this measured expectation may occur and are always possible. So it is not wise to rest too extensively within the cradle of familiar symbols since certain cuing may be coming, positively or negatively, from a future event or obscure belief system, as in the surrealist talismans presented anonymously to this reporter over a period of several years in the 1990's.

In the province of the Prince/ess of Darkness, there may be somewhat of a competition in feats of cunning. For example, Ira Einhorn of the infamous 1977 until

2002 peripatetic murder case involving mummified remains of a lover discovered in Einhorn's hall closet,[73]may not actually have committed this specific murder for which he was convicted. On the other hand, judicial proceedings brought forth the dual identity of "Guru Einhorn" who evidently had been smooth in neo-tech and philosophical discussions but rough and beastly in certain personal relationships. Until the conventional murder trial in Pennsylvania in 2002, Einhorn's duality had not been clearly detected and might never have been publicly discussed—typical as this duality was of neo-shamanic dabblers in the 1970's and 1980's as detailed in the book *The Stargate Conspiracy*" discussed earlier in this text.. Had the murder not been committed and the mummified remains, as Einhorn alleges, been placed inside his premises with the intent of incriminating him, this issue of "abuse by the guru"might not have been an issue for public discussion beyond very limited circumstances..

In this context, one can easily speculate that if there exist neo-shamanic persons more cunning than Einhorn and with more subtle evil talents these persons may indeed have introduced a mangled corpse into a scenario otherwise successfully manipulated to show only the mystic mind power of Einhorn and his close associates   Might the source of this hyper-cunning strategy .be the Atlantean-inspired "Thantatos" organization? Or a lone practitioner of "Al Kemi" with similar, power-oriented characteristics?

Recall in this context the "Commander Hataan" transmissions published in 1970-80's editions by *American West* press (not the 1990's airline by the same name) about accessing the knowledge of the Egyptian deity "Aton" in the present day to assist in combating the global strategies of the U.N. and world banking systems. Militant Afro-American leader Louis Farrahkan claims to have seen a ufo "wheel" in September of 1985 while traveling in Mexico and to have been "beamed up" into this circular aircraft. This vision or "sighting" was partly telepathic and coincided with the September 19, 1995 earthquake in Mexico. Involved with this experience was also a "scroll rolled down" in the mind's eye which contained esoteric instructions. Farrahkan, who claims to be guided by Advanced Intelligence from outer space or similar spirit worlds, saw the ufo wheels as having something to do with the "New Jeruselem" or "New Wisdom", a"City in the Sky". Since Rev.Louis Farrahkan also has met with Arabic leaders and has expressed independently anti-Semitic views, it is appropriate to wonder about the possible connection between the extremist black militant faction in the United States and those Arabic Fundamentalists who wish to use terrorist tactics to implement their agenda.

Farrahkan mentions in his talk[74]both a well-known Japanese sighting of ufos and the fact that U.S. President Jimmy Carter, a ufo witness, had promised to reveal more about U.S. government research in that area, but ultimately   was not forthcoming.

So a subtle agenda is revolving here about ufo contact, and specifically ufo contact in Mexico, where some of the "Commander Hataan" communications had taken place also. The very existence of this obscure agenda may seem surreal to the reader. So let us once again return to the topic of surrealism as an art form used to startle the experiencer onto new levels of awareness.

During the video presentation "*Washing the Baby*" by artist Teresa Margollen [75]hands in surgical gloves are seen washing the mummified corpse of an infant identified as being the "premature birth by an associate of Margollen, given to her for this purpose. Your present correspondent found this artistic video, during which the corpse is dissected by scissors and pliers, to be distasteful and did not stay in front of it to watch the complete showing. However, what the very existence of such an artwork does demonstrate is the reality of human sacrifice among some extreme practitioners of the South American .Santoria and Umbanda sects, specifically often those who worship the god Exu, prince of darkness and trickster in that particular tradition. Recall here the rogue Sufism with actual impact experienced at times by this writer in investigations into anomalous events. This is the same type of rogue practice cited by Shiek Gilani in his counsel to Western reporters and investigators that there are powers of the mind and of spirit contact which have been underestimated or misunderstood by Western correspondents. Perhaps the gruesome, avante guarde art video by artist Teresa Margollen is for the purpose of opening the mind to possibilities unacceptable to the global folkways of "cool-cult" electronic media.. Practices of ritual human sacrifice for purposes of obtaining "power" do continue to exist, beyond archeological anecdotes.[76] Sometimes these practices may work for the practitioners, and be concealed, simply because these rogue practitioners are actually tapping a vital patterning not accessible to the conscious human mind.

In an email correspondence with then notorious fugitive guru Ira Einhorn prior to his 2002 extradition from France and subsequent conviction for a bizarre murder he may not have committed , this reporter brought up the "supernatural" possibility of shamanic participation in ritual activities involving actual, bloodthirsty spirit presences. The image of a triangular mask worn by such a modern shaman had come into my mind clairvoyantly while meditating on Einhorn's situation.

By co-incidence there was at that time a Chilean artist renting the studio opposite the Magick Mirror Space in a building in Soho—NYC near the Hudson River. I had simply been standing is this artist's studio chatting socially at the time of a Studio Open House in the gallery building, when I suddenly noticed in one of the paintings done by the Chilean artist the exact triangular mask I had remembered from my meditations on the controversial Einhorn murder situation. This was in 2000. I asked this artist about the mask and she told me it was a traditional mask from Tierra del Fuego, Chile. She also told me that it was included in the painting to represent peace and friendship, understanding between cultures. I had a visceral doubt about this interpretation but did not express my misgivings. Later, I looked up shamanic practices in Tierra Del Fuego in the book "*Way Of The Animal Powers*" by Joseph Campbell where I found a photo of a shaman wearing the same mask, but with a different interpretation appended.

When questioned, the intellectually-oriented Einhorn had nothing to report about these Chilean possibilities , remarking only that there had been a statue of a "laughing Buddha" in the yard of psychical researcher Andrea Puharich during the 1970's and that he did not recall any specific South American artifacts from that situation, where "Star Children" gatherings were held by Dr. Puharich.

This reporter, however, was struck, in context of the existence of the "Friendship" commune in Tierra Del Fuego which claims both contact with the Third Reich before World War Two and with extraterrestrials.[77], by the Chilean artist's idea that the shamanic mask, traditionally used used in austere initiation ceremonies, was for "friendship" in the sense of international understanding. According to anthropologist Joseph Campbell, [78] the exact mask depicted in the Chilean artist's painting, a large triangular structure covering the entire face and neck with a striped robe attached to the lower side of the triangle, was used in male initiation rites of the Ona tribe in Tierra del Fuego. These rites, whish tested the mental and physical fortitude of the initiate, involved shamans impersonating terrifying apparitions.

But the ceremonies also involved displays of actual spirit materialization phenomena, mixed in with obvious trickster sleight of hand. The object of this activity was to test the initiate. Was the initiate honest? Was he playing tricks? Rationalizing what he had experienced in the ceremonies? Could he discern the tricks from the actual materializations? The members of this lodge believe that the spirits employed by the shamans have the power to materialize "insects, tiny mice, mud, sharp flints or even a jelly fish or baby octopus into the anatomy of those who had incurred its master's displeasure."

Here it is necessary to directly confront the possibility that, in experiments by psychical researchers involving the employment of actual shamans, all is not necessarily a matter of the "laughing Buddha". Companions of the Chilean artist had told me at the time I was asking her about the shamanic "friendship" mask in her painting that Native Tierra del Fuegans had visited the U.N. for a ceremony in the 1980's. They were the guests of diplomats who were politely distressed at their odd use of food in the house, and by a story of cannibalism cited by one shaman who told them he had "eaten his grandmother". This all sounds simply like a matter of cultural dietary differences humorously enhanced by a sarcastic remark. But the reference may be literal.

This particular shamanic focus would, of course, not be the style of all Tierra del Fuegans. It is a matter of individual ability and experience, as in the discipline of the more urbane and sophisticated "Al Kemi" described by Andre VandenBroeck, who discovered that his aristocratic mentor actually held elitist anti-Semetic views. These are the same views which led to the attempted mass extermination of the European Jewish population by Axis forces during World War Two. So it is clear across the boards that the development of extraordinary, arcane skills does not preclude blood sacrifice as an arcane propitiation ritual.

On October 21, 2001 I noticed while packaging a small, gold cardboard chevron found in my working loft in Woodstock prior to September 23, 2001 that there is the number 37 printed on the back of it in small, regular numerals. This accords with my feeling that some sort of "black magick" neo-tech organization may be using "micro effects" as a form of sorcery. I wondered how the small bit of cardboard got into the workspace, which is private. Possibly, the "37 chevron" is a positive, warning apport.

For shortly after finding this item inside the loft at noontime, I found outside the building an odd butterfly-shaped and/or folded wide-V shape of thick, metal gold-like foil nearby a piece of moss which had been regularly sliced into a square-cornered turf chunk, as with a sharp knife or sword. During the early hours of the morning previous to finding the cut turf, there had been a notable effect to the loft smoke alarm, which kept ringing for about ten minutes off and on after suddenly activating in a situation of no smoke, no fire and no electrical power flux. So the gold foil talisman could have been set and the turf cut at just the time the smoke alarm was malfunctioning. This reporter's journal subsequent to this finding is occupied with observations of various "suspicious people". Indeed, there was quite a bit of nervous activity in the vicinity, including the obvious use of a talismanic "pointer stick" as a signal by persons who had evidently arranged to meet at a bridge intersection on Ohayo Mountain road just as this reporter

DOING BUSINESS IN THE ADIRONDACKS by E. Macer-Story

was approaching that location on her customary, constitutional walk. Part of this stick signaling tableau included a border collie-sized, lame black dog sitting smack in the middle of the road with a man and boy hunkered down beside it. These rose to meet a white van with a New York State license plate which hesitated until the man flashed his pointer stick to the driver as he entered the front passenger seat of the van.

Of course, the viewing of this incident could have been a picturesque accident. But there is also the possibility it was staged for some obscure reason. The butterfly is a symbol in a type of physics speculation termed "chaos theory". One of the witches with whom I have chatted during the last few years felt I had been impacted by individuals practicing "chaos magick". Possibly. The Thantatos organization may dabble occasionally with the symbology of known systems in order to create the impression that some known religious or cult belief in being utilized. Perhaps also the Thantatos adepts may use known tags from technical or media systems so that it seems that such business are "complicit" in covert shenanigans.

Or these persons may actually have developed extraordinary abilities. On January 28, 2001 at about 7:45 in the evening this reporter had been holding a video tape of an episode from FOX-TV's *X-Files* series concerning a crippled East Indian fakir with paranormal powers who was taking revenge on Western people who had participated in the killing of his son in India. Each of the individuals involved in the killing had, in the fictional television show, met a mysterious and catastrophic death where they lived in the United States, far from the site of the son's death in India. Thoughts of extraordinary abilities of Fakirs were on my mind when the bell rang outside the front door and I discovered a mistaken pizza delivery. When I closed the front door, the video tape had disappeared. I searched the entire house but could not find it.

It was the new moon. Thoughts of sorcery and the supernatural passed through my mind briefly in context of a nationally-publicized murder in Vermont and were jotted in my journal. The victims had been ex-patriot Germans active in intellectual circles as asking restitution for Nazi war crimes.[79]

On February 1, 2001, when activating the VCR to insert a new, blank video tape just bought at the store, I found the "Fakir tape" I had sought three days before inside the tape machine, where I had originally searched after the pizza interruption and found nothing. It seemed this was an indication of "real" paranormal powers perhaps active in my vicinity. Some entity or force was perhaps signaling me about the possibility that the scenario depicted in the fictional show might possibly actualize in some form.

During an interview on the Larry King television show,[80] convicted serial killer David Berkowitz talked about being possessed by Satan so that his will was not his own, and about the fact that more than one person was involved in the "Son of Sam" killings in 1977

"KING: We're back. By the way, did you always act alone?

BERKOWITZ: Well, not really. Not totally like that.

KING: Were other people caught?

BERKOWITZ: No.

DOING BUSINESS IN THE ADIRONDACKS by E. Macer-Story

KING: They're still out there?

BERKOWITZ: Most have passed on. And...

KING: But they were involved in killing as well?

BERKOWITZ: They were...

KING: They got away with it?

BERKOWITZ: Well, no, they haven't gotten away with it and they won't. I -- I...

KING: Do you think they're in hell?

BERKOWITZ: Some have lost their lives. And...

KING: Are you going to go to heaven?

BERKOWITZ: I know I'm going to go to heaven. I don't deserve it, but that's God's mercy, because that's the promise. You know, I know that the blood of Jesus has washed away my sins.

KING: What kind of prayer do you want to do for us?

BERKOWITZ: I'd just like to pray in general if that's OK.

KING: OK. We have a couple of minutes.

BERKOWITZ: Thank you so much, Larry, for, you know, this opportunity. And it says in Second Chronicles, Chapter Seven that the Lord is speaking. He says, "If I shut up heaven, that there be no rain, or if I command the locusts to devour the land or if I send pestilence among my people."
It says, "If my people, which are called by my name, shall humble themselves and pray and seek my face and turn from their wicked ways, then I will hear from heaven and forgive their sin and I will heal their land.

KING: Do you feel sad as to how you will be remembered?

BERKOWITZ: Yes. Because I have regret over that. I...

KING: Your obituaries will not have pluses in it, while you in your heart may have done lots of good for lots of people since all of this.

DOING BUSINESS IN THE ADIRONDACKS by E. Macer-Story

BERKOWITZ: Of course, I know because of my past they will always remember the bad. But God has had mercy on me and he'll have mercy on anyone who calls upon him."

There are several investigative studies of the "Son of Sam" serial murders[81] which support the allegations of David Berkowitz that he was a member of a "Satanic" cult though police forensic experts allege that Berkowitz was the sole traceable perpetrator in terms of physical evidence. Berkowitz claims that he was possessed by a force which made him feel both "invincible" while committing the murders and "blank" or empty of ordinary feeling when reading about the murders in the newspaper or going about his daily routines before he was apprehended. The duality of this situation has puzzled investigators.

Here it is constructive to recall the actions of the suicide hijackers who demolished the World Trade Center towers on September 11, 2001 in context of the remarks of Shiek Gilani about the "djinn" entities, powerful demonic intelligences, causing people to take action against their will or better understanding. It is generally acknowledged that the individual hijackers were dupes of a larger organization, induced to their doom by tales of a sensually-oriented heaven into which they would be transported after their violent deaths. Subsequent to the disaster, the United States forces thus went after the Al Quaida terrorist network in Afghanistan, perceived to be the actual perpetrators who had financed and empowered the terrorist hijackers. Obviously, mental persuasion had been exerted on the pawns who lost their lives in carrying out the violent objective.

It may be a failure of perception that the "Son of Sam" serial murder case was not handled in the same way by authorities. When apprehended, David Berkowitz claimed, among other statements about demonic influence, that "Druids" had influenced his behavior. Druids?

People in long white robes with triangular, pointed masks? The stereotypical KKK? Or some other group less well known but resembling the Ku Klux Klan? Folk singer Richard Farina, who had a fatal motorcycle accident subsequent to the release of a record album containing the song "*Bold Marauder*" which describes secret "Grottos, Caves and Sacrificial Altars" of the "White Destroyer". comes to mind here. Had Farina actually seen these locations, or directly heard of them from a witness?

This is difficult to discern exactly as the would-be "Destroyers" or "Avengers" may wear a variety of masks to obtain power. Recall, dear reader, the previous mention of masks in this text. There was the director Stanley Kubrick who died just as his film *MASKS* about a wealthy, covert cult was about to be released. The masks worn by Papa Legba, powerful voodoo trickster demi-god. who controls the keys to the Other Worlds entered at the crossroads, visible and invisible, between material and spiritual dimensions are seen as similar to the masks which may be worn by other forms of Advanced Intelligence both human and non-human. But the heavy face makeup of an unusual woman with evidently material characteristics who stepped into line behind me during the afternoon prior to hearing a lecture at Princeton University on psychic research and trickster shenanigans could also be construed to be a mask, perhaps a ritual protection which was inadvert or compulsive, a visible sign of unusual stress. It has been claimed

DOING BUSINESS IN THE ADIRONDACKS by E. Macer-Story

by individuals such as Dr. Bernardo Canė of SENASA investigative organization in Argentina that the livestock and poultry mutilations in the Southwest U.S., Puerto Rico, and South America are somewhat of a masque, a macabre charade to draw attention from drug smuggling and other black market activities.

It is also claimed by certain individuals such as neo-Nazi apologist Frederich Mattern andf Dr. Carol Rosen, a former assistant to repatriated German rocket scientist Dr.Werner Von Braun, that the "*UFO: Nazi Secret Weapon*" theme is used in the modern day for a similar purpose, to distract the mind into speculative historical circumstances whilst contemporary espionage is taking place under the noses of the historians. The mask of the Atlantean Pharoah worn by a variety of individuals seemingly fascinated with ancient Egypt might also be used for similar purposes.

But the demonic mask of smoke spewing out from the collapsing World Trade Center towers as seen in a still from one CNN news clip serves exactly the opposite purpose and, like the iron Masks of Shame in the Rothenberg, Germany Kriminal Museum, is the exterior representation of inner mental attitude and intent, as are a variety of shamanic masks from all cultures which depict powerful demonic forces or deities. These forces do not have conventional organic bodies and must therefore be depicted by means of masks worn by the shamans who wish to invoke or represent them.

It was a mask of exactly this fantastic design which occurred to this reporter intuitively while thinking about the bizarre murder of Holly Maddux, the companion of 1970's "psi research" guru Ira Einhorn, who was convicted of this murder during a trial in Pennsylvania in 2002. Like convicted serial killer David Berkowitz, Einhorn has consistently claimed that "other people" were involved in the crime for which he was convicted. But the drug-befuddled and/or schizophrenic pawns may have been the mask or screen[82] for sophisticated ritual crimes orchestrated by "adepts" with financial means..

The origin of the particular type of ritual mask seen by this reporter during a clairvoyant "brainstorming" of the Einhorn enigma was found later to be Tierra del Fuego, Chile, where the neo-Nazi "Friendship" commune is also located and a photo of this type of ritual mask exists in the book "*The Way of the Animal Powers*" compiled by Joseph Campbell and published in 1984.Suppose for purposes of argument that Ira Einhorn did not commit the bizarre murder of which he has been convicted. Who might have done this as a ritual act of "black magick"? The evidence against Einhorn, which is extremely convincing, consists of anecdotes about his previous episodes of violent behavior against a girlfriend and a poem hew ha had written advocating use of violence. Overlooked in this situation is the fact that surrounding "new age" guru Einhorn at the time were numerous people with bizarre beliefs related to their assumptions that they were "special" due to their use of LSD and other consciousness expansion substances. One or more of these persons could have felt they were "special" enough to try ritual murder for occult effect.

Here it should be commented that the actual meaning of the word "occult" in reference to philosophical systems is simply "subtle" or "non-apparent" and not "hidden". The adept occultist is working not "in secret" or with cryptic mumbo jumbo but right out in the open, with an added, non-apparent level to the proceedings. It is classic in the development of esp/pk and spirit contact skills that the neophyte, thinking to be too "special", will attempt to enact rituals and use directives which are unintelligible to anyone but a "select" group of people. But this is not wise because such

DOING BUSINESS IN THE ADIRONDACKS by E. Macer-Story

activity can be easily detected and encircled by more positive attention and/or a rival dark sorcerer.

Here recall the Alfred Hitchcock film "*Remains To Be Seen*" which depicts a group of college students who have committed the ritual murder of a friend and placed his coffin covered with a linen tablecloth in the midst of a holiday reception as the draped buffet counter. Recall here also the bizarre tales now circulating about the "Skull & Bones" Society at Yale University.

As an overt mental exercise and recipe, dear reader, kindly contrast the sophomoric charades with skulls and prostitutes as alleged of Yale's Skull & Bones Society and other nominal "Order of the Colonialist Oriental Pooh Ba" organizations with the clever strategy suggested in the Hitchcock film. Here, in the concealing of a victim's body at a holiday reception, there is no flaunting of the superficial "robe, mask and cryptic statement" stereotype. For "*Remains To Be Seen*" depicts very deep ritual sorcery wherein the mask is no mask, as in the martial arts teaching that the true adept will be in a condition of deception//no deception. A hypnotist, for example, in the case of David Berkowitz might exactly suggest the identity "Son of Sam" and criminal acts to be committed as a sort of ritual bloodletting without being physically present at these events. Such a hypnotist might wear the mask of a Druid for such an emotionally vulnerable individual as Berkowitz, who has claimed to be inspired by Druids.

Yet the original purpose of the shamanic mask is not to trick but to present the visage of a non-human or superhuman Intelligence thought to be animating the human practitioner who is wearing the mask. Might these "Masks of the Gods", a term coined by anthropologist Joseph Campbell, then come to operate independently in the human mind, but seeming in memory to have a trickster human body supporting them?

In a recent Internet communication, ufo activist Dr. Steven Greer asserted that Dr. Werner Von Braun, a Nazi V-2 rocket specialist brought to the United States subsequent to World War Two, had warned that there might be an effort by Axis loyalists to pull off an Outer Space charade of some sort. According to Greer:

" A former high official at the NSA (National Security Agency) told me about a protocol informally dubbed DDT - that old poisonous chemical long-banned in much of the world. In this application, it stands for Decoy, Distract and Trash - which is what sophisticated intelligence operatives use to set up some person or group, take them off the trail of something real and important, and trash the person or the subject. This pretty much sums up the lion's share of all things UFOlogical, with the latest example being the much-hyped Sci-Fi channel roll-out of Spielberg's mini-series, 'Taken'....
You will recall that no less a figure than Wernher Von Braun warned to his personal spokesperson Dr. Carol Rosin in 1974 that after the cold war, those operating behind the scenes would roll out global terrorism and then, finally, a hoaxed alien threat from outer space. Dr. Rosin gave this testimony before [the Al Quaida terrorist action of] 9/11, by the way...".

Would Dr. Werner Von Braun have known about secret SS ahnenerbe experimentation with actual sorcery and contact with interdimensional intelligence? Not

DOING BUSINESS IN THE ADIRONDACKS by E. Macer-Story

necessarily, no more than special operative Col. James "Bo" Gritz knew about the U.S. double agentry already implanted within the Cambodian opium trade before he encountered this situation in Cambodia and interpreted it simply as "American officers trafficking in narcotics".

In naïve context, the prominent German rocket scientist is in substantial agreement with Frederich Mattern, author of the paperback book:"*UFO: Nazi Secret Weapon*" only Von Braun seemed to be indicating that the "Secret Weapon" was not a specially designed spaceship but a sophisticated disinformation game much like the "Delta Green" game discussed in context of the "real" Col. James "Bo" Gritz which actually does involve German-English word salad and thinly veiled references to the 1986 Golden Triangle narcotics sting operation involving the controversial U.S. military officer, Col. Bo Gritz.

At that time, Col. Gritz was claiming that there were double operatives within the military organization, acting as drug smugglers or couriers. This, of course, is shopworn "James Bond" stuff. You remember, dear reader, how quickly the name of a suspected neo-Nazi government employee became also the name of a character in a James Bond film shortly after being web searched by the "Black Kabbalist? In fact, didn't the subject of "James Bond" also come up in discussing KGB veterans who had allegedly been paid to impersonate themselves in a semi-fictional documentary about UFO research in the former Soviet Union?

STRANGE TALES AND TALENTS

Recall here Dr. Eric Ross Koss who met a strange fate in 1990 after claiming that errors were being inserted into a "Trojan Horse" computer program he was designing for the NSA. Shortly after complaining of this interference, Dr. Ross Koss was seen walking naked down the center divider of a major highway near his office in Virginia, where he veered into oncoming traffic and was killed. In light of the previous discussion, it seems plausible that Eric Ross Koss had been drugged and/or hypnotized as well as having been subjected to negative behavioral conditioning through the injection of errors into his meticulous programming. Who on Earth would do this? Certainly we are not talking about Intelligences from Outer Space.

The only individuals who would care to block a naïve NSA hired specialist in this way would clearly be rogue specialists of equal expertise. The issue here then becomes rogue use of such "backdoor" cyber technology as Ross Koss was alleged to be developing. But this is not the only issue in this situation. The fact is that whatever mental sabotage techniques were used against this individual were effective. Maybe someone slipped Dr. Ross Koss a PCP-laced confection. Perhaps this confection was prepared like certain meth-amphetimenes "Nazi style"[83] inside the "Eternity Enamel" cookware trick root page which is slipped beneath the legitimate cyber announcement, or similar. One does not deal in specifics when doing effective tracing of this type of subterfuge. A web page, like an assumed identity, is here today and gone tomorrow. This type of deceptive and malleable identity hides most easily behind icons or masks which seem stable and well-known .

For example, this reporter recently received several crank emails, one having sources in Austria, which identified Santa Claus with Satan and the British nursery rhyme about "Humpty Dumpy" the indecisive egg who fell from a wall and shattered, with sado-masochistic reconstructive surgery. One might suppose that some tracing or

DOING BUSINESS IN THE ADIRONDACKS by E. Macer-Story

response to these provocative emails might be made by the recipient. But this use of the familiar icons is a trick. For if one tries to trace Santa Claus or Humpty Dumpty one finds only the mask of the trickster. It is not "Santa" who is "Satan" but the trickster who is playing games with both masks.

Therefore, it is not wise to follow the trickster into a masquerade which s/he has actually organized by suggesting or supplying the stereotypical masks to be used for debate. Shortly after receiving these provocative communications, I ignored the suggestive fact that the Christmas Ornament and Hummel figurine stores are a tourist feature of Rothenburg, Germany where the Kriminal Museum containing the medieval, iron "masks of shame" is also located Instead, I requested the resident Catskill mountain spirit intelligences previously cited as having "fetching" and boomerang ability to bring the perpetrator closer within my circle, that I might be able to grasp the actual identity. I was not disappointed. About three days after beginning to think in this way, I heard the sound of a motorcycle outside my house in the early morning hours of November 10, 2002. The next morning I found that a thin, jagged streamer of tar, resembling a lightning bolt, had been placed onto the asphalt of my front driveway, just outside the garage door windows through which a car is visible. One tire track from a motorcycle crossed this swatch of tar, as if the bike had accidentally run across the swatch after it was laid on the driveway. On one side of this tar streamer was a whitish residue which had dried. Perhaps salt or other substances such as mud or herbs had been poured over the tar to cool it or as some sort of ritual act. I photographed this stuff on the driveway with a digital camera. The next day, after a rain, the design was partly washed away.

November 9th and 20th of 2002 were no particular lunar events but a half moon did occur on November 11th. Some months previous to the tar streamer incident I had found a rectangle of roofing material in the yard, worked so that pale gray pebbly asphalt was exactly half of the rectangle and black tar was the other exact half of the rectangle. I had felt odd about this but put it aside on my desk rather than storing it in my talisman box because I thought it was a "zauba zeitel" of some sort[84] . I had thought that if I kept the object out and visible some meaning might attach to it. I wondered now if this meaning related to "half bad/ half good"or "half black//half white" as in the "gray witch" philosophy. As previously mentioned, one of the anecdotes I had heard about observed sorcery in the Ozarks was the discovery of a naked young man in the road, his face painted half white and half black. He was incoherent and had no exact memory of what had happened to him. I have no proof of this incident but the fact that the tale would be told is significant. Possibly both this young man from the Ozarks and Dr. Ross Koss had been subjected to the same type of hypno-narcotic sorcery. An interpretation of the Ross Kiss incident as being this type of technique, of course, is "not permitted" within the academic and law enforcement presuppositions as these exist at the time of this writing. This is the reason that a number of murders and assaults have not been solved by authorities. Of course, allies of the perpetrators might work subtly within academic and media situations to assure that such a viewpoint on certain crimes was taken as being only a "folk tale" or sensational invention.

.On New Years Day 1999, I had been intuitively motivated to check the front driveway and found a motorcycle track outside in the snow but also thought of the "untraceable" gris gris type of hex item made of ice, food scraps or ordinary plaster.. I had connected this track associatively with some sort of motorcycle club resembling the neo-Nazi Gray Wolves and wondered why I might be visited. Images in my mind on that occasion were sexual although it was early in the morning on a cold, winter day and I thought of "Liz Taylor playing Tennessee Williams".Why? Was I intuiting sexual intentions in the mind of someone drunk on New Years Eve? Or was I picking up telepathically a Southern location or identity?

Recall here the "baby's burial expenses" literature mentioned at the very beginning of this book which this reporter found carefully laid out in the front yard of her country house in context of a death in the family involving Southern locations. There was also, of course, an anomalous "car insurance" call .from Melville, Long Island in 2001 which, traced by the *69 method, seemed simply to be synchronous or spirit guided coincidence with an Internet discussion on the author Herman Melville and did not mention a Southern location but came in as if on cue just as I had moved the Magick Mirror business location in New York City. More recently, closer in time to the tar streamer incident, there had been the odd call to the Magick Mirror cell phone voice mail about "insurance on the Lee Spahn" property, which reminded me associatively of the Spahn ranch of Charles Manson lore.

Like convicted serial killer David Berkowitz, Charles Manson is alive in jail at this writing. Whereas Berkowitz claims "born again Christian" status, Manson has an active association with far right elements masquerading as "environmental" and "nature religion" activists.[85] Might these folks also be masquerading as "insurance agents" and the classic "vacuum cleaner" sales people we take for granted as simple nuisances of modern life? In my play "The Redecoration According To Currier"[86] the Devil, Sam Suado, is an appliances salesman, named from a rearrangement of the letters of the Latin demon's name Asmodeus.

Along this same thread of inquiry, might the alert investigator look for the anonymous perpetrators of ritual nuisance interference as hiding behind banal and/or nominally "good" religious and ethical facades? A book entitled "Beyond Duality" written by Laurence Galian, stresses the importance of recognizing the innate duality of nature (good angel//bad angel) as essential to occult practice.[87] Galian himself is employed as a professional musician and professor of witchcraft and other occult topics by Hofstra University in New York.

November 10, 2002

The driveway vandalism shown above has nothing to do with Laurence Galiani .But two lightning bolts in thick black, jagged form and a triangle divided equally into areas of black and white in Galian's book also significantly resemble the talismanic sigils found outside this writer's Magick Mirror Space in New York City and on her property in upstate New York, as described in "the lightning bolt connection" later in this narration. .So, although the creator or creatrix of these sigils is probably not the public professor, the source of the problem may be a rogue student of chaos magick. A lightning bolt is just a lightning bolt. But this is a tarbaby zig zag. That's for sure.

Galian suggests in his book that transcendence is obtained by a recognition of "opposites" and a resolution of these opposites in the sense of Hegelian philosophy. Yet another practitioner following this same thread of reasoning might not be so philosophical in orientation.

Since I am a practitioner of mental magick who has also used a half moon image in a pamphlet published and copyrighted about twenty years previous to the publication date of Galian's book [88] It is worth noting, since Laurence Galian is a pianist, that this booklet also contains an original guitar tablature invented for those who play kinetically by ear.

So since we are at the apex of overwhelming co-incidence, I shall include here the lyrics of my own song from the 1973 happening: "Lady Video and the Ecosensor":

> Half moon, I'm split in two
> > Dark and light, just blending it new
> Half moon, the sky is clear

> Half moon, where's the edge of your light?
> > Blending into deepest night, still
> Half moon, the sky is clear

> Half moon, there's a breeze in the trees
> > Blowing clouds across your face
> Half moon, the sky is clear

> Half moon, always split in two
> > Dark and light, even when you're full
> Half moon, the sky is clear.

Recall now, dear reader, the type of "Hollywood" spirit guide associated with a small "sorcerer's shop" in Los Angeles who also mysteriously manifested much later in time in Rosendale, New York as ozone on the commuter bus with a rock music reminder that significant sorcery may be practiced also by the Captain Midnights of the interdimensional dreamshop. I had written of my semi-fictional pirate spirit guide in a short story entitled "*The Captain Midnight Transmissions*"[89]

Here, perhaps, we should also begin to call upon the expertise of Captain Midnight in collecting the many and diverse references to "lightning" included in this present text. Captain Midnight's assistance is essential because here we are dealing with

DOING BUSINESS IN THE ADIRONDACKS by E. Macer-Story

the interface between fact and fiction created by trickster magicians and spirit entities. Just as your present correspondent can take on the personae of a variety of characters in writing plays or putting on a costume and/or mask for a poetical performance, so also the tricksters may play a dramatic game in order to make the mind susceptible to a rogue agenda.

However, in actual history as far as we know this in New York State, the ship of the Dutch explorer Hendrick Hudson was also named the "Half-Moon". So since Captain Hudson 's ghostly crew are mythologized in folk tales as bowling in the Catskill and Adirondack mountain sky whenever the thunder is rolling above, perhaps it is once again these phantom pirate accountants who should be asked to total up references to lightning, and tell the reader what this rebus[90] might mean.

Since the lightning bolt of tar evidently meant something to the person who took the trouble to race up my driveway in the early hours of the morning and place it there, it might be that my adversary and/or devotee had a "lightning bolt" connection which will prove illuminating. So let us now, dear reader, join together certain illuminating bits and pieces from the previous narration.

LIGHTNING REBUS, the unexplained visitor:
On July first, the smoke alarm at he house in Woodstock, which had previously been disabled in a lightning storm, blatted twice at 5:34 in the morning and then ceased. Thinking this number somehow significant, I web-searched and located a professor Henry D.I. Alarbarel who was resident at Scripps Oceanographic Institute doing research into chaos theory. I was later informed that Alarbarel 's research on reflections from a shark's skin is actually in the bibliography of the Ph.D. dissertation of a Turkish physicist with an interest in numerology to whom I had sent the original email inquiring about the possible significance of 5:34 a.m.
It is the mental lightning of our interpretations which jumps the conventional alarm system. Yet is what might be allowed by our measuring instruments actually the limitation of material Nature? I corresponded in September of 1997 with Michael Theroux of *Borderlands* magazine about his efforts to link biodynamic signals to the larger celestial movement of stars and the etheric (as Theroux terms it) movement of weather patterning.
According to our intellectual resource on the Trickster Deity, in the traditional Caribbean prayer to Papa Legba "Sonde miroir, O Legba" means literally "Fathom the mirror" or figuratively: "Uncover the secrets". So I asked this question of the living spirit of Legba, who replied with a well-known Lightning Hopkins blues music couplet:
"Don't let your left hand know
What your right hand do:
An unseen eye is watching you"
It is worth commenting that after directly challenging Aexus under an email alias your present correspondent found that the Magick Mirror desktop publishing computer had been infected by the "god/shit" virus mentioned in the opening passages of this book. I make this connection most forcefully since when the alias was identified as being connected with knowledge of Shakespeare's play *Hamlet* in some way the "events calendar" page of the YankeeOracle.org performance site originating from the Magick Mirror computer received a number of unusual posts containing executable files which

were not opened. Give these people fifty cents for guessing the source of the email alias correctly.It is indeed very tempting to jest a bit with these concepts.

So here it is interesting to locate reference to the Axis Inner Order's belief in the talismanic significance of ancient ceramic artifacts and the ancient name of Troy, termed "Hissarlik" by archeologist Schlieman[91]. which resembles somewhat the untraceable name "Haioimr" in the tracking signature of the deliberate viral email which arrived onto this reporter's queue during Memorial Day weekend of May 2002.

Memorial Day in the USA commemorates the soldiers in all Wars who fought for the Allied cause and for Free Enterprise. Heinrich Schlieman , who interpreted the swastika symbol as uniting Teutons, Homeric Greeks and Vedic India, had found the actual site of the ancient Greek city in the country of modern Turkey by inspired, literal interpretation of ancient Greek epic poetry.

So let us now apply this same literal inspiration to conjurations made in 2002 by your present correspondent in order to unravel certain elements of this present enigma. In the same conjuration diagram which provided the word "Faince" the scribbled note "Strategy-Open Sesame-Boston-Sect-Tantra misunderstood" precedes that underlined word, which is prefaced by a lightning bolt leading into the F of "Faince". The double lightning bolt was of course the symbol of the elite Nazi SS. But this is a single lightning bolt, which is the symbol of the Nordic gods Zeus and Wotan, and of the Voodoo god Shango, independently-existing entities who may be mighty angry at having been identified recently with the limited cause of National Socialism and drug gang rituals during a number of quaisi-antiquarian charades.

In a limited distribution video produced by Iciris Productions in 1993 there is an interview with Gunter Richter, a man who claims that he witnessed the flight of a "ufo" at Pennemunde research base in Germany when he was a child. On this video, there are also diagrams of theoretical ufos without the exact structural plans. These diagrams are marked with the double lightning bolt of the elite Nazi SS. Peenemunde base, destroyed in 1943 by Allied bombers, was the location where the V-2 rockets, the first pilotless "guided missiles", were first developed by Nazi scientists during World War Two. Nothing is publically known about these alleged "ufo endeavors" except that there does exist an obvious blank in historical knowledge about the whereabouts of certain Axis scientists after World War Two, as pointed out by UK reporter Nick Cook in his 2002 book *"The Hunt For Zero Point"*.

Therefore, it is not wise to follow the trickster into a masquerade which s/he has actually organized by suggesting or supplying the stereotypical masks to be used for debate. Shortly after receiving these provocative communications, I ignored the suggestive fact that the Christmas Ornament and Hummel figurine stores are a tourist feature of Rothenburg, Germany where the Kriminal Museum containing the medieval, iron "masks of shame" is also located Instead, I requested the resident Catskill mountain intelligences (once regarded by the Ontcora tribe of the Iroquois Confederacy as vampiric :"flying heads" but not limited in function to this designation) to bring the perpetrator closer within my circle, that I might be able to grasp the actual identity. I was not disappointed. About three days after begiuning to think in this way, I heard the sound of a motorcycle outside my house in the early morning hours of November 10, 2002. The next morning I found that a thin, jagged streamer of tar, resembling a lightning bolt, had been placed onto the asphalt of my front driveway, just outside the garage door windows through which a car is visible. One tire track from a motorcycle crossed this swatch of tar, as if the bike had accidentally run across the swatch after it was laid on the driveway. On one side of this tar streamer was a whitish residue which had dried. Perhaps salt or other substances such as mud or herbs had been poured over the tar to cool it or as some sort of ritual act. I photographed this stuff on the driveway with a digital camera. The next day, after a rain, the design was partly washed away.

So far, the rebus seems to indicate occult activity of the controlling sort which may or may-not be inspired by the Thantatos sorcerers. Departing somewhat from the "lightning bolt" motif, one can enter the "Christmas" theme and recall email correspondence about a talismanic motorcycle happening in exactly the same driveway location at New Years 2001, as previously described:

"This is about one specific "talisman" which was found in my driveway on New Years Day of 2001:It seems, after a probing of this talisman by various means, that some attempt has been made by user(s) of esp/pk to block my psi abilities so that the operations of their craft are not evident to me. I link this to the quaisi-martial arts group using Japanese ethos which I mention in a previous article published in 2000 and 2001 both by Magonia Magazine Online and in hard copy by Alternate Perceptions magazine. This covert but inept organization has, among other charades, managed to annoy the controversial neo-Fascist "Temple of Set" by impersonating conventional and/or "published"neo-Nazi and "Golden Dawn" occult groups in various contexts .Apparently, these practitioners have successfully been using hypnosis and spell-casting as part of some illegal venture."

[Auth.Note in 2003: These are not all of Japanese nationality but are using the Shinto, Buddhist deity and Zen facade. Here it is wise to remember that General Karl Haushofer[92], founder of the Ahnenerbe occult research organization during the Third Reich in Germany, had traveled to Japan to study esoteric Shinto and Zen concepts, though Axis probing into Tibetan and Vedic lore is better known in historical accounts.]

Back to 2001 again: " A crank call was left on the message machine at my Magick Mirror studio space late on the night of Thursday, Jan 4th. This was a charade during which Reggae-like music was played in the background whilst children's voices made vaguely obscene nonsense statements. I saved the tape. I emphasize: this was a charade. These were not actual "voodoo" or similar practitioners. Once again, an attempt is being made to "set up" a known occult group as the culprit."

[Auth. Note in 2003: Whereas in use of "behavior modification" via crank calling the actual "Thantatos" black magicians may have managed thus far to slip through the cracks of historical analysis, yet they have left absurdist traces.. The circumstances of finding one of these strange yet micro-subtle talismans has been narrated previously in the following email sent on January 2, 2001, and ending with the question.:]

"But I followed my inner guidance & found the bike track. What next? "

In re-reading this naïve but jovial communication, keep in mind that, among other annoyances, what was "next" after this awk-cult souvenir was a very palpable lightning bolt of tar in the driveway:

"Just to keep you up to date: I found a discernably awk-cult talisman at the foot of my back driveway this afternoon. It was very small so I had not seen it from the porch. I felt like walking around the house at 4:30 EST, and there it was! Just as an aside: sometimes my inner guidance

DOING BUSINESS IN THE ADIRONDACKS by E. Macer-Story

cam be very specific. My inner voice instructed me: "don't put on heavy socks under your boots. You won't be outside long." I wasn't out long. It was neat. I walked up to the talisman, plucked it up with gloved hand and went back inside. I am deliberately not describing the form of this thing by email. It is a traditional spell-casting shape.

At any rate, I now have this tiny awk-cult thing in my possession. I don't think I was supposed to notice it. So I will query it sometime tomorrow. I do feel, holding it, that the origin is Cambridge, Mass and environs. The entire awk-cult situation is much weirder than I have yet narrated in my articles."

[Auth. Note: I had anticipated there might be some occult shenanigans in an email sent prior to the New Year celebrations, as follows.]

" Happy New Year --
This is actually the first new year of the Millennium. I have had a few
new talismanic occurrences in Woodstock during the past few days. I am
deliberately not giving a specific description as these were definitely of
human construction and who knows who's tapping the email:-)"

[Auth.Note: The expert talismanic objects are also worked cleverly from natural materials so that reproductions may look like someone simply picked up a twig or a stone and thought it "looked like" a talisman. The significance of these items is in the subtle energy, which may not be visible in a photo. Here follows a continuation of the original email, which was triggered by esp perception of telepathic, subtle energy of an obstructive nature as attached to these clever talismans.]

" I think—and co-witnesses also think--that somewhere "out there" is an actual adept in the martial and/or magickal arts who has either gone crazy about my probings into sorcery or is being paid &/or cajoled into this hexing activity. I am keeping a journal as this evolves. The key to understanding these events is that the talismancer actually is gifted, and the talismans left outside my place have multidimensional resonance. So for me it's like playing martial arts chess. Something is going to be attempted on the turn of the Millennium here, as I intuit and I hope the poker face above my poker hand is absolutely inscrutable. "

As documented in news reports after the fact,[93] there was a foiled terrorist plot to disrupt the Times Square New Years Eve celebration in both New York City and Seattle, Washington in the year 2000. This reporter had abstained from these festivities because of a clear premonition there was danger in traversing the midtown Manhattan area Yet upon seeing the "worked twig" in the driveway one year later on the same date, only an amused perception of "awk cult" efforts crossed this same reporter's mind.

Maybe the elusive night motorcyclist of the "worked twig" and "lightning" signs is a solid state phantom, like the Hollywood sorcery shop elevator encounter with a man dressed in black carrying an armload of groceries, warning the percipient of interdimensional intrigues described earlier in this book. Or, if these are real people dressed and behaving according to occult rationale, perhaps the Thantatos sorcerers sought for a "blanking" effect they did not fully achieve, and created a "shadow puppet" which clearly could be discerned. This shadow of a biker marked the year 2001 with a

DOING BUSINESS IN THE ADIRONDACKS by E. Macer-Story

warning of "witchcraft" and this was the year of terrorist action at the World Trade Center in New York on September 11 which has precipitated continual guerilla war and game playing in the Mideast and Afghanistan since that time, as well as heightened economic stress in the United States, and globally.

Oddly, when this reporter web searched Hendrick Hudson's ship, the "Half Moon" simply for reference documentation a quote from Lenni Lenape, a chief of the Delaware Indians, was part of the historical summary about the massacre of that tribe in Stockbridge, Massachusetts. This reporter had just come back to upstate New York from giving a talk for a salon in Stockbridge about "DemiGods and Demons", the reality of spirit presences.

The quote from Chief Lenni Lenape was:" *I know the Long Knives. They are not to be trusted.*". Certainly, the premonitions of Chief Lenape were correct. This connection of the fate of the Delaware Indians with Yankee pirate activity, as perceived by the Indians, reminded this reporter that the Tobyhanna, Pennsylvania area where "ufo" activity was reported near an Army Materiels base in 1980[94]was also an area from which the Delaware Indians had been removed by American settlers. At the time of the "ufo" sightings there in 1980, the Army information officer claimed in a letter to this reporter that the military had no knowledge of the "ufo" activity which had been witnessed by several local residents.

However, this reporter had gone to the area with one of the witnesses and had seen "energy forms" which were not conventional aircraft take various forms over a small pond on the materials base property. The conclusion reached at that time was that the U.S. military had no official knowledge of the phenomena and were relatively innocent of any subterfuge. What, then, was happening? In Pennsylvania, in 1980, this was an obscure and murky situation, involving investigative leads as diverse as the U.S. military, the owners of a Mid Eastern restaurant, local tales of the supernatural, Delaware Indian lore , an avowed second generation Nazi sympathizer then employed as a civilian "health physicist" by the Navy,[95] and a lady hustler who gave a variety of false identities and at times wore a red feather boa when focusing professionally on her psychic readings of ufo craft and related topics.

Here in the Catskill mountains of New York State in the year 2002, the question raised by finding the oracular quote from Delaware chief Lenni Lenape becomes exact and basic: " *Who* is not to be trusted?" What might this oracular reference to the 'Long Knives" of yore really mean in this present context?

Shortly after telepathically requesting my spirit "business associates" to answer this tactical question, I received an email forwarded to me by Andrew Microwski of the Planetary Association for Clean Energy in Ottowa,Canada.

Although neither Microwski nor the author of the forwarded email had any knowledge of this reporter's current research in specific, the following email from a researcher in Russia substantially corroborates the findings of this reporter in identifying a covert "Thantatos" organization of sorcerers aka "researchers into mind/matter connections and psychotronics" who may be attempting to affect World politics by directing their telekinetic energy toward specific World leaders and other individuals they may regard as key players. Though Dr. Constantin I. Ivanenko of St. Petersburg, Russia did not identify the group by "Thantatos" or any other specific organizational name, he stated:

DOING BUSINESS IN THE ADIRONDACKS by E. Macer-Story

" Now we're discussing with colleagues necessity to accept for all heads of nuclear powers internationally standardized protocol of operating "nuclear buttons" in cases of emergency - as there exist real danger of psychotronic attacks on these heads of states which might render them physically incapable to perform their constitutional duties (A spectacular example was a temporal loss of consciousness by US President Bush on 13 Jan 2002, demonstrated via CNN to millions of people around the globe in real time. As think Russian experts in psychotronic defense, this incident might be caused by psychotronic attack - which could be launched by Chinese via Internet: during 2001 there was released strictly controlled by authorities Chinese Internet an "amusing electronic game" featuring President Bush as a "cute but helpless computer animal" which ought to be fed with "virtual grass" only in reward for complete obedience. A hidden group of trained meditation experts might precisely focus & direct - using Internet as an efficient device for precision control of mind rhythms -tremendous amounts of psi-energies generated by millions of participants of this game; - aiming them at their selected "human target" in a moment of their choice. Such experiments - without, of course, use of Internet – are known to have been performed already more than a century ago by Aleister Crowley & other black magicians. Thus the need for elaboration of such protocols seems to be really important & urgent; - as such technologies may become accessible also to less disciplined regimes of "outlaw states", increasing global instability in our already stressful time. (Of course, of even greater importance will be development of efficient techniques of defending heads of state, operators of defense installations & other sensitive people against such attacks; - but it belongs to area of national defense policy which every nation wishing to preserve its sovereignty must solve for itself (and perhaps its close allies). A parallel here may be drawn with universally accepted encryption protocols - where each user does select his/her own encryption key unknown to other users of this protocol.)Hope that you & your colleagues also recognize importance of this problem -which can be resolved only through international cooperation of responsible experts"

A commentary on Dr. Constantine I. Ivanenko's opinion by James W. Black of Toronto, Canada provided in a subsequent email by Andrew Microwski provides the crucial "corroborating opinion" on the Thantatos theory. The commentary was sent to Dr. Ivanenko independently of any prior contact with this reporter:

"Dear Dr. Ivanenko,
I received the enclosure from my friend, Dr. Andrew Michrowski, of the Planetary Association for Clean Energy (P.A.C.E.),Ottawa, Ontario, Canada a short while ago this evening. I am very interested in the subject matter of your article and have been familiar with psychic warfare for a number of decades.
Do you have a web site where I may read more about your research? I have some friends from Russia and one of my earlier partners was the late Dr. Borys Polyachenko, Ph.D., Physics, then, First Secretary, Science and Technology, Embassy of Ukraine in Canada. My other partner was Eldon A. Byrd, USNR, Ret. (United States Naval Reserve)[96], a medical scientist who is a friend of Uri Geller, the Israeli psychic, among others. Eldon was called in on behalf of the U.S. Military and Intelligence Community when Russian scientists introduced Mind Control technology to the U.S.

DOING BUSINESS IN THE ADIRONDACKS by E. Macer-Story

government, e.g., Reverse Speech. Later, although Eldon had no involvement whatsoever, the devices were used against Mr. David Koreas at Waco, Texas.

[Auth. Note: In context of this assertion about "devices" of a psychotronic, "mind control" nature, it is worth noting that the late Dr. Eldon Byrd once confided to this reporter that he had experienced a romantic relationship with a very human woman who was able to "change shape" and was interested in sadomasochistic sex. Yet these shape-shifting abilities were not due to "psychotronic devices" but unique capacities of this person, as was her hypnotic ability to induct the at first reluctant Dr. Byrd into sadomasochistic practices, which may have begun when Byrd suddenly felt motivated to double cross a mutual psychotronics associate by dating her though she was the associate's long term girlfriend. "I thought he wouldn't mind because he was so aware, so expanded about these things."commented the unfortunate Eldon Byrd.

The type of ability manifested by this hypnotic "shape changer" is called in Western witchcraft terminology "glamour" and sometimes is thought to be due to the linkage of the person with a djinn or demon. Of course, the person may not actually change shape but the hypnotized victim may believe the appearance has changed. David Kirsch had an interest in demonology and ritualized sexual practices, and may have unwittingly invited the presence of destructive or diabolic energy.]

Dr. Constantine I. Ivanenko continues:

" A friend of my music teacher when I studied piano years ago in Hollywood,California was Ingo Swann who had been involved with experiments funded by the U.S. C.I.A. at the Stanford Research Institute of Stanford University.Ingo Swann was also involved with Scientology at this time. The brother of another friend of mine in the Los Angeles area who I worked with years ago was a special Psychic Agent of the Mexican Federal Police who guarded the President of Mexico. I do not work for nor have I ever represented any government, military or intelligence agency or private organization, e.g., church. I believe in God. I have previously trained myself in this field and another friend and Ph.D.,originally from Ukraine, trained students on the weekends in Los Angeles in Psychic Espionage, including the psychic training to locate underground military bases in Russia.

I understand what you are talking about. I have looked at the changes in health of other individuals in our world and have determined that some deterioration in their health may very well be due to psychic attacks. Use of the Internet to focus a concerted attack is a very real and potentially ominous possibility. I have dealt with some of these things myself. The attacks or influences are directed not only at the individual target's mind and physical being (body), but also directly at the intrinsic essence of the soul which is who and what every being truly is. This is an Eternal warfare and it is going on right now. The activities extend well beyond the realms of philosophy and religion to very real, concerted and organized events. Thank you for pointing this out. I am interested in your theories and in co-operating with you as much as I can. I have enjoyed the friendships of many in our world from Russia, the United States of America, China, the Middle East, Europe, Taiwan, Japan and Mexico, et al.. St. Petersburg is a very beautiful and historic city. My grandmother who was from Ukraine, still remembered the Russian Revolution until she passed away a number of years ago."

Aside from the mental persuasiveness of those who have studied spirit contact and Zen skills as a form of combat weapon, the ill-fated reporter Daniel Pearl referred to in the initial section of this book may have been successfully kidnapped by a renegade

DOING BUSINESS IN THE ADIRONDACKS by E. Macer-Story

group because he did not bring corroborating companions into the situation both on site and by correspondence. Or Mr. Pearl should have refused a "no companions" demand by his potential terrorist informants. In this way, certain "mind games" enacted on the Internet may be very effective in seducing and blocking opponents unaware of their personal isolation whilst playing the strategy game. In addition, as James W. Black points out in his commentary, an esp/pk link established via Internet contact may be a powerful mind control tool in such situations.

Into the psychical investigation situation will enter a variety of people claiming to be ex-intelligence agents and whatnot else, who serve to complicate matters. Mr. Black makes no such questionable claims. He does claim that mind control technology was used against David Koresch during the Waco, Texas siege by the FBI.

This reporter has a slightly differing view. There is no proof that the U.S. government or the FBI was using such telepathic or psychotronic techniques. The facts which do exist [97] document that the USSR was more seriously developing these techniques during the 1970-80's than was the United States. Similarly, documentation suggests[98] that Chinese psychical and ufo researchers have been seriously researching these techniques for over two decades. If there was a deliberate kindling of the Waco catastrophe and/or other bizarre acts of terrorism by enhanced telepathic influence, this kindling may have originated with the developers of a mercenary and/or "black hat" version of emotional telepathic techniques such as those employed by a "shape shifting" sorcerer of yore, perhaps directed to upset Koresch and/or the FBI representatives into extreme behavior. One hexagram of the I Ching cites this mindstate as being when: "One perceives one's best friend as a wagonload of devils." Recall here the use as previously described in this book with reference to the work of Dr. Jack Sarfatti and the "Black Kabbalist" of the pornographic parodies of a variety of actual websites and email communications in conjunction with rogue viral attacks by cyber strategists evidently interested in bolexing legitimate public "ufo research" and neo-tech physics speculation.

The answer to this conundrum of "which renegade is the deceptive Long Knife?" may lie in plain view. In fact, the expert criminal disinformer does place the contradictory evidence in plain view, attached to multiple interpretations, including the parsing of "work of genius", "simple" or "idiotic". It is the belief of this reporter that persons following standard investigative paradigms and job instructions will inevitably be deceived by this type of mercenary disinfo operation, as the Native Americans— governed by strict tribal taboos and caste-oriented levels of command—were fooled by the "Long Knives" coming from an entirely different tribal set of behaviors learned in England and Europe. One should not confuse either set of learned tribal taboos with absolute ethics or morality. Beyond rational analysis, there is sorcery for convenience.

The answer, of course, is individual discernment. One is free, of course, to make the wrong decision. In the case of reporter Daniel Pearl, the treacherous "Long Knives" were apparent intellectuals masquerading as religious idealists but acting in cynical, mercenary context. All is not seen in the overt comparison of accounting totals . Good business is sometimes not to do business , regardless of loss of revenue. For the loyalty of the djinn is not for sale, and sometimes may be surprising.

Recall here the unquiet ghost of Fredrick Von Mieres, the gem magick sorcerer mentioned briefly at the beginning of this book, who committed suicide in 1992. His live interlocutor, contractor Tom Walker, relates that Von Mieres'wealthy devotees, then

DOING BUSINESS IN THE ADIRONDACKS by E. Macer-Story

living somewhere in the East midtown area of New York City, each sported a sorcerer's ring set with a diamond, an emerald and a "cat's eye" gem. Walker also claims that an article about Frederick Von Mieres' activities, which mentioned his book on the occult and Christianity, appeared in Vanity Fair magazine shortly before his death. Though Von Mieres' activities evidently brought him some fortune, or at least some income when living, no trace of him remains in conventional reference works except that some unknown "initiate" in 1998 had marked the alphabetic place in the Woodstock, N.Y. library card catalog drawer where normally his surname might appear with a card out of sequence alphabetically but referring to the art of making very small sculptures or carvings upon gemstones. The technique of "mirror intaglio" can be used with very fine instruments to create a small, printable seal, sometimes used for the purpose of sorcery or encrypted identification.[99]

   Distrust, of course, dear Reader, any fabrications about this gem magician which may be presented subsequent to the publication of this book. For such may be the attempts of the "Thantatos" sorcerers to once again re-rig the catalog of public information.

#30#

GUIDE TO TOPICS

DOING BUSINESS IN THE ADIRONDACKS by E. Macer-Story

DOING BUSINESS IN THE ADIRONDACKS by E. Macer-Story

---

[1] ." From Frank Edwards' book, "Strange World", Lyle Stewart, New York, 1964, pp. 209 - 210

[2] Originally reported to the Institute of Hispanic Ufology by Gloria R. Coluchi

[3] "The Stargate Conspiracy".Lynn Picknett, Clive Prince.Berkley Publishing Group 2001.

[4] Steven Levy."The Unicorn's Secret: Murder in the Age of Aquarius"Onyx Books.1999.

[5] PARANOIA magazine. Winter 2003.

[6] Symbol rebus and alias are pseudonymed here to prevent the trickster from easily harming the curious reader.

DOING BUSINESS IN THE ADIRONDACKS by E. Macer-Story

[7] "Four Major Mysteries of Mainland China.Paul Dong Chinese "UFO god" is seen in the countryside as wearing a coolie hat.

[8] *AP Washingston,D.C. February 13, 2003.They[FBI] also interviewed a witness who had aided government prosecutors in other white supremacist cases. John Shults told agents in 1997 he was ``sure beyond a shadow of a doubt'' he saw McVeigh at Elohim City[White Supremicist gang compound] in 1994 at a meeting about a mysterious delivery and the use of a Ryder truck. Shults ``felt strongly the delivery may have been a reference to the bombing,'' according to one federal agent's interview report.Within a few days of the bombing, FBI officials received intelligence suggesting members of Elohim City had information relevant to the investigation.A federal informant talked with one compound member who ``discussed alibis for April 19, 1995, and the components of'' McVeigh's bomb, investigative memos show. The same member had claimed, before McVeigh's bombing, that he had detonated a 500-pound fertilizer bomb, similar to the one McVeigh later used.That compound member also discussed the name of a munitions dealer that McVeigh's phone records showed the bomber called more than two dozen times in the weeks before the attack. McVeigh had the dealer's phone number in his wallet when he was captured."*

[9] "Destiny Matrix".Jack Sarfatti. First Books.2002.

[10] Niels Bohr, *"The Causality Problem in Atomic Physics,"* in *New Theories in Physics,* 1939, page 19.

[11] CNN still frame. http://www.yankeeoracle.org/archive.html.

[12] "The Jefferson Market Triangle" E.Macer-Story. Borderlands magazine. 1993.

[13] Citation by E,Macer-Story and Riley Crabbe of similarity between Klepoth and certain alleged ET contacts.Appendix. *Extraterrestrial Friends and Foes.* George C. Andrews. Illuminet Press. 1993.

[14] "The UFO/FBI Connection." Bruce Maccabee. Llewllyn Press. 2000.

[15] E.Macer-Story.S.P.A.C.E. Seminars 2001.Paranoia Magaine Online 2002.

[16] In echo of the "black hat" tradition of power meditations practiced by certain Tibetan adepts, there exists a type of cyber technician who is extremely sensitive and skilled but is for hire to covert or warlike interests as well as above board business firms. The "black hat" practitioners were said to use martial arts meditation techniques in their practice which more idealistic monks may spurn. This is justified on the basis of the necessity for Advanced Intelligence simply to survive in unjust and/or adversarial circumstances.

[17] :"Operation Paperclip" Lieutenant Colonel William L. Howard. Web posting.1993.

[18] "The Satanic Bible" Anton Szandor LeVey.

[19] Interview with Kreskin."Alternate Perceptions" magazine 1999..

[20] Bulldozer dematerialization. Curt Sutherly. *Strange Encounters.* Llewllyn Press.1996.

[21] *Ufo Mind Games.* E.Macer-Story. Borderlands magazine 1995.

[22] Page 42.*Doing Business in the Adirondacks: True Tales of the Bizarre and Supernatural.*2003.

[23] *Diario La Arena* (La Pampa, Argentina) April 29, Translation (C) 2002. Institute of Hispanic Ufology. Special thanks to Gloria Coluchi.

[24] *"What's Up At The South Tip?"*Austin Anomaly TV.Scripted by E.Macer-Story.

[25] Michael Theroux, editor Borderlands magazine 1994.

[26] *Legacy of Daedalus, E.Macer-Story.Magick Mirror Press. 1995.*

[27] Angus Fraser, *The Gypsies*, Blackwell Publishers, Oxford UK 1992, 1995 .

[28]Nicholas Goodrick-Clark *Hitler's Priestess, Savitri Devi, the Hindu-Aryan Myth, and Neo-Nazism*; New York University Press, New York and London, 1998.

[29] Colin Wilson *"A Criminal History of Mankind"*.Carroll & Graf.New York. 1984.

[30] GeorgeAdamski. *Behind The Flying Saucer Mystery.*Paperback Library.New York.1967.

[31] *Translation (C) 2002. Institute of Hispanic Ufology. Special thanks to Gloria Coluchi*

[32] *"Ancient Beasts of Light"*. E. Macer-Story. Body, Mind, Spirit magazine. 1991.

[33] *The Search For The Manchurian Candidate* John Marks. N.Y. Times Press.

[34] *La Nacion*, Argentina. July 2, 2002.

[35] Photo of clean incision on animal found at Berroteran, Argentina. *Institute of Hispanic Ufology.*June 2002. Scott Corrales and Alicia Rossi.

[36] George P. Hansen. *The Trickster and the Paranormal.* Xlibris Corporation.2002.

[37] E. Macer-Story .*Dark Frontier.* Magick Mirror Press. 1998..

[38] E. Macer-Story .*The Philosophical Double Cross "*. Magonia Magazine online 1998.

[39] *Planetary Association For Clean Energy.* Ottawa, Canada. pacenet@ Canada.com

[40] http://stardrive.org

[41] http://fluidice.com

[42] *The FBI-UFO Connection.* Dr. Bruce Maccabee. Llewllyn Publications.2000

[43] *Fluidice Transformation Matrix: A Living Model For Mass Structure..* E.Macer-Story. Proceedings.U.S. Psychotronics Association.2002.

[44] Term for unknown but technologically sophisticated culture destroyed in antiquity.

[45] Contract between Jack Sarfatti and CIA-op Harold Chipman .Magick Mirror Archives.

[46] Stephan A. Schwartz. Features & obituary reporter . San Francisco Chronicle.1970's..Author of book *Two Faces of Islam.* Doubleday 2002.

[47] Photos :Artifact Arcade Appendix. *"Dark Frontier"*.E.Macer-Story. 1997.

[48] Michael Christie.*"Inconstant Speed of Light May Debunk Einstein"*Reuters. August 7,2002..

[49] Term for "haunted land" used in British Isles in antiquity.

[50] Archives of the Quantum Mind internet postings.University of Arizona.

[51] Interview with Ms. Jane Doe about harassment.Woodstock,N.Y. 1996.

[52] Peter Levenda.*Unholy Alliance.*History of the Nazi Involvement With the Occult..2000.

[53] From Radio National.*"In The Spirit of Things "* .Rachael Kohn,moderator January 30,2000.

[54] Week In Review.Sunday N.Y. Times September 8, 2002 . Section 4-page 1.

[55] Quotes from *Delta Green* in this book preserve copyright but pseudonym respondent.

[56] *"Called To Serve"* Bo Gritz 1989.Center For Action. Las Vegas, Nevada.

[57] *A New World Order For The New Millenium"* Unpublished monograph. J. Grimes c/o S. Parker.*United Fascist Union.*2001.

[58] Released during the mid-1970's in California.

DOING BUSINESS IN THE ADIRONDACKS by E. Macer-Story

[59] *The Art of War* of Sun Tzu. Stephen F. Kaufman,Hanshi 10th Dan 1996.

[60] *The Japanese Art of War*. Thomas Cleary.Shambhala Press 1992.

[61] New York Times Archives.1980's.

[62] Joseph E. Persico."*Roosevelt's Secret War*".Random House.2002.

[63] E.Macer-Story"*The Art of Making Wolves From Human Skulls:The Binding of Fenris*". And "*The Philosophical Double Cross*" Magonia magazine 1999 & 2000.

[64] "*The Art of Making Wolves From Human Skulls:The Binding of Fenris*" Alternate Perceptions magazine.2000 The white wolf beside the white mushroom as a powerful, protective guide"..

[65] Ibid. This would be the natural, primal wolf guardian of spirit tradition rather than the ferocious wolf demon, Fenris. Recall the legend of Romulus & Remus of Rome, who were suckled by a mother wolf.

[66] *The Bookseller Daily*. Frankfurt, Germany October 9, 2002.

[67] Which would attract unwanted attention as curiosities?

[68] E. Macer-Story. "Dr. Fu Man Chu Meets The lonesome Cowboy:Sorcery And The UFO Experience". Advanced Sciences 1991.

[69] *The FBI-UFO Connection.* Dr. Bruce Maccabee. Llewllyn Publications.2000

[70] CNN network. 9/11/01. Posted to http://yankeeoracle.org 9/13/01.

[71] Edwin Black .*"The IBM Link to Auschwitz: Researchers Uncover Records of the Company's Work at Death-Camp Complex "*VillageVoice.com 2002.

[72] *International Display Forum.*. Frankfurt, Germany Book Fair 2002

[73] Philadelphia, Pa. newspaper archives 1977-2002.

[74] http://play.rbn.com/?url=fcn/fcn/g2demand/dayofatonement2002.rm&proto=rtsp RealPlayer required.(Fast forward over the poorly recorded introduction.) go to about 20 minutes in to get to ufo sighting.

[75] ACE INVITATIONAL 2002. ACE Art Gallery.275 Hudson Street,NYC.USA.

[76] "Matamoros Cult".1988.Associated Press. Mexico City. Brownsville, Texas.

[77] "Tecnologia, OVNIs y Ciencia" CD 2002. Chile.

[78] Joseph Campbell."*The Way of the Animal Powers*" Harper & Row. 1983.

[79] Later, two teenaged boys were arrested in Vermont for the murders of Half and Suzanne Zantop and no Nazi or cult association was attached to the killings beyond far right magazine articles found in one boy's room.. But, in the area of the "supernatural",were these murders extraordinarily inspiued by suggestion?

[80] CNN.Rebodcast of David Berkowitz interview. October 26, 2002.

[81] Maury Terry."*The Ultimate Evil*"Dolphin Books.New York.1987.

[82] "*The Screens*".play by Jean Genet 1965 about Algerian colonialism.

[83] "*Nazi style*" is street slang for a quick way to make methamphetimenes using household ammonia and/or ammonia fertilizer in a casserole on the stove burner. This type of home cooking was used to keep Nazi foot soldiers pepped up during World War Two.

[84] German-American folk magic practice. See E.Macer-Story." *Dark Frontier*" 1997 for discussion of the oral tradition "Besprechen".

[85] Adam Gorightly."*Shadow Over Santa Susanna*""2000.

[86] Gallery 313. NYC. March 2001.

[87] Laurence Galian."*Beyond Duality*".New Falcon Publications.1995.

[88] E,.Macer-story"*Half Moon, a song and How To Play It*"1973.Funk Fest Booklet.Boston.

[89] E.Macer-Story"*Troll & Other Interdimensional Invasions*" Magick Mirror Press.2000.

[90] E.Macer-Story."*The Astrebus: An Intergalactic Language*". 1977.Pursuit magazine.

[91] In 1870, the German archeologist Heinrich Schlieman discovered the ruins of Troy (and several cities above and beneath it) in northwest Turkey.

[92] A frequent visitor to Landsberg prison where Hitler was writing *Mein Kampf* with the help of Rudolf Hess, was General Karl Haushofer, a university professor and director of the Munich Institute of Geopolitics. Haushofer, Hitler, and Hess had long conversations together. Hess also kept records of these conversations. Hitler's demands for German 'living space' in the east at the expense of the Slavic nations were based on the geopolitical theories of the learned professor. Haushofer was also inclined toward the esoteric. As military attache in Japan, he had studied Zen-Buddhism. He had also gone through initiations at the hands of Tibetan lamas. He became Hitler's second 'esoteric mentor', replacing Dietrich Eckart." - Wulf Schwartzwaller, *The Unknown Hitler*

[93] Diane Francis .*Financial Post* .Canada.Tuesday, January 04, 2000

[94] E.Macer-Story"*Dr.Fu Man Chu Meets The Lonesome Cowboy: Sorcery and the UFO Experience*". Advanced Sciences.1991.

[95] E.Macer-Story. "*Men In Black*"Mufon Ufo Journal 1990.

[96] Eldon A. Byrd passed away in December 2002 of cancer after an extended battle with this disease.

[97] Sheila Ostrander and Lynn Schroeder "*Psychic Discoveries Behind The Iron Curtain*". Bantam Books G.P. Putnam's Sons. 1987.

[98] Walter Uphoff."*Mind Over Matter*" 1985.

[99] Gemstone carving has a long and ancient history. The begining of carving or engraving in the Orient can be dated to the early Chow Dynasty (1122-49 B.C) in China. In ancient Egypt, artisan craftsmen worked with steatite and colored quartzes such as *amethyst* and also with *carnelian* and *jasper* In the East, carving art reached its zenith during the Mughal period (1508-1707 A.D.). One of the wonders of the world, *TAJ MAHAL*, fantastically beautiful, built in pure white ornamented marble by artisans from India, Paris, Central Asia and beyond, during 1632-54, still glitters with its exquisitely carved gemstones. Generation after generation of these artisans are in gemcarving vocation. *Many of them migrated to Pakistan in 1940s at the time of partition of Indian sub-Continent and since then they are pursuing their vocation in this country. http://asiangems.com/carving.htm*

[100] George Adamski *Behind The Flying Saucer Mystery*.Paperback Library.New York.1967.

[101] Term for "haunted land" used in British Isles in antiquity